BUFORD PUSSER: "The Other Story"

As told by the people who were there

Author

Michael Elam

I hope you enjoy the Real Story of "Walking Tall" Sheriff Buford Pusser As the truth isn't for Sissies.

Best Wishes

Mike Elam

Acknowledgments & Credits

Barbara Anderson Mitchell
Dennis Hathcock
Wain Snyder
Ghostnote Studio, Memphis TN
Ward Moore
Jackie Prather
Paul David English
Paul Ervin
Lavon Plunk Sullivan
Beverly Maxwell
Camilla Wilson
James Opal Gray
Bill McPeters
Barbara Bivins
McNairy County Sheriffs Office
The Jackson Sun Newspaper, Jackson TN
The Commercial Appeal, Memphis TN
Daily Corinthian Newspaper, Corinth MS
Dr Jerry Francisco
Loyd Tatum
Theresa Smith
Memphis Press-Scimitar, Memphis TN
Bill Way
Edwin Lovell
Juanita Richardson
University of Memphis, McWherter Library, Memphis TN
Tennessee River News Graphic, Selmer TN
Oneal Moffett
Brenda Moffett
Robert Farish
Office of the Chief Medical Examiner, Nashville TN
Ewing "Skeets" Adkins
Adamsville Newspaper, Adamsville TN
The Tishomingo County News/Vidette, Iuka MS
Independent Appeal Newspaper, Selmer, TN
Betty Sparks Gee
The Condo News
Jerry Heacock
Eddie Bond
United States Archives, Washington DC
Tennessee Bureau of Investigations, Nashville TN
The Memphis Tennessean Newspaper/Magazine, Nashville TN
Federal Bureau of Investigation, Washington DC
Wayne Edgins
Earl McCoy
Kenneth Wayne McCoy Jr.
Jeffery McCleese
McNairy County General Hospital
W.T. Yarbrough
Paul Moore
Shirley Smith
Synova Cantrell
Jack Kennington
Kenny Rose

BUFORD PUSSER: The Other Story
1st Edition
Copyright © 2020
As told by those who lived the real story
1937-1974
McNairy County TN, Alcorn County MS
Author: Mike Elam
Editor: Jackie Prather
Cover: Wain Snyder

DEDICATION

Connie Elam   Dennis Hathcock   Bobby Anderson   Barbara Anderson Mitchell

It was with the encouragement of my wife Connie that I authored this book. Without her continuing encouragement and support, this book may never have seen the light of day. She alone understood why I was so compelled to research and finally tell this story as she saw the time and effort I placed on research and conducting interviews to learn the true story of the Walking tall Sheriff and the state line. I will forever be thankful for her insistence that I tell this story.

I will be forever grateful to Dennis Hathcock as well as he became, first a source of information about the state line and then became a friend as well. He was instrumental in introducing me to people from the state line side of this very real story as well as law enforcement personnel in McNairy and Alcorn Counties, all of which were people who lived their own parts in Buford Pusser's story.

I also want to dedicate this story to Bobby Anderson, whose part of the story was given to me by Barbara Anderson after her brother's death. Bobby was close to many of the main characters in this story. Bobby passed along a lot of valuable information to make this book possible.

Barbara Anderson Mitchell, like Dennis Hathcock, was instumental in helping me to understand the story from both the state line prospective as well as that of the law enforcement community in the area. She was there and she lived it and wanted the real story to be told, therefore this book is dedicated to her as well.

Finally, I would like to include the surviving family members from both sides of this story as they are the ones who have suffered great loss as the real story unfolded. These people shared with me, their experiences, both good and bad. They made this book possible. I thank all of you for your assistance in telling the real story of Buford Pusser and the state line.

Mike Elam

Buford Pusser: There Other Story

Extras

Hathcock Documents

Photos
Remembering McNairy County and the
state line as it once was

The Smith Deposition

Interesting Items about Towhead and Lousie

Forget everything you think you know about Buford Pusser and start with a clean slate.

Forget everything you think you know about the Buford Pusser and his legend as this is a very different story as told to me by people who were actually there and lived their own parts of the "Pusser Legend."

The story of Buford Pusser and his fight against the state line mob is an amazing tale. Unfortunately, the tale we have been given by writers and movie makers over the years is most often incorrect, thus it gives us a narrative with little truth. Why? Because their agenda was to create a hero.

As a former law enforcement officer myself, I had an interest in Buford's story and started to research it. I have made several trips to McNairy County Tennessee and Alcorn County Mississippi to find and interview the people who lived their own part of Buford's legend. I learned that while Buford did a lot of good for McNairy County, most writers and movie makers have chosen to ignore the true story in many events, as my research indicates there was also a very dark side to the story in which Buford was said to be involved in accepting payoffs and possibly murder.

In this book I will present what I have learned from people on the law enforcement side of the story as well as those from the state line side. Their stories are often very much alike rather than opposing points of view.

Clear your mind and start with a clean slate as you read the information in this book. Read the stories as told to me by the people who were there. Examine for yourself the documents, photos, reports and newspaper clippings and then decide for yourself if Buford was the hero that books and movies made him out to be, or if he was simply part of the problem, not the solution as he served as Sheriff of McNairy County

Did Buford accept payoffs and line his pockets as I have always been told? More importantly was he involved with the murder of his wife Pauline as so much evidence suggests? Read "The Other Story" and decide for yourself. Remember this as you read…, "The truth has no agenda".

NOTE: When viewing some of the photos in this book, please keep in mind that most were made several decades ago and the images were made by various cameras of equal various qualities. As a result, some of the images may appear to be a bit blurry or out of focus. This is the result of the photographic process of each individual camera. The image quality is not related to the printing of the book itself.

Chapter One
"The Other Story"

Ignoring the small but growing crowd, a young photographer snaps photos of the exterior of a car which is covered in blood spatter. His concentration is keen on detail, realizing the importance of the photos he has been asked to take.

Earlier that same morning, a young Bill Way had received a call about a shooting, or ambush as it had been described to him. Warren Jones of the Tennessee Bureau of Investigation had asked the young photographer to go with him to a crime scene in a neighboring McNairy County. Way knew what Jones really wanted was for him to take some crime scene photographs, with the high-quality camera Way used in his job as a Memphis newspaper photographer. His camera would take far superior photos than the camera than the TBI issued camera Jones used. Still, Way was glad that the TBI Investigator had asked his assistance.

Now, more than an hour after having left Jackson Tennessee, where both Way and Jones lived, Way begins to take the photos that both he and Jones need..., Jones for his case file and Way for his newspaper.

The location is at Allen McCoy's store, an unassuming country store which had two gas pumps out front where they sold "Gulf" brand gasoline and carried some very basic grocery items. The store was on highway 45 in Eastview Tennessee, a small town which lies midway between Selmer, McNairy's county seat, and the infamous state line. This is the location where the ambushed car finally stopped.

Way immediately gets down to business, taking photos of the late model Plymouth Fury which had been shot up in the predawn ambush. The young photographer first takes pictures of the exterior of the car, which has all the side windows shot out. He takes photos of blood spatter on the grill, hood, outside of the windshield and top of the car. He photographs the vehicle from every possible angle.

After he is satisfied with the first photos he has snapped, he moves to the passenger's side of the vehicle to make some images of a now deceased body lying in the front seat. These will be important photos for the case file Jones will compile during his investigation. TBI Investigator Jones had informed Way during their drive from Jackson, that one of the parties who had been shot during the ambush had not survived, so Way knew he would have to photographically document the victim for Jones.

Way, by the very nature of his job as a newspaperman, has seen some horrific scenes over the past few years, accidents, murders, all kinds of nightmarish sights, but nothing he had witnessed in his past work had even remotely prepared him for what he would see this day.

As young Bill Way peers in the window from the passenger's side front window, he can see the body of a young woman lying in the front seat, her body semi stretched over toward the driver's side of the vehicle. As he snaps his photos, he thinks about her dying at such an early age... and dying in such a violent and tragic way.

Way takes several photos from this position, then decides a better angle might be possible from the driver's side of the car. Circling around the big Plymouth, Way raises his camera as he looks in the driver's window and prepares to snap the camera's shutter once again..., then he stops in total shock and paralysis, staring intensely at what he sees inside the car. He is stunned into almost total horror as about the only thing left of the young woman's head is her face. The top and back of her head are missing having been blown away by the blast of a high-powered rifle.

McNairy County Coroner Ward Moore, who also worked at the Shackelford Funeral Home, would later be the one to prepare the young woman's body for an open casket funeral ceremony. Moore would concur with Way's assessment of the woman's head trauma as he would tell that it took eight hours of labor-intensive work, using cotton and plaster of Paris to build something on which to place a wig as so much of her head was missing.

Sickened by the sight of the head trauma, Way somehow manages to regain his composure and continues to photograph the scene for Jones as well as his newspaper. All the photos would be given to Jones, many however, will be far too gruesome to be printed in a newspaper. Never again will the young photographer see a wound so devastating as the one he sees today.

Way now examines and photographs the inside of the car and how it is covered in blood. Blood was everywhere, along with bits of the victim's brain matter. It is on the seats, the car's interior headliner, the door panels, and the inside of the windshield. Everywhere Way looks there are the signs of death.

Attempting to put his emotions aside, Way documents everything. He photographs the bullet hole in the dash as well as the one in the windshield on the passenger side of the vehicle. He photographs some loose ammunition that was in the back floorboard of the car, the empty handgun holster that lays in the front seat, the young woman's shoes that lay neatly positioned on the passenger's side floorboard. He takes photos of authorities as they examine the vehicle... he shoots photographic images of everything Jones requests.

Eventually, the young woman's body is removed from the car and taken to Shackleford's Funeral Home. The Plymouth Fury will be towed to a location in Selmer for further examination by authorities investigating the shooting. The other victim has been taken to the hospital in Selmer before being transported on to Baptist Hospital in Memphis. The male victim has been shot in the chin but has survived thus far. The small medical facility in Selmer was ill equipped to handle a gunshot wound of this nature making it necessary to transport him to the more adequately staffed and equipped facility approximately ninety miles away.

Way's job is not finished here however, as this was simply where the driver had stopped after being shot. Way and Jones would now head several miles down highway 45, before turning back to the north on New Hope Road. The intersection where they make this turn is in the very heart of the infamous state line area. Jones and Way will now drive approximately four miles through the sparsely populated countryside to the site where the ambush is believed to have taken place.

As the two men arrive at the ambush site, a small crowd has gathered here as well, mostly law enforcement officials as well as a few onlookers, all curious about the shooting. The scene is that of a short and narrow bridge on a remote country road.

At this point in the investigation, law enforcement personnel have few details about the ambush and how it occurred. A couple of different caliber shell casings have been found on the bridge itself, but it is unclear if these have any connection to this morning's shooting. A McNairy County deputy is treading through weeds approximately ten yards west of the small bridge and declares that he has discovered what appears to be a "sniper's nest" from where he believes shots had been fired at the Plymouth Fury. It is little more than wishful and mistaken thinking on his part.

Way begins to photograph this scene even though there is not much to see. He photographs the bridge, the straightaway leading up to the bridge as well as the road on the south side of the bridge.

While taking these images, Way listens to investigators as they try to make sense of the ambush. The car itself had been hit several times while one victim had a facial wound and the young woman had been shot in the head twice. Investigators had found only two shell casings thus far and again they were not sure if these particular casings were even connected to this incident as they were different in caliber.

The tone of some of the investigators is beginning to change, Bill Way thinks to himself. All the law enforcement officers on site are familiar with the young couple who had been ambushed. Some think the ambush was real, while others disagreed, suggesting it was marital dispute gone bad, one that ended in murder. One of those suggesting the latter is Clifford Coleman, a former McNairy County Sheriff, who knew both the victims well.

Way then notices two young boys talking with one of the investigators, wondering why the officer is even giving them the time of day given the circumstances. He overhears one of the boys as he tries to convince the investigator that this is not where the ambush took place, saying there is another site down the road with broken glass and several shell casings on the shoulder of the roadway. While the officer seems dismissive of the young man's story, TBI Investigator Jones has his curiosity aroused. He has not seen much at this site to hold his interest and instinctively knows there is simply too much missing at this site for all of the ambush to have taken place here. Jones asks the young men to show him the site they are describing as just maybe, they are onto something.

A few minutes later, Jones, Way and a couple of the other investigators find themselves, along with the two boys, just a few yards north of the intersection of New Hope and Davis Yancy Roads. The location is two and one tenths miles south of the bridge, near Saint Rest Cemetery. Broken glass and several shell casings are there just as the boys said they would be, shifting the focus of the investigation to this site.

Way and others notice that the road has been recently maintained as the surface has been coated with a fresh layer of oil and chat. There is no shoulder on this country road, and it is clear to everyone that the ditches on each side of the road had recently been bladed out with heavy equipment leaving the ditches in an almost clean and pristine condition.

One of the boys points out to the investigators something he had found earlier. A piece of scalp with bloodied blond hair attached and, what appeared to be a piece of skull lying on top of it.

As investigators walk down the roadway visually scanning the road's surface and the surrounding area for other evidence when one of them spots something peculiar. In the ditch on the west side of the road was a small pile of human brains. Jones and others including former sheriff Clifford Coleman and County Coroner Ward Moore cannot help but think the brains had "been stacked," as if they had been intentionally placed there.

Also found on the roadway, about a foot from the ditch, is a matchbook cover from Hernando's Hideaway, a club located in Memphis. This was a night club that both victims were known to frequent, often not as a couple. Investigators wondered how and when the matchbook cover got to this particular spot and if it had anything to do with the shooting as it seemed so out of place on the freshly maintained road.

It does not take investigators long to check with the county road department to learn that the roadway had been maintained in just the last day or so, meaning the matchbook cover was left at this location very recently.

Way grabs his camera and begins to photograph everything at this site. One photograph is of a McNairy County Deputy looking at blood on the leaves of a roadside bush. It is obvious to everyone that this location is indeed a true crime scene.

It soon becomes clear to everyone present that this is the location where most, if not all, of the shooting took place. Details are sketchy as the victim who was shot in the chin has yet to be interviewed about the incident, leaving investigators to do guess work to figure out what had happened. Due to the nature and severity of the wound, it will be several hours before they can speak to the victim. Until then, all the investigators have to work with currently are the victim's car and the two possible ambush sites.

As you may have guessed by now, this is the story of McNairy County Sheriff Buford Hayes Pusser. The date is Saturday, August 12, 1967. This event will eventually propel Sheriff Buford Pusser to national fame. Books will be written, several movies and even a TV series will be made about this young sheriff. Most people consider this event, an alleged ambush that resulted in the death of his wife Pauline Pusser, as the pivotal moment that made his fame possible.

While the book "The Twelfth of August" launched Buford to fame, it was the movie "Walking Tall" that created a national sensation about the young sheriff's life and law enforcement career. More books would follow, and more movies would be made, but you simply must ask yourself if any of them tell the real story? The answer to that question will be quite surprising.

If you visit McNairy County, most of the people, especially those who lived there at the time when all of this happened, will tell you that the story you have always heard from the media has little or nothing to do with the truth. Many will tell you that lots of local people believe that Buford murdered his wife.

Many of these people will tell you that Buford was as corrupt as any of those he has vowed to arrest. Vowed to arrest, you ask? You see, many locals are quick to accurately point out that for all of the talk and hype about how Buford was supposed to have "cleaned up the state line," they can't name a single club he shut down or a major player he arrested and sent to prison. They will tell you that the young sheriff was part of the problem in McNairy County rather than being part of the solution.

any of the people involved in the law enforcement community at that time will point out the myths, legends and lies regarding Sheriff Pusser's law enforcement accomplishments. Many did not like Pusser, and some law enforcement agencies refused to work with him as they had grown wise to his ways and did not trust him. One local sheriff, Grady Bingham of Alcorn County Mississippi, would later publicly refer to Buford as a "thug."

So, what is the real story? Was he the great sheriff the books and movies made him out to be, or was he simply a county sheriff that had few checks and balances to monitor a man in his position, in a time when the sheriff was "King of the County"?

Many of the locals say Pusser was a bully, that he not only accepted payoffs from those he was supposed to arrest, but that he "demanded" such payments from them. It is said that he took the practice of shakedowns to a whole new level, which none of the locals had ever seen before or since. Did all of this have anything to do with Pauline Pusser's death?

"BUFORD PUSSER: The Other Story" is a tale told by people who lived their own parts of Buford's "real-life story." Many were friends of Buford's. Many are from the law enforcement community while others are from the "State Line" side of the story.

As you read this account, there is one piece of advice you should follow...., Forget EVERYTHING you think you know about the story, keep an open mind, and start with a clean slate regarding Sheriff Pusser and the "State Line Mob".

The real story is nothing like what you have read in books or seen in movies and this story comes from people who were there and lived it.

Bill Way, about the time frame in which I interviewed him about his story.

Chapter Two
The Legend and the Timeline

Most of us probably became fans of Buford Pusser due to the 1973 movie "Walking Tall". I became an instant admirer of Buford's after seeing this movie. To be clear, I of course, realized that there had to be a certain level of "creative licensing" when the film was made as some scenes were overly dramatic. It was however, an incredible and allegedly "true story" about the young Tennessee sheriff.

Having been in law enforcement myself, I had to wonder just how much of Buford's incredible story could be true. I started digging, looking on the internet for information, researching old newspaper stories and magazine articles as I found them, even joining forums that dealt with his story.

One of these forums led me to my first good contact with the real story. I was on a forum called "Firing Line" where a lot of law enforcement officers and gun enthusiasts go to discuss firearms. The topic I became involved in one evening was one about a .25 caliber semiautomatic handgun. One police officer on the forum proclaimed it was like the one Pauline Pusser had often carried. The name Pusser grabbed my attention. As I read the thread, just about everyone on the forum began to post about Buford and what a magnificent sheriff he had been.

Finally, I decided to post a little information on this forum that I had learned about Buford and compare that to what we saw in the movie "Walking Tall." There simply is extraordinarily little comparison between the facts and the movie. I suspect, some of the readers were intrigued by what I had to say, while others were belligerent toward my posts, some insisting he was a true national hero.

Shortly after I had posted this, my phone rang displaying an out of state number that I did not recognize. Even though it was quite late in the evening I answered the call. The caller was asking where I got my information about Buford. He said it was as close to the truth as he had heard anyone speak. I explained that I had been researching the Pusser legend for some time and had some profoundly serious doubts about its accuracy. Having been somewhat coy about his identity, the caller finally gave me his name..., Dennis Hathcock. You may not be familiar with his name, but you may have heard of his father, W.O. Hathcock, who had owned the Plantation Club where Buford claimed to have been beaten, carved up, robbed and thrown out into the rain to die.

Over the next couple of weeks Dennis and I would speak, almost nightly, as I interviewed him about Pusser and events at the state line. I would finally travel to Selmer to meet with him.

We met at the courthouse where Pusser's office and jail had once been.

I felt Dennis had to be authentic as he soon began to introduce me to others who, much like himself, were a part of Buford's story. These were people from both sides of the story. There was a host of players from the state line side as well as many people from the law enforcement side of the story.

As I interviewed several of these people over time, I couldn't help but notice just how much their stories seemed to agree. Odd, I thought, that both sides would be telling stories that so closely matched. I spent four days with Hathcock and learned a great deal from him and others. I must admit that at one point while investigating Buford's story, I became disillusioned by what I was learning, and almost stopped researching this story.

Suddenly however, I realized that each of these people I was interviewing had such interesting stories of their own that I began building a timeline. Each of these people had lived their own part in Buford's incredible legend. Their stories developed into a pattern and I started connecting the dots to pull all of this into a much larger story than just Buford's.

For you to better understand "BUFORD PUSSER: The Other Story," you need to look at how he became a legend through erroneous books and movies. The real story is quite different. Once you compare the books and movies to real events you may have a different view about Buford.

The Legend...

The legend of Buford Pusser is one of those that absolutely holds your attention.

*   An under aged Buford, at a bar, witnessed Louise Hathcock kill a sailor.
*   Buford was a Marine for 3 years.
*   Buford was attacked, cut up and left for dead at a state line club.
*   Buford barely defeated a dead sheriff in the 1964 Sheriff's race.
*   Buford, almost single handedly, "cleaned up the state line."
*   Buford carried a "big stick."
*   He "couldn't be bought" by the criminals as other sheriffs had been.
*   Destroyed 88 moonshine stills in 1965. Made 7,500 arrests in his six years as sheriff
*   Seven attempts were made on his life while sheriff.
*   He was shot eight times while sheriff of McNairy County and stabbed seven times
*   Had his jaw blown away during the August 12th ambush.
*   Required 16 surgeries to repair the damage to his face from the ambush.
*   Killed three of the four men who ambushed him and killed his wife.
*   Was killed in a car accident at the hands of the state liners.

The dynamics of "The Other Story", or what I have been told is the real story by those who actually lived it with Buford, is one where I suggest you take a step back and take a hard look at the story's timeline. You need to understand the early years that shaped his life and move forward to the time of his death, and for that matter, even after that as the legend does not really end there.

When we examine the writings of W.R. Morris in "The Twelfth of August" and compare that to what we saw in the movie "Walking Tall," you see the glaring difference in the story lines, leaving you to wonder which story, if either, were actually true. Now, you have an opportunity to compare that to the real story as told by many others who were there and lived it as well. When you make these comparisons with an open mind; the legend quickly begins to fade.

Timeline....

Born December 12, 1937 between Finger and Leapwood Tennessee, a small farming community in northeast McNairy County, Buford Hayes Pusser was the youngest of Carl and Helen Pusser's three children. He had a brother, John Howard, and a sister Gaylia.
Life could be tough for the Pusser family in the economically depressed county in which they lived. Wages in the area were low and few good jobs were to be found in an area that depended on farming and moonshining for most people to make a simple bare bones living. To say the area was desperately poor would have been seen as a compliment to many who lived there. Just about everyone in the area was "dirt Poor," including the Pusser's.

Carl Pusser had a family to support so he farmed, worked at a sawmill, and occasionally did some day work whenever it was available. Stories told by those who knew Carl, suggest that He did a fair amount of moonshining as well. The Pussers eventually moved to Adamsville while Buford was still in elementary school. Helen landed a job at a local shirt manufacturing facility and after a while she also served as a union steward there. The family was now making the small town of Adamsville their home.

As a child, Buford had the reputation of being a bit of a mama's boy. He didn't let Helen out of his sight. Helen Pusser would even tell in one interview that when Buford was about ten or eleven years old, he liked to dress up in woman's clothing, even wearing high heel shoes. Buford finally seemed to be developing into a typical kid, however, there were other early warning signs of trouble that were missed by those close to him, signs that Buford had a very dark side which indicated a propensity toward acts of violence and cruelty.

As an example, as a youngster, one of Buford's favorite activities was to ride around Adamsville on his bicycle and shoot "stray dogs" with his CO_2 pistol, so said a museum placard by the display of the gun that he is said to have used. That gun used to be available for viewing at The Pusser Home and Museum in Adamsville. The museum used to have Buford's CO_2 pistol housed in one of the many display cases along with the placard explaining this particular practice of young Buford. It has since been removed.

Psychology Today, a magazine written by mental health professionals, has reported that studies done since the 1970's, have established a link between cruelty to animals as a youth, often lead to far more serious acts of violence as an adult. In fact, they report that a vast majority of the worst criminals in our nation's recent history, those involved in murder, many of them serial killers, all have in their profiles, information stating that their acts of violence commenced during their youth, with acts of cruelty to animals.

One must wonder just how many "stray dogs" Buford shot and how many were actually someone's household pet? Just how many stray dogs were there to be found in such a small community, as Adamsville had a small population of less than a thousand people at that time. Enough about this for now, as you will later see how this behavior pattern of Buford's comes into play in his life as an adult.

During his high school years, Buford seemed to be academically challenged and described as a very mediocre student, something that his report cards at the museum would confirm. He was however a standout athletically, playing on both the high school's football and basketball teams. Even in his high school years, he was said to be quite the physical specimen and he did excel in sports. Newspaper clippings and his yearbook show that he did his school and the town of Adamsville proud.

As a high school student, Buford would work for Charlie Duren, one of the local merchants in Adamsville. Ironically, this very building where Buford worked as a teen aged store clerk, would later house his office when he became Adamsville's Chief of Police.

Stories have been written about Buford's teenage years, one suggesting that Buford's first exposure to the infamous state line was when he and some high school buddies wanted a little taste of adventure and excitement and made a visit to the state line's infamous "White Iris." The state line was an area along the Tennessee and Mississippi border.

Busy highway 45 in the southernmost part of the county. It had the reputation as the place to go, if you were looking for a little booze, entertainment..., or trouble. W.R. Morris would write in his book "The Twelfth of August" that Buford would visit the White Iris where he and his friends would see Louise Hathcock kill a young sailor with a ball peen hammer. The time frame on this event would be about 1955 or 1956. Is the story true? Oddly enough, the White Iris wasn't even operating until the early 60's.

Lt Kenneth Wayne McCoy

Lt McCoy in his aircraft

1st Lt Kenneth McCoy in his aircraft circa 55-56

McCoy in flight School

Prior to his death 2012

Kenneth Wayne McCoy would tell his sons about that day when he was attacked at a state line joint. He would tell them that he observed some cheating going on in a dice game. His son Earl would tell me that his dad was a self described cocky Naval Aviator.

McCoy confronted the cheater of his observations. McCoy was then himself confronted by a man who was later identified as Towhead White. White wanted to settle their difference so they drove to a lonely county road. As McCoy was getting out of his car Towhead hit the unsuspecting aviator in the back of the head knocking him unconscious, after which McCoy was unmercifully kicked and beaten. McCoy was taken to a Memphis hospital for care and recovery. Contrary to Buford's story about this event, McCoy recalled the location as being The 45 Grill and Louise Hathcock was nowhere to be seen during the attack. Kenneth McCoy lived until November 6, 2012, showing that Buford's story about this incident was just another lie to embellish his own story as well as the reputations of the state liners.

There was an investigation and Towhead would allegedly be arrested and serve three months of a six months sentence in the McNairy County Jail, his jail time however has not been confirmed to be true. It is important to note that Louise Hathcock was not arrested or charged as she was never implicated in this violent act. Pusser advocates will say a young Buford Pusser was simply mistaken that McCoy was dead. If this was the case, why did Buford never correct his story. This was the beginning of a long list if lies and embellishments simply meant to create a bigger legend than Buford actually earned.

W.R. Morris claimed that during the two years he was writing "The Twelfth of August," he spent much of his time with Buford as the young Pusser, now the Sheriff of McNairy County, was telling Morris his life's story. Buford would eventually claim however, that he hardly even knew Morris, even though Morris would claim his book was Buford's official authorized biography and a contract allowing Morris to write about Pusser's life would soon surface. Once again Buford was caught in yet another lie.

Stories such as Buford's visit to the state line and the White Iris in particular is far different than the one Morris told. Stories such as these however became the cornerstones for building a reputation for not only what a hero Buford was, but to add to and exaggerate the existing reputation of the state line's history of violence as well. This would all later serve to build Buford's legend. Unfortunately, many of us would believe this and other stories like it, as being factual.

It has been established that Buford dropped out of school for a while during his junior year, taking a job on the pipeline in Oklahoma to make some "good money." This job however, turned out to be far more than he had bargained for, so he returned to Adamsville and school, graduating in 1956.

After graduation, Buford thought a military career might be where he was destined to be. In the movie "Walking Tall" there is a scene where Buford's wife, Pauline, references that Buford had spent three years in the Marine Corp. Many would of course accept this as fact; however, his actual discharge papers would show that he received a medical discharge due to asthma and that he left Paris Island in South Carolina before he even completed boot camp. He never really was a full-fledged Marine. It is difficult to say exactly why the movie company chose to make such a misrepresentation about his military service. One can only assume that this intentional embellishment was meant to bolster his character in the movie.

After his early discharge from the Marine Corp in 1956, comes another one of those stories that are entirely baseless and without fact. This story was also used to build his image even more in both books and movies.

W.R. Morris would write in his book "The Twelfth of August" about Buford arriving home after being discharged from the Marine Corp and making a visit to the "Plantation Club" on the Mississippi side of the state line, to do a little gambling. This club was owned by W.O. Hathcock.

The story goes that on a night in late February 1957, Buford had become involved in a game of dice, when he accused the game's operator of cheating. Buford was allegedly attacked by multiple assailants and was beaten, kicked in the head, cut up and thrown out the door of the club in a pouring rain, where he lay bleeding on the gravel parking lot. He was robbed of three hundred dollars of his mustering out pay from his short stint with the Marine Corp.

Finally summoning enough strength to get up, Morris would write that Buford would drive himself to a clinic in McNairy County. The story continues, saying he was injured so badly that it required one hundred and ninety-two stitches to close the wounds on his face and head. This story differs however, from the version as shown in the movie "Walking Tall" where Buford makes a visit to the state line with his old high school buddy Lutie McVeigh. They go into a club called the "Lucky Spot" (Plantation Club) where Lutie tries to impress Buford with his gambling skills.

Losing at the game of chance however, Lutie borrows money from Buford to stay in a dice game. Buford is watching the game operator closely since it is his money on the table. Buford sees the man switch dice and Lutie loses, leading Buford to confront the games operator. A fight breaks out and state liners come from every direction to fight Buford.

The movie version shows that Buford holds his own for a while but is finally too outnumbered to win the brawl. He is pinned to a table by multiple attackers, his shirt ripped open and his chest is savagely carved up with a switchblade by one of the club's thug employees at the behest of the club's owner. The movie next shows Buford laying on the roadside in the pouring rain, his clothing soaked in blood from the wounds in his chest, as he attempts to flag down passing motorists for help.

Much like W.R. Morris' version of the story, there is no evidence that this ever happened either. We will also visit this alleged incident in far more detail in another chapter as well. These tall tales appear to be nothing more than stories told to enhance Pusser's reputation. In this day in age, if either story were true, we would surely find some proof on the internet. Even the Pusser Home and Museum in Adamsville has no proof to back either version of these stories.

In Pusser's real story, Buford soon found work as an ambulance driver, and helped with funerals during his employment with Shackelford Funeral Home. The job at the funeral home was one Buford was said to have enjoyed, as some of those who knew him said death seemed to somehow intrigue and fascinate Buford.

He in fact, was suddenly be terminated from his job in September 1957 for reasons that still are unclear. Many locals suggest the reason for his termination, involved some inappropriate behavior with bodies, however since they offer no proof to back these accusations, there is no point in dwelling on the subject as even those who worked with Buford at that time refused to comment or define this "inappropriate behavior" as I interviewed them.

Once again looking for employment and wanting more than McNairy County could seem to offer at the time. Buford would leave home and head for Chicago, following many other young men who had left McNairy County and the surrounding area. His hope was to find better paying jobs and more opportunities in the distant city while he followed yet another dream of attending morticians school.

Buford went to work at the Union Bag Company, where some of his friends from McNairy County were employed. He was hired to operate a die cutting machine. This job paid approximately three times what he was paid working at Shackleford Funeral Home bank in McNairy County. It certainly helped pay the bills while he attended morticians school at Worsham College of Mortuary Science in Wheeling Illinois, a suburb of Chicago.

Despite the attack he had allegedly experienced at the Plantation Club back at the state line, Buford still enjoyed the excitement of the night life and everything it had to offer. The nightlife in Chicago was unlike anything he had seen at the state line and he was drawn to it. He is even said to have worked as a bouncer in an establishment there.

Rumor has it that another young man from the state line area also worked at the same bar. Make no mistake, as while this rumor has not been fully vetted or confirmed, records do show that Buford and a young man named Carl Douglas White did indeed live in the area at that time. This was verified through information contained in White's FBI file. Ironically, the same Carl Douglas "Towhead" White would one day be known as "The Al Capone of the South" and would operate a business at the state line in McNairy County ..., while Buford served as sheriff.

Wanting to increase his income even further and being the physical specimen that he was along with his natural athletic abilities, Buford took an interest in professional wrestling. His interest in mortician school soon waned, with Buford eventually dropping out.

He wrestled under the name of "Buford the Bull" and was said to be one of the top wrestlers on the Chicago circuit. It is said that it was during his wrestling career in Chicago that Buford met his future wife, Pauline Mullins Vance. Pauline was an attractive, petite woman and a mother of two children, Diane and Mike, from an earlier marriage to Pete Vance.

Rumors persist however, that Pauline was an exotic dancer at the establishment where Buford was employed as a bouncer. Regardless of which, if either, might be correct, their romance was short as the two were married just a few weeks later in December of 1959.

Buford now had a wife and a ready made family with two children. He has a steady job at the Union Bag Company..., it is now just weeks before Christmas in 1959. This is the same period in which the Plantation Club back on the Mississippi side of the state line is robbed and the club's owner, W.O. Hathcock is almost murdered by three men.

Keep in mind that it has been almost three years since Buford was allegedly beaten, cut up and robbed at this same club. The movie "Walking Tall" suggests that Buford, acting alone, returned to and robbed the "Lucky Spot" (Plantation Club) using nothing but a big stick as a weapon as he took back the money he alleged they had once stolen from him in February 1957.

The facts of the real story indicate however, that Buford Pusser and two other men would be arrested in Chicago, just weeks later, in January of 1960 for the robbery of the club and attempted murder of its owner. So, why did the movie show Buford as acting alone?

Most people have never heard the names, Jerry Wright or that of Marvin King Jr, yes, the same Jerry Wright and Marvin King Jr that also worked with Buford at the Union Bag & Paper Company. These were Buford's two accomplices in the robbery and attempted murder that Walking Tall never mentioned. Likewise, most people do not know that the club's owner suggested that it was actually Marvin King Jr, not Buford Pusser, that struck Hathcock with a blunt object, possibly the butt of a gun rather than a "big stick" as was shown in the movie.

These three men would stand trial together in Corinth Mississippi, the county seat of Alcorn County where the crime had occurred, not in McNairy County as the movie suggested.

Once again, all of this will be covered in far more detail in another chapter as all I am attempting to do here is correct the timeline of the story.

Hopefully, you now have a far better understanding of how the timeline of events played out and how so many stories have been scrambled and embellished.

I suggest that you should "forget everything you THINK you know" about Buford Pusser and the state line, as you can see the real story is quite different from the legend as told in books and movies.

In "BUFORD PUSSER: The Other Story," I will give you a more exact timeline as well as a lot of new information obtained from people who were there and lived their own part of this story. You will be asking yourself why Buford's story differs so much from others who were there with him, people from both sides of the story.

There well may be some new evidence disseminated in the hope that you will better understand what actually occurred in McNairy County and at the state line. You will hopefully see just how easy it is for this legend to be manufactured while being misconstrued as a "true story." You will have information to help you understand how all these false and or highly overstated stories were used to turn Buford Pusser into a national hero.

Chapter 3
Robbery at the Plantation Club

It is Saturday in Chicago Illinois, the date is December 12th, 1959. Buford, and two friends from the Union Bag Company have a road trip planned, one that will take Buford, Marvin king Jr, both of Adamsville and Jerry Wright of Selmer back home to the Tennessee / Mississippi state line. (Source, local newspapers).

Not wanting to miss a day's pay, they made arrangements for a friend at work to punch their time cards in their absence from their workplace.

This will not be a pleasure trip for the three men. Their plan is to be in and out of the state line area in a very brief amount of time. They don't want to be seen while they are back in Buford's home territory. Why? Because the three men plan to rob W.O. Hathcock's Plantation Club.

This Mississippi club is a popular place at the state line. Each night there is music and dancing, plenty to drink and the club is known as the place to be at the state line. There are of course, other places at the state line..., such as the Shamrock which was almost directly across the highway.

One, if not the only photo of the Plantation Club.

The Shamrock Restaurant is also on the Mississippi side of the border while the Shamrock Motel is just a few feet away, barely inside Tennessee. The Shamrock was built by Jack and Louise Hathcock..., W.O.'s aunt and uncle. It is a different operation than the Plantation Club, as the Plantation is where live entertainment and dancing is a draw on weekend nights. The Shamrock Restaurant and Motel is known by locals as a place where hard liquor can be bought even though the sale of hard liquor is illegal in McNairy County. It generally draws a different kind of crowd than the Plantation Club, especially on those weekend nights.

Yes, if you are looking for entertainment, the Plantation Club is indeed the place to be and Buford knows this. He has been there a few times and has seen the crowds that visit the Plantation Club. He has seen with his own eyes the club's overflowing parking lot with a line of cars, often a quarter of a mile long parked on the shoulder of highway 45. He has seen people walking the distance to get inside the club, just as he has also watched them later, often staggering their way back to their vehicles. Buford knows that W.O. must be taking in a small fortune each night the club's doors were open, and Buford has decided he needs some of that fortune.

His plan is a simple one. Drive down to the state line at night, avoid seeing anyone you might know, or who might know or recognize you. Buford knows he can avoid people by arriving at the club just before it closes for the night. He and his two buddies will go in just before the place locks up for the night, and they plan to be the last ones out..., with W.O.'s money.

Following Buford's plan, the three men leave Chicago early on Saturday evening, driving more than five hundred miles through the night to arrive at the state line between 2:00 and 3:00 am Sunday morning. The trip will take about eight and half hours to drive each way. They intend to be back in Chicago by Sunday afternoon.

After driving for several hours, the three finally reach their destination and pull into the now almost empty parking lot as most of the patrons have left for the night. Buford and his two friends walk inside the club, surveying it as they proceed to a table on the dance floor, each ordering something to drink as they wait for the few remaining customers to filter out of the building. In the meantime, Buford strikes up a conversation with W.O.

Buford, eventually leaving his table and moving to the bar area with his two friends as he examines and buys a .32 caliber handgun from Hathcock for $25.00.

While W.O. has operated the club for some time now, he is actually a watchmaker by trade. As such, he knows the value of watches, jewelry, coins, antiques, and many other items, including guns. He is known by many in the community as a "trader of fine things" as he is often dealing in these various items.

By this time, it is just the four of them left in the club..., Buford, Wright, King and of course W.O.. It is nearing 5:00 am. and everyone one else had gone for the night. Larece, W.O.'s wife, retired a little earlier to the Hathcock's personal living quarters in the back of the club. Two of Hathcock's employees, Nita Godwin and Billy Joe Robinson have just left as well.

It has been a long evening for W.O., and he is tired, after all it is late, or very early depending on your point of view, but his three remaining guests are still sitting in the bar. The inside of the Plantation Club is shaped in a rectangle form, with the bar area on one side with a four-foot pony wall which separates it from the dance floor. There is only a tiny backroom to store supplies for the bar. It is barely big enough to hold the supplies the Plantation Club can go through on a busy weekend. The club's restrooms are accessed from the outside of the building. Of course, in the back of the building is the Hathcock's small onsite living quarters. Competition could be fierce in the state line area, forcing club owners to keep someone on location at all times. If you left your place unattended for any length of time, one of your friendly competitors might just burn you out.... thus, the need for onsite living accommodations.

There is no casino area in the club as was shown in Walking Tall. This alleged casino area was a complete fabrication for the purpose of spicing up the movie and adding drama.

Seeing that his last three guests are in no hurry to leave, W.O. decides to give them a subtle hint as he leaves the three men at the bar where they are now seated, to walk over to the jukebox on the far end of the dance floor.

As W.O. grabs the music machine's power cord and pulls it from the electrical outlet, the music slows as the volume fades to silence. He turns to walk back to the bar area, he immediately notices that only Pusser and Wright remain at the bar. As Hathcock walks past the four-foot pony wall, he feels a crushing blow to the back of his head as he crumples to the floor.

As the bar owner slowly regains consciousness, he realizes he is now alone in the room, lying in a pool of his own blood. His shoulder and neck are in excruciating pain. His thinking process still impaired by the blow to his head, W.O. slowly becomes aware that he was unable to move his arms and legs.

As his mind begins to clear, he realizes that his three assailants have hogtied his hands and feet behind his back. He calls out to Larece for help, but he can't make enough noise to get her attention as he has been gagged with his own handkerchief. W.O. wiggles and twists his wrists but it seems as if it takes an eternity for him to free himself from his bindings. In great pain, and feeling somewhat exhausted, he simply lays there on the floor, all beaten and bloodied before trying to untie his legs which are bound at the ankles. Finally, he is free.
The injured club owner attempts to get on his feet but his body rebels against these efforts. Still lying on the floor and in extreme pain, he slowly starts to drag his body toward his living

quarters and his wife Larece. It was an extremely slow process as he has the use of only one arm as his neck and shoulder injury prohibited the use of his other limb. He realizes now, that during the assault, someone had stepped on his neck in a failed attempt to break it.

He leaves a dark red trail across the floor as he pulls his torso and legs through the blood which is still gushing from the gash in the back of his head. Finally, he reaches his living quarters. All he has to do now is make his way up the three steps to get to the door and get Larece's attention and aid. In his weakened and injured state, this is more of a task than he had first anticipated. He slowly conquers the first step, then manages to drag himself up the second step. Almost there, he reaches for the door that separates himself from help, when he hears a welcome sound, that of his Pomeranian barking incessantly at the noise it hears on the opposite side of the front door.

A photo of the bar area inside the Plantation Club with W.O. behind the bar. A young Dennis Hathcock is in the foreground of the photo.

Suddenly, the door opens and Larece sees her husband laying on the steps.

Wasting no time, she helps him get inside the living quarters, examines his injuries, and quickly gives him what little care she can. Fully understanding that W.O. is in need of immediate medical attention, she calls Doctor Frank Davis, who tells her to get W.O. to the hospital as soon as possible, telling the frantic Larece that he will meet her and W.O. there.

Larece rushes outside to their car and cranks on the cold engine of their 1957 Oldsmobile 98 until it starts on this frozen December morning. With the engine now running, she turns on the defroster to clear the frozen mist that covers the windshield. Rushing back inside she somehow manages to help her husband to the car. Larece, still unclear about exactly what had happened to W.O., heads to the hospital in nearby Corinth.

Dr. Davis is already waiting at the hospital when his patient arrives. W.O. would be treated for injuries to his neck and shoulder and would be hospitalized for two weeks as the result of his injuries from the brutal attack.

Meanwhile, Alcorn County Constable Cleveland Marlar, upon learning of the robbery and assault, starts his investigation into the incident. He travels the short distance from Corinth to the Plantation Club to get a look at the scene. There, he finds the pull cord to the hanging electric light in the bar area that had been used to bind W.O.'s hand and feet. In the middle of the floor lay what may be his best clue however, a handkerchief with a laundry marker still attached. Ironically, the marker would be linked back to a Chicago laundry and his assailants.

W.O. is in no condition to leave the hospital, so as Marlar finds suspects he takes them to the hospital for possible identification. One such suspect is a local man who is back in from working on the pipeline and has not been back to the state line area for quite some time. He was at the Shamrock Restaurant having a cup of coffee when he was summarily taken to the hospital to see if W.O. could identify him as one of the assailants.

He enters W.O.'s room and is surprised to see W.O. appearing so battered. W.O. gives him a slight smile, something a little unusual for W.O. to do, and greets the man, telling the officer that this individual was not involved in the robbery and assault. Constable Marlar will be tenacious in his investigation, continuing to bring suspects to W.O. for identification.

Rumor has it however, that it was actually one of Pusser's own relatives who informed authorities that Buford and his two friends had robbed W.O. and attempted to kill him, but like so many other state line stories, this has been difficult to confirm, especially after so many years have passed.

Regardless, on the evening of January 4, 1960, there is a knock on the door at 4754 North

Magnolia Street in Chicago. When Pauline answered the door, there stood two Chicago
law enforcement officers asking to speak with Buford. Buford steps to the door and asks why
they were there? The officers explain they were there to take him into custody for Alcorn County
Mississippi on charges of robbery as well as assault with intent to murder. Buford is handcuffed
and taken to the city jail where he goes through the usual booking process, including being
photographed and fingerprinted. Wright and King would go through the same process.
The three suspects are held in separate cells for the next three days, until Alcorn County Sheriff
Hillie Coleman and his brother Deputy L.W. Coleman arrive from Corinth on Jan7, 1960 to
transport the three men back to Mississippi to stand trial.

The Plantation Club robbery was big news in the local newspaper.

Marvin King Jr 26, Buford Pusser 22, and Jerry Wright arrested for Plantation club
robbery. A week and a half later, on January 19th, Pusser, Wright and King have a hearing
before Alcorn County Mississippi Judge T Raymond Jarvis regarding the charges pending
against them.

All three men answer "not guilty" when asked how they wish to plead to the charges filed against them. All three men are "true billed" that same day and held over for trial.

Hold Three Men Corinth Robbery

CORINTH, Miss. (AP) — Three men charged in the Dec. 12 armed robbery of an Alcorn County nightclub owner were under arrest in Corinth today.

Sheriff Hillie Coleman said he has brought back the three from Chicago, where they were arrested by police Jan. 4.

The three are Marvin King Jr., 26, and Buford Pusser, 22, both of Adamsville, Tenn., and Jerry Wright, 22, of Selmer, Tenn.

The three have denied the charges, their attorney, Carey Stovall of Corinth, reported.

In the robbery, W. O. Hathcock Jr., owner of the nightspot, was badly beaten and robbed of $1,000 hospitalized for two weeks.

The three were bound over to the Jan. 18 session of the Alcorn County grand jury.

Judge Jarvis would prove to be benevolent however, considering the nature of the charges against each of the men, setting bail at $4500 on the robbery charge and only $3000 on the charge of assault with the intent to murder.

Carl Pusser is quick to arrange for Buford's bail. The older Pusser had contacted George and Clyde King, a couple of farming implement dealers in Corinth who agree to post bail for Buford.

During Buford's trial, the charge of robbery is the first to be addressed by the court, with the charge of assault with the intent to murder to be heard later. As the trial on the robbery charge begins, the three defendants were represented by Attorneys Carey Stovall and Jimmie Price. Prosecution will handle by District Attorney N.S. "Soggy" Sweat and County Attorney H.M. Ray. The trial that was about to take place will be absolutely nothing like the dramatic one you saw in Walking Tall.

The prosecution lays out its case with Hathcock giving details of what had happened on the night in question. They tell the court that the three men stole a metal box containing the night's receipts. $1,176.00 was taken. W.O. Hathcock on the stand states that the three defendants took $100.00 he had in his pocket; the rest was in the metal box.

W.O. goes on to tell that he knew Wright and Pusser as both had been to the club previously. He says that he had not seen King before that night. W.O. would tell friends later that he would have remembered Pusser due to his almost freakish size. He would also tell friends and family that he had no idea why Pusser hated him so much.

Buford's attorney Stovall, asks W.O. during cross examination, how he could know who bound and gagged him if he had already been rendered unconscious? Hathcock replies, "because they were the only persons in the club who could have done it," causing a little laughter from those in the crowded courtroom at Stovall's expense.

Larece Hathcock would tell what she knew about that night, that Pusser, Wright and King had arrived at the club around 3:00 am. She, like W.O., would testify that she knew Pusser and Wright from previous visits. She knew however that she had never laid eyes on King according to newspaper reports.

Larece stated that the three came in and sat at a table on the dance floor. She said that she retired to the living quarters around 4:30 am and the three men were still in the club at that time. She was unaware of the assault and robbery until she found her battered husband. Stovall did not cross examine Larece Hathcock.

Next, the District Attorney calls Doctor Frank Davis. The doctor describes the nature of Hathcock's injuries adding that W.O. had been confined to the hospital for two weeks because of the injuries he received from the assault.

Hillie Coleman is the next to take the stand. He testifies that at the time of the robbery and assault that he was a deputy for Alcorn County (he has since become Sheriff), and that he had been in the club prior to the incident and saw the three defendants there.

He stated that he recognized only Pusser, but not Wright or King. When asked, he replies he has never arrested Pusser before, though he thought of him as a troublemaker.

During cross examination, Defense Attorney Stovall asks if he thought it strange that Hathcock would sell a gun to Pusser. Coleman doesn't seem to offer an opinion.

Alcorn County Courthouse where Pusser, Wright and King stood trial

Finally, the last two witnesses for the prosecution, Billy Joe Robinson, and Nita Godwin, are called to the stand and both place Pusser, Wright and King as being at the club during the early morning hours just before the robbery and assault, testifying that Pusser was the only one of the three they knew.

Defense attorney Stovall is quick to ask each if they were employed at the Plantation Club, knowing full well that they were. This of course is just a calculated move on Stovall's part to try and disqualify their testimony in the eyes of the jury as they are "loyal employees" of Hathcock's.

The prosecution believes they had made their case for the jury. They had shown that the three who stood accused, even by their own admissions, were nowhere near Chicago at the time of the robbery and assault, that they had in fact traveled southward from Chicago to Anna Illinois.

The prosecution has shown that even with the accused family members and friends vouching for the three men's whereabouts , there is still a sixteen hour window where no one can say exactly where Pusser, Wright and King actually were...., except for John Pusser, Buford's older brother who claims to have accompanied them on the trip. Oddly however, if the older Pusser had been with them and could he now vouch for their whereabouts as so many others placed the three defendants inside the club..., the question lingered as to where was John Pusser at the time of the robbery as no one has mentioned him being at the Plantation Club?

The prosecutors pointed out that these witness's statements matched up a little too well and appeared to have been contrived. They also had questions regarding the alibi that the three men were "visiting a friend" in Anna Illinois, questioning why anyone would make a round trip of over 600 miles without first verifying that friend would be home?

Even the accused have admitted they did not see the friend they had gone to visit, seemingly nullifying this story as well. The list goes on with the prosecutors having established that Pusser and his friends were indeed at the state line through the testimony of W.O. and Larece Hathcock as well as that of employees Robinson and Godwin, and more importantly, then Alcorn Deputy Sheriff Hillie Coleman who also placed them inside the establishment on the morning in question.

Then there is the handkerchief, the one with the laundry marker from Chicago, found on the floor of the Plantation Club where the assault had taken place. Their case seems almost air tight. Surely, they think, this will be enough evidence to convince a jury from the buckle of the bible belt, that the three men are guilty of the crimes they have been charged with.

Finally, it is time for the defense to present their case and their own witnesses. Buford, of course, repeats his story that they made the trip to Anna Illinois, not the state line and more specifically the Plantation Club, as they had been accused of. He indicates that he was accompanied by his wife Pauline, to whom he had been married for about a week at the time of the robbery. Also, with him were his older brother John Pusser along with Wright and King. He says that they had left Chicago around 6:00pm, arriving in Anna around 2:00 am. He testifies they had planned the trip to Anna for several days, but never mentioned why they had failed to notify their friend that they were coming for a visit. Pusser indicated that upon not finding his friend at home, they returned to Chicago.

When asked, Buford also admits he had been to the Plantation Club previously, the last time being in mid-October with Jerry Wright, when they were on vacation. Buford would continue to deny that he or the others were anywhere near the state line when the December 13th robbery occurred.

Of course, the other defense witnesses back every word has Buford said. They are in such perfect harmony; it is if they are singing in a concert. It is as if their many voices seem as though they are one.

Both the prosecutors and the defense attorneys are watching the jury closely, searching their faces and their body language for any sign which might give them a hint as to which way they are leaning with their impending verdict.

Finally, the three men's time cards from the Union Bag Company are presented into evidence. The cards indicate that all three men had worked their full shift before they left Chicago on their trip, making it nearly impossible for them to have driven to the state line and then back to Chicago as the prosecution team want the jury to believe the three had done.

During closing arguments, District Attorney Sweat reminds the jurors that the accused's stories simply seemed "too pat" to be believable. He suggested that the defendants had collaborated on the story about going to Anna Illinois, to "visit a friend," driving 300 miles each way to visit a someone that wasn't home and wasn't even expecting them. Sweat points out that the defendants had been seen by several people at the Plantation Club, one of them being Hillie Coleman..., a man who wore a badge and one who had dedicated his life to enforcing the law. Could so many eyewitnesses possibly be so wrong?

He reminded the jurors that W.O. Hathcock was injured so severely that he spent two weeks in the hospital recovering from the beating he took.

Sweat now wishes that he had earlier made a case that the robbery and the assault were an act of revenge for the alleged beating Pusser had allegedly been subjected to back in February 1957. He knows however, he can not make this argument as he had no evidence that it ever happened. There are no police reports, no medical records or evidence, no photos of an injured Buford Pusser and no witnesses to the alleged event. To mention it might only serve to play into the defendant's hands.

Finally, Sweat asks the jurors to do the right thing, suggesting that in view of the insurmountable evidence against the three men, he can't see how twelve honest, law-abiding people can do anything but return a verdict of guilty.

Stovall on the other hand, has to do little more than point to the time cards of the three men, reminding the jurors it is nearly impossible for the three men to have been near the state line.

It is around 6:00 pm when Judge Jarvis gives the case to the jury. The jurors meet for a couple of hours before taking a dinner break. Shortly afterwards they give their verdict to the judge on the robbery charge. Sitting on pins and needles the gallery finally hears the verdict.

NOT GUILTY...

In this trial, there were no dramatic courtroom scenes as were shown in the movie Walking Tall, such as the one where Buford ripped off his shirt, showing the jurors a chest full of scars..., why? Because he had no such scars.

Buford never raised his voice to the jurors as he did in the movie version of the trial, telling them "if you let them do this to me and get away with it, you give the eternal right to do the same damn thing to any one of you." Instead, Buford was well behaved..., just hoping to avoid serving time at Parchman..., Mississippi's infamous state prison.

` There was of course, the pending charge for assault with the intent to murder that had not been heard yet, but the prosecution team had to be realistic. If they could not convince a jury that Buford and his friends had robbed the Plantation Club, just how could they, using the same evidence, convince a jury that the three men had tried to kill W.O. Hathcock? As such, the charges on this case were dropped.

Years later, newspaper reporter Ellie Grossman would tell how Buford was singing a different tune, admitting that he, Wright and King had a friend punch their time cards at the Union Bag Company on the day in question, also admitting they did indeed go to the Plantation Club and committed the acts they had been accused of. By then, nobody really cared about the truth as the movie Walking Tall had made Buford a living legend.

Three photos of Buford with none showing any scar tissue from the alleged attack at the Plantation Club in February 1957. These Photos expose another embellishment or lie that so many people still wish to believe.

W.O. Hathcock (left) Operated the Plantation Club with Walter Flanigan (Right) who managed the Rustic Inn located in Corinth MS.. Flanigan, contrary to the popular beliefs of some novel writers, was one of only two people known to have relocated to Corinth after illegal activities in Phenix City Alabama were shut down.

Fannie Belle Barker, 'The Queen of Hearts of Phenix City" was once involved in the prostitution industry in Phenix City Alabama. Like Flanigan, she too came home to Corinth Mississippi after Phenix City was shut down by authorities.

Staff of the Humphrey-Phillips Clinic in Selmer were Buford allegedly drove himself to get 192 stitches after the alleged attack on him at the Plantation Club in February 1957. Dr. Humphrey is second from the left, Phillips is fourth from the left and Dr Harry Peeler is far right. No evidence has ever been produced to show that any of these doctors actually took care of Buford's alleged wounds.

THE STATE OF TENNESSEE)

COUNTY OF McNAIRY   )
)

THIS CONTRACT AND AGREEMENT by and between Buford Pusser, herein called Mr. Pusser, as FIRST PARTY, and W.R. Morris, herein called Mr. Morris, as SECOND PARTY, shall hereinafter conclusively evidence the following:

Mr. Pusser, who at this date is Sheriff of McNairy County, Tennessee, does hereby give and grant unto Mr. Morris the sole and exclusive right to write, issue and cause to be published under appropriate titles; book or books pertaining to the life of Mr. Pusser which is to include stories and photographs on the life of Mr. Pusser.

For the same consideration, Mr. Pusser agrees to grant unto Mr. Morris the sole and exclusive right to write manuscripts and to publish photographs for the said books, the first to be a hard-back edition.

It is understood that Mr. Morris may later write, issue and cause to be published paper-back editions of books pertaining to the life of Mr. Pusser, and that Mr. Pusser grants Mr. Morris the sole and exclusive right to publish such books.

Mr. Pusser agrees to furnish and provide Mr. Morris with pictures, information and interviews and other matters deemed necessary for publication of above mentioned books.

FOR AND IN CONSIDERATION of the foregoing, the said W.R. Morris agrees to immediately commence to write and cause to be written and published a hard-back book upon the life of said Buford Pusser.

BE IT ALSO UNDERSTOOD that Mr. Morris shall have the right to decide if and when paper-back editions of books on Mr. Pusser's life shall be written and published.

IN CONSIDERATION OF THE FOREGOING, it is mutually agreed by the parties that all net profits from the foregoing enterprise shall be divided by paying the parties the percentage thereof shown opposite their names:

TO W.R. MORRIS   Sixty-Five Percent thereof.

TO BUFORD PUSSER Thirty-Five Percent thereof.

—More—

W.R Morris and Buford's contract for the printed version of Buford's story. This contract caught Buford in yet another lie when he said he hardly knew Morris.

This agreement shall be binding upon the parties thereof, their heirs, successors and assigns.

WITNESS OUR HANDS at Selmer, Tennessee, this 31st day of January A.D. 19___.

_____
Buford Pusser---First Party

_____
W. R. Morris---Second Party

Both Pusser and Morris signed this contract allowing Morris to write about Buford's life. Obviously, Pusser lied when he said he hardly knew Morris. Pusser not only knew Morris, but they were business partners in a corporation they formed.

W.O. Hathcock a few years after his state line days of running the Plantation Club.
Hathcock would tell people he had no idea why Buford Pusser hated him so much.
(Private Collection)

W. O. Hathcock Being Treated For Injuries

The owner of the Plantation Club is being treated at Corinth Hospital for injuries suffered during an alleged beating and robbery at the Club Saturday night.

W. O. Hathcock was reported somewhat improved at the hospital this morning, where he is being treated for deep scalp lacerations from a severe blow to the back of the head.

The unidentified assailants allegedly stole approximately $1,000 from the cash register after rendering Hathcock unconscious.

The Plantation Club is located just inside Alcorn County near the Mississippi-Tennessee state line on Highway 45 north.

Cleveland Marlar, an Alcorn County bailiff, investigated the robbery and said a handkerchief with a laundry mark is the only clue to the identity of the assailants.

Marlar said the handkerchief was found on the floor of the club shortly after the incident occurred.

Alcorn County Sheriff's Department was not called to investigate the robbery, and the investigation is being done entirely by the bailiff.

Court Bailiff Cleveland Marlar investigates robbery at Plantation Club. Found handkerchief on floor with Chicago laundry marker as best clue.

CORINTHIAN

MMUNITY SERVICE

The motto of a group of citizens protesting atomic tests because of radioactive fallout — "Drink plenty of milk and get your daily supply of Strontium 90."

AY-SUNDAY, JANUARY 30-31, 1960.

TWELVE PAGES

PRICE TEN CENTS

SIDES RUNNING EVEN

Plantation Robbery Trial Battle Between Witnesses

W. O. Hathcock took the stand in Circuit Court here yesterday and told a jury how three men allegedly beat and robbed him on the morning of Dec. 13.

Owner of the Plantation Club on Highway 45 North, Hathcock claims that the three men now on trial knocked him in the head — injuring him seriously—and robbed him of over $1,000.

Buford Pusser, 22, son of a McNairy County, Tenn., constable, is one of the trio being tried for robbery and assault and battery with intent to kill in the incident.

Pusser was arrested in Chicago on Jan. 4 along with Marvin King Jr., 26, and Jerry Wright, 22 on a warrant issued here by Justice of the Peace Buck Sorrell.

Both Pusser and Wright, originally from McNairy County, Tenn., testified that they had been to the Plantation Club near the middle of October while on vacation from Union Bag and Paper Corp., in Chicago where all three defendants are now employed.

But all three denied having been anywhere near the establishment on the night of the alleged assault and robbery.

Prosecuting attorneys are attempting to prove that the three came here from Chicago on the weekend of Dec. 13, as-

saulted and robbed Hathcock and then returned to Chicago.

The defense has produced a number of witnesses who claim they can vouch for the presence of the three in Chicago except for a 16-hour period between 6 p. m. on Jan. 12 and approximately 10 a. m. on Jan. 13.

Taking the stand on behalf of the defendants yesterday were Pusser's wife, Mrs. Pauline Pusser; Wright's mother and sister, Mrs. Margaret Wright and Patsy Wright; and a friend, E. J. Surrett, formerly of Shiloh Park, Tenn.

The three claim to have left Chicago for Anna, Ill., approximately 300 miles south of Chicago at about 6 p. m. on Jan. 12.

They said they went to Anna for the purpose of visiting a friend, and, when arriving there between 1 and 2 a. m. on Jan. 13 found him away from home, and headed back for Chicago—arriving there at about 10 a. m.

Buford Pusser's brother, John testified that he had accompanied the three on the trip to Anna, and said he could account for their whereabouts throughout the time in question.

Mrs. Wright testified that they actually did leave Chicago at approximately 6 p. m. on Jan. 12, and, along with the other defense witnesses, placed the time of their return at about 10 a. m. on Jan. 13

District Attorney N. S. "Soggy" Sweat, in cross examination, suggested that the stories presented by the witnesses were a little too pat, and that they may have gotten together after the arrests to reconstruct the happenings of the weekend in question.

Hathcock stated that the three men entered his establishment at about 3 a. m. on Jan. 13 and took seats in the dance hall section of the club.

He said that both Buford Pusser and Jerry Wright had been there "several times" prior to that night.

According to Hathcock, there were several other people in the dance hall at the time.

"After the others left," he said, "the three came up to the bar and bought a pistol from me."

He said that Pusser and Wright were standing in front of him talking, and that King got behind him and hit him over the head, knocking him unconscious.

He claims that after gagging him with his handkerchief, the men looted the pockets of his clothes, and stole a small money box from the bar.

After recovering from the blow, Hathcock testified, he made his way to the living quarters adjoining the club and woke his wife, who called a doc-

tor and rushed her husband to Corinth Hospital.

Hathcock's wife, Lorise, told the jury that her husband had blood all over his head, face, and clothing when he reached the bedroom, and that his handkerchief was still tied around his neck.

She also testified that she had seen the three men enter the club about 3 a. m. and that she recognized Pusser and Wright.

Two witnesses for the prosecution took the stand to testify that they had seen the defendants enter the Plantation Club on the morning in question.

Billy Joe Robinson and Mrs. Nita Godwin said that they were in the club when the three entered.

Robinson identified all three men, but Mrs. Godwin said the only one she recognized was Pusser.

Prosecuting the case is District Attorney N. S. "Soggy" Sweat and County Attorney H. M. Ray, along with attorney W. C. Sweat, Sr., and W. C. Sweat, Jr., who were hired by Hathcock to assist.

Defense council is composed of attorneys Cary Stovall and Jimmy Price

Judge Raymond T. Jarvis recessed the trial until 9 a. m. this morning.

(Photo credit to Daily Corinthian)

36

ROBBERY SUSPECTS

Defense Witnesses Supply Good Alibi

TRIO SAID STILL IN ILLINOIS AT TIME OF ROBBERY, ASSAULT

Three men charged with the alleged Dec. 13 robbery of W. O. Hathcock, owner of the Plantation Club on Highway 45 North, were acquitted by a jury here Saturday in Circuit Court.

Charged with robbery and assault and battery with intent to kill in the case were Buford Pusser, 22, Marvin King, Jr., 26, and Jerry Wright, 22.

The trio was acquitted on the robbery count only and still face charges of assault and battery with intent to kill. However, defense attorneys Cary Stovall and Jimmy Price have made a motion that these charges be dropped.

A hearing on the motion will be heard today by Judge Raymond T. Jarvis.

Prosecuting attorneys made no effort to prove that the trio, all employees of a Chicago, Ill., bag company, drove from Chicago to the Plantatoin Club, beat and robbed Hathcock, and then returned to Chicago.

However, several defense witnesses took the stand and testified that they could account for the presence of all three except for a 16-hour period between 6 p.m. on Dec. 12 and 10 a.m. on Dec. 13.

Pusser and Wright, originally from McNairy County admitted being in the club about the middle of October while on vacation from their Chicago jobs. But all three of the men charged denied being anywhere near the Plantation Club on the night of the alleged robbery.

Hathcock and his wife, Loriae, along with two other witnesses for the prosecution, took the stand Saturday and said they positively saw the three men in the club about 3 a.m. Dec. 13.

Hathcock said the three men, two of whom he had seen several times before, entered the club about 3 a.m. on Dec. 13.

He said that after all other customers had gone, Pusser and Wright engaged him in conversation while King knocked him in the head from the rear.

Over $1,000 was reported stolen in the robbery.

Pusser, Wright and King escaped prison by committing perjury

Adamsville News

THREE MEN GET AN AQUITTAL ON ROBBERY CHARGE AT CORINTH

Three men charged with the alleged December 13 robbery of W. O. Hathcock owner of the Plantation Club on Highway 15 North of Corinth, were acquitted by a jury at Corinth last Saturday in Circuit Court.

Charged with robbery and assault and battery with intent to kill in the case were Buford Pusser 22, Marvin King, Jr., 26, and Jerry Wright 22.

The trio was acquitted on the robbery count only and still face charges of assault and battery with intent to kill. However, defense attorneys Cary Stovall and Jimmie Price have made a motion that these charges be dropped.

Prosecuting attorneys made no effort to prove that the trio all employees by a Chicago, Ill. Bag Company, drove from Chicago to the Plantation Club beat and robbed Hathcock and then returned to Chicago.

However several defense witnesses took the stand and testified that they could account for the presence of all three except for a 16-hour period between 6 P. M. on December 12 and 10 A. M. on December 13.

Pusser and Wright, originally from McNairy County admitted being in the club about the middle of October while on vacation from their Chicago jobs. But all three of the men charged denied being anywhere near the Plantation Club on the night of the alleged robbery.

Hathcock and his wife, Lorise, along with two other witnesses for the prosecution took the stand Saturday and said they positively saw the three men in the club about 3 A. M. December 13.

Hathcock said the three men, two of them he had seen several times before, entered the club about 3 A. M. on December 13.

He said that after all other customers had gone Pusser and Wright engaged him in a conversation while King knocked him in the head from the rear.

Over $1,000 was reported stolen in the robbery.

(from the Daily Corinthian)

————o————

Adamsville News

Pusser was just 22 years when he was arrested for robbery and assault with intent to kill. His true story is unlike those told by novel writers or movie makers.

IS BUFORD PUSSER FOR REAL OR
VIOLENCE LOVING BRUTE?
BY Ellie Grossman
Tuscaloosa News 3/28/74

dice and beaten to the tune of 192 stitches. Pusser stews about being framed, pleads innocent, and is acquitted.

In "Walking Tall," Pusser, home from Chicago with his family, reluctantly visits one of the cheap clubs that have sprung up in the area since he left, aids a friend being cheated, and is beaten severely. When the sheriff refuses to act, Pusser later returns with his hickory stick and fractures bones. The jury acquits him.

Nowadays, Pusser verifies the book's version, then goes on to admit that he and his friends lied to the jury in Mississippi under cover of a pre-arranged alibi in Chicago.

In her story for the Dayton Daily News, Cammy Wilson alleges Pusser extorted

Reporter Ellie Grossman reports how Buford would tell that he Wright and King all lied to the Alcorn County Jury about the robbery and how they had per-arranged for an alibi in Chicago. Grossman also mentioned Cammy Wilson who I interviewed. Her story "WALKING SHORT" is included later in the book.

(Tuscaloosa News)

Chapter 4
Moving Home to McNairy County

After his trial for the robbery at the Plantation Club, Buford returned to Chicago and his life with his new wife Pauline as well her two children Mike and Diane. Somehow, things just weren't the same. He was not only a husband now, but a father as well..., and soon there would be another to join the family at the Pusser's four room apartment at 7454 N Magnolia as on January 9, 1961 Pauline gave birth to nine-pound, four-ounce Dwana Atoyia Pusser at Chicago's Ravenswood Hospital.

All of this made Buford examine his life and his priorities. His work at the Union Bag Company offered little chance for advancement, not to mention that even though the job paid fairly well, it was repetitive and boring. The job as a bouncer at a local club had become much the same and interfered with his wrestling schedule.

Yes, of course there was always wrestling, but Buford had slowly come to realize that this too was a dead end. He had watched the top draws of the circuit and had noticed that the top earners, the wrestlers who drew the big crowds, the ones which people came to see and the ones who made the real money, were more than just wrestlers..., they were showmen. They were loud, flamboyant, and bigger than life and this was not Buford's way. Although Buford was a formidable physical being, he was not the entertainer, the showman that the top wrestlers were. He had long realized professional wrestling was more show than a serious competition. This was a business where the organizers told you when you could win, when you had to lose and most often even choreographed the matches for maximum entertainment excitement for the spectators.

Buford had also grown tired of the travel that wrestling required. On weekends he would find himself in cities like Philadelphia, St Louis, or Pittsburgh among others He wanted more out of life, something more than what he had found in Chicago. Finally, he discussed with Pauline the idea of moving home to McNairy County. Pauline however, had her concerns about making a move to rural Tennessee. She heard Buford talk about the lack of good employment there..., after all, that is why he had moved to Chicago. She wondered if Buford could earn enough in this economically depressed area to support their family. Still, Pauline followed Buford's wishes.

In 1962, the Pusser's loaded up their belongings and moved to McNairy County and into a mobile home not too far from Buford's Parents. Buford looked for work for a brief time before he realized just how little work was to be found. Buford reflected on his past and started wrestling in the west Tennessee circuit just to have an income. While wrestling wasn't what he wanted to do, it did help pay the bills.

Carl Pusser, Buford's father, had been serving as Adamsville's Chief of Police for some time. He managed to get Buford a job as a patrolman with the now two-man department.

Carl, being somewhat of a politician, had a plan. He had recently been suffering from leg pains from an auto accident he was involved in back in 1957. Carl had crushed a hip in the accident, and he would never again be the same physically, and he knew it. Now that he had Buford in the department, Carl contacted Adamsville Mayor Leonard Blanton and made arrangements for Buford to take his place as Chief of Police so he could retire.

It was really quite simple as Mayor Blanton and the city council, which included local businessmen J.D. Abernathy and George Tidwell, agreed to make Buford Chief. Adamsville was just a small town of a few hundred people. It was a town where everyone knew everyone else and their business. There wasn't any real crime in Adamsville, yet Buford was happy to have the job.

While serving as Adamsville's Chief of Police, Buford got to know several of the areas other law enforcement officers and constables. James Dickey was the County Sheriff at the time and to his credit he mentored Buford to a great degree. As Buford learned more about his new trade, his ambitions naturally began to grow. The city limits of Adamsville were so confining, he thought as he looked for a way to expand his horizons. He began to think about running for the Constable position in the 3rd civil district of McNairy County, a position that Tommy Morris had held for years. Buford filed for the position and campaigned for the job. With Adamsville being so small, Buford knew he could serve both Adamsville and the rural area of the 3rd district at the same time.

Buford campaigned hard for the position, visiting most of the residents in the area and asking for their votes. When the election came late in 1962, Buford had bested the incumbent Morris by more than a hundred votes. This gave Buford the opportunity to expand his authority and he was soon out looking for moonshiners in his newly acquired rural area. Being new at this part of his trade, Buford received some valuable assistance and training from his friend James Dickey. Not only would Sheriff Dickey assist Buford with moonshine raids in his 3rd district, but the Sheriff would ask Buford to assist him with raids in other parts of the county as well. This gave Buford the opportunity to see the scope of the moon shining operations in McNairy County.

Truth be known, Buford already knew how vast the problem was as his own father Carl Pusser is said to have been involved in making moonshine himself at one time. You must keep in mind the southern culture of McNairy County back in those days. Jobs were hard to find and many in the area made the illegal brew to support their families. While most made enough to sell locally, a few of the larger operations made enough to send shipments out of state. In turn, a lot of law enforcement officers of the time took advantage of this situation.

A Sheriff's salary back then was really low..., about six thousand dollars a year and that was with the Sheriff often providing his own car and firearms. Sheriffs often followed a long practiced and long held tradition of accepting payoffs from those who ran these illegal stills. For a little cash, sheriffs would look the other way. No harm, no foul.

It wasn't just the moonshiners that could put a little cash in a lawman's pocket as there were also bootleggers hauling hard liquor into McNairy County where only beer could be sold. Then there was the clubs and beer joints. McNairy County had more than thirty of these places spread across the county. Butler's, Donna's Place, Catherine's Club, Frank's Place, The Anchor Club, Moore's Place, Jourdan's Place and many more, each said willing to pay to be allowed to operate illegally.

The most infamous of these places however, during Buford's reign as sheriff were found at the state line that separated Tennessee from Mississippi. As already mentioned, the Shamrock Motel and White Iris were on the Tennessee side of the state while the Plantation Club and Shamrock Restaurant sat on the Mississippi side. These places gained more notoriety than the others for several reasons, but most are more familiar with these as they were made famous in the movie about Buford. The Plantation Club was called "The Lucky Spot" in the movies while The Shamrock was referred to as "The Pine Ridge Club".

Make no mistake as crimes did occur at these locations..., mostly the sale of hard liquor at the Shamrock Motel and White Iris. Sure, there was some gambling that went on, mostly a "razzle game".

Oftentimes, when tourists ate breakfast at the Shamrock Restaurant, they would be given the opportunity to win a free meal. The "razzle game", which was played openly at the restaurant's cash register, involved three cups with dice. Each dot on the dice equaled a half a point. All you had to do was roll the dice until they added up to a predetermined number... say 29. It's almost mathematically impossible to accomplish this, but many victims didn't know this. The first roll would be "on the house." Each roll of the dice after that would cost the tourist a little cash. Many of the victims would roll until they were out of money and still not win.

The Shamrock was infamous for swindling patrons, especially those from out of state. FBI reports would reveal that there was often someone stationed outside the Shamrock who would look for out of state tags as cars pulled in the parking lot. This information would then be transferred inside the restaurant where these customers would be treated graciously by the staff as they were targeted for swindling by the "razzle game."

These victims would often drive to the Sheriff's Office and report the gambling operation to the sheriff, who would assure them he could arrest the operators for their illegal enterprise, but he would then inform the victim that he would have to arrest the victim as well, as they too were gambling.

There wasn't any big scale gambling at the state line as was shown in "Walking Tall". It was all on a much smaller scale. The "razzle game" was played out in the open at the Shamrock Restaurant and a card game or a dice game could often be found in these establishments, similar to what you might find in many of today's VFW clubs. Still, the state line did indeed take advantage of tourists passing through the area.

My point is, yes, they sold illegal alcohol and had some gambling, but it was embellished to include a small casino in a back room in the movie . The movies about Buford relied more on stories of gambling and prostitution from the 30's 40's and 50's than what actually happened while he was Sheriff from 1964 -1970.

Most Sheriffs never got too greedy. They would take the payoffs that were offered, and in some cases, there may have been some negotiations, but such activities didn't get out of hand until James Dickey's term as McNairy County Sheriff. Somehow, local and federal prosecutors became aware that Sheriff Dickey was on the take from club owners and was suspected of being involved in moonshine operations as well. This led to investigations into Sheriff Dickey's dealings at the state line and in McNairy County.

Yes, Sheriff Dickey's actions had brought unwanted attention to the state line area again. I'm told that this was troublesome for some, especially Towhead White. It is now 1964 and the state line and McNairy County Sheriff Dickey have the attention of and is under investigation by authorities. This is where Buford Pusser comes into the picture.

McNairy County Sheriff James Dickey

Willie B's

Shamrock Motel

Old Hickory Grill

White Iris

The Infamous State Line

44

Chapter 5
Without the Hathcock Family, There Would Be No "Pusser Legend" ...

To understand "The Other Story" and Buford Pusser's tale about cleaning up the state line, you first need to more accurately acquaint yourself with and understand the complex cast of characters that were there as this story played itself out. It is also important to have a good understanding of the history of the area as it is very different from what you saw in the movies or read in novels written about Sheriff Pusser. We will begin with the state line's infamous Hathcock family.

When you actually think about it, if it wasn't for the Hathcock family, there would probably not be a "Pusser Legend", at least not as we know it today. It really is just that simple. If you take the Hathcocks out of the story..., there is not much of a story left at all. Every good crime story needs a "good guy", and of equal importance, it needs a "bad guy" to balance the story. Ask yourself, if there was moonshining, bootlegging and clubs all over McNairy County, why is the "Pusser Legend's" focus only on what took place at the state line, rather than what happened county wide? The answer is really pretty simple...., The Hathcocks.

Over the years several books and movies have focused on the state line and the Hathcocks in particular, making them the "evil" that Pusser had to fight. The truth is by the time Buford was elected sheriff, Louise Hathcock was the only member of the family still operating at the state line.

Of course, novel writers and movie makers do not really care much about the truth as they are often nothing more than storytellers who bend and twist the real story any way they can to make their story more interesting for their audiences. For that reason, the Pusser Legend exists today.

It was so disappointing for me to learn that the real story is so far removed from the Pusser Legend. Like so many others, I would, for a very long time, hope that my research was wrong as I held Buford in such high regard. The truth however, could not be denied.

Jack Hathcock...

Jack Hathcock....

Buford Pusser, W.R. Morris, Bing Crosby Productions, Eddie Bond and fictional novel writers of today, found the "bad guys" they needed to balance Buford's false narrative of events at the state line. Thus, you have Jack, W.O. and Louise Hathcock, which were somehow morphed into a state line crime syndicate for Buford to clean up, in order to build the legend into what it has become.

Many will ask, what about Jack Hathcock and his involvement at the state line? The short answer to that question is that he was dead before Buford Pusser ever became sheriff, and the two men basically had little to no interaction, eliminating Jack from the time frame of Pusser's reign as Sheriff of McNairy County.

Still, many authors, especially some who write novels about Buford today, will use Jack Hathcock's name in their stories as a means of manipulating their tales in order to embellish Buford's accomplishments as a crime busting sheriff. When you look at the story in a realistic way however, you realize that Jack Hathcock was actually killed months before Buford became sheriff of McNairy County and was never actually involved in the "Pusser Legend" itself. Jack Hathcock's history was simply used to make Buford Pusser out to be much more of a crime fighter than he ever really was, by manipulating people into thinking Jack was somehow still involved at the state line.

Once you have eliminated Jack Hathcock from the Pusser legend, you are left with the remaining two members of the alleged state line syndicate.., W.O. Hathcock, who owned the Plantation Club on the Mississippi side of the state line, and W.O.'s aunt, Louise Anderson Hathcock, who operated the Shamrock Restaurant which also sat on the Mississippi side of the state line as well as the Shamrock Motel that was located just a few short feet away on the Tennessee side of the line. Of course, Louise also had control, but full not ownership, of the Jack Hathcock estate after Jack's death, as Jack had left half of his estate to their minor aged and adopted daughter Jeanette Susan. This estate included the Shamrock Motel and Restaurant, the White Iris and other properties along highway 45 at the state line.

W.O. Hathcock....

William Odell (W.O.) Hathcock

It was easy for writers and movie producers to try and make W.O. out to be a real "bad guy" for Buford to deal with, however, when you put W.O.'s story into its proper context and examine it closely, it does a lot to eliminate much of his involvement in the Pusser legend. Sure, WALKING TALL told a tale of Buford being beat up, cut up and left for dead outside a mythical club the movie called the "Lucky Spot" which was operated by an equally mythical character named Buell Jaggers. This is a tall tale which came from Buford Pusser himself and the movie production company ran with it, changing the club's name as well as the proprietors name, probably because they suspected that Buford's story was a lie and wanted to avoid any possible legal entanglements with W.O. Hathcock over the false narrative. One must ask, where is any evidence to support this tall tale, which Buford would repeat time after time again in newspaper and magazine articles? Have you ever seen any police reports to back his story? What about medical reports to support his claims of having been carved up as the movie claimed? What about photos of Buford's wounds and scars or statements from witnesses regarding this alleged attack? Oddly, none of this seems to exist and not even the Buford Pusser Home and Museum has anything to validate Buford's story regarding this event. In this age of the internet, where most information is so easy to search for and find, why does it seem so impossible to find this evidence? The simple answer..., because the event never happened as Buford told it, if it ever happened at all.

Of course the movie WALKING TALL would also show Buford going back to the Lucky Spot (Plantation Club) to collect the money that had previously been stolen from him, as well as to dispense a little of his own brand of justice on the ten or so state liners in the club, while using only a stick as a weapon.

Of course, the real-life story tells us that Pusser and two friends allegedly came down from Chicago one December day in 1959 to rob the Plantation Club and attempt to kill W.O. Hathcock. Buford and his two friends were arrested in early January of 1960 in Chicago where they lived at the time and were extradited back to Alcorn County to stand trial. The real trial was nothing like what the movie indicated as Buford was described as quiet, controlled and even timid during the proceedings during the court proceedings. He knew there was a good chance he could end up in prison, so he was on his best behavior.

Of course, this was not enough for Hollywood, so movie makers saw the need to spice things up a bit, making up a mythical buddy for Buford, Lutie McVeigh, who was with Buford when he was cut up and saw the attack. In the movie, Lutie was found dead before he could testify in Buford's behalf, an apparent victim of the state liners.

In another movie scene, Buford is shown ripping off his shirt to expose his bare chest so the jurors could see the scars left from the attack on him at the "Lucky Spot". As the jurors looked on at the horror of this sight, Buford yelled, " If you let them do this to me and get away with it, you give them the eternal right to do the same damn thing to anyone of you"! Of course, this never happened in the real-life story, but it made for good movie fare, as some people, still today, think the movie version is true.

In the real story, the three men beat the charges however, by showing they were at work in several hundred miles away in Chicago just before the robbery occurred, seemingly making it impossible for them to have been at the state line.

Buford would later admit in a magazine article that he and his accomplices had a friend punch their time cards at the Union Bag Company where all three were employed, to provide the three with an alibi and of course a days pay.

To go a step further in making Buford Pusser a legend, the movie production company had a scene near the end of the film, showing Buford leaving Pauline's funeral in a Sheriff's patrol car, crashing in into the "Lucky Spot" (Plantation Club), with local citizens stripping the club of its gambling paraphernalia and furniture and burning it out in the parking lot as an injured Buford looked on. This, of course never happened either.

What really did happen to W.O.'s Plantation Club, you ask? Records show that in March of 1964 Alcorn County officials decided not to renew most of the liquor licenses in the county, effectively forcing clubs to cease operations. This is what happened to W.O. Hathcock's Plantation Club, which of course was in the county of Alcorn and the state of Mississippi. More importantly however, this event took place six months before Buford Pusser became Sheriff of McNairy County, meaning the Plantation Club was never even open during Buford's tenure as sheriff.

So ask yourself, if Pusser was never robbed at the Plantation Club as he claimed to have been, and the Plantation Club was actually in Mississippi, not Tennessee as the movie would falsely show, and better yet, had closed down well before Buford was sheriff, exactly how was W.O. Hathcock ever such a real life nemesis to Buford as books and movies have made him out to be? It is simple, if you are a writer..., you merely lie, embellish and twist the facts to make the story meet your agenda. Once you have eliminated Jack Hathcock as well as his nephew W.O. from the Pusser legend, you are left with the only remaining member of the alleged family syndicate..., Louise Hathcock.

Louise Hathcock...

Laura Louise Hathcock

49

Laura Louise Anderson was born on March 19, 1919 in the West Point area of Clay County Mississippi, about 105 miles south of the state line area. The Anderson family, like most others in the area, and to no fault of their own, was dirt poor as the economically depressed area in which they lived offered few good job opportunities. No one could blame a young teen age Louise for leaving Clay County to look for employment elsewhere.

She arrived in Corinth Mississippi and was looking for employment when she met "Shug" (pronounced Shug, as in short for Sugar) Timlake. Shug Timlake helped manage several establishments owned primarily by his brother, businessman Nelson Timlake. When Shug Timlake met the teen aged Louise, he obviously saw some potential that others had not recognized in her. She was young, fairly attractive, smart and above all self-confident.

Timlake offered her a job waiting tables and so on at the Rainbow Inn at the state line, where she went to work for another under aged teenager, Jack Hathcock. Jack soon became attracted to his new employee but was said to be somewhat intimidated by her as she was a mature young woman, and more than a year older than Jack. To a sixteen-year-old Jack, being more than a year younger than Louise, must have proved to be daunting for him. Somehow, the two finally connected romantically and were married on October 2, 1937.

Now, just for the sake of reference and keeping a proper timeline, it would be another two months before Buford Pusser was even born, as Buford didn't arrive in this world until December 12, 1937. I mention this time disparity only to show that it would be more than two decades before Buford would take on situations at the state line, and Louise Hathcock in particular.

It wasn't long before Timlake had Jack and Louise running the State Line Club at the state line. The State Line Club would one day be reinvented into the 45 Grill. While working for Timlake, Jack and Louise would hone and refine their business skills.

Timlake would eventually decide to divest himself of several properties, selling the 45 Grill to Jack. Jack was now living his dream of operating a club of his own and it was doing so well that he and Louise bought a new home on Proper Street in Corinth.

After a time however, the 45 Grill mysteriously burned to the ground one night and Jack decided to replace it with a new and modern restaurant on the Mississippi side of the line and an equally modern motel just a few feet away in the Tennessee side, with only a driveway separating the two businesses. It is now 1957 and the Shamrock facilities are under construction when marital discord strikes Jack and Louise.

Stories go that Jack was a jealous man. He had decided that Louise was seeing a friend of his named Pee Wee Walker. It would not be long before Walker was found murdered, when his body was discovered in an open field in the Corinth area.

Of course, many suspected Jack to be involved in Walker's death and soon Jack and some of his friends would be arrested for the crime. No one knows if Jack was really involved, as authorities would not find enough evidence to make charges stick and the entire matter was soon dropped. This of course took a further toll on the Hathcock's already strained relationship and they would divorce in 1957, before the Shamrock's construction was completed. Jack would take the state line properties in their divorce settlement and complete the construction of the restaurant and motel, while Louise would keep their new home in Corinth.

Most people would of course expect that this would be the end of their relationship, but what many do not know is that Jack and Louise opened the Shamrock for business together, with Louise running the operation.

Jack kept a small room in the back of the restaurant where he lived for the next seven years. The room was so small that he could hardly fit as bed inside it's walls. Living on the premises as he did, created a situation where he and Louise would see each other almost daily. And this would bring us to another problem of Jack's own making.... Towhead White.

Back in the days of the State Line Club and the 45 Grill, Jack had hired this young man to provide some muscle, for when things got a little ugly and out of hand with rowdy patrons. Towhead served this purpose well as he was physically fit and fearless as well. When a fight broke out Towhead was there to handle the problem.

Carl Douglas "Towhead" White had built quite a reputation for himself through those years as he was said to have worked at one time as a driver for New Orleans Mafia Kingpin Carlos Marcelo. He was also reputed to have connections with Dallas crime boss R.D. Mathews as well. I cannot say with any real certainty that either of these stories are true, but I do know he was indeed, at one time, on the Texas "Ten Most Wanted" list for crimes he had committed in that state. Over the years his exploits created a voluminous FBI file.

White was also tied in with the alleged "Dixie Mafia" as well. The Dixie Mafia was unlike, and no part of, the Italian Mafia that so many are familiar with. It was a just name or tag given by Investigator Rex Armisted to categorize a group of unorganized criminals, who were knowledgeable and often dangerous outlaws in the south, who would sometimes work together on a job when it benefited them individually. The "Dixie Mafia" had no real hierarchy over the entire group as the Italian Mafia families do.

Towhead White was a young and ambitious renegade who aspired to be "The Al Capone of the South" and he saw the state line a place to build his own empire. His only problem was his old boss, Jack Hathcock. While Jack Hathcock owned the state line properties, it was Louise that ran them, and she relied heavily on Towhead, who not only helped manage the Shamrock, but also spent some of his time at the new "White Iris" just down and across the highway from the Shamrock. This was an establishment that Jack had built after his divorce from Louise. Towhead knew how much these establishments were making and saw them as a good opportunity.

According to some, Towhead saw Jack as an obstacle to his plans of developing his own empire. Sources suggest, and again it is simply conjecture, that if Jack were eliminated from the picture, Towhead and Louise could take over all of Jack's properties and Towhead could run them as his own. It is rumored that Towhead and Louise were lovers and some unverified stories say they were secretly married.

Regardless, what we do know for a fact, is that Jack was shot and killed on May 22, 1964. He was shot several times in the neck and chest, while in Louise Hathcock's living quarters in room #1 at the Shamrock Motel. Jack is said to have left the room after being shot, making his way toward the restaurant and his room there, before collapsing on the driveway in between the restaurant and motel, just inside the Tennessee State line.

Since Jack was shot in Tennessee and his body found on the Tennessee side of the state line, the crime would be investigated by McNairy County Sheriff James Dickey. Sources say that Louise had Dickey on her payroll and as such, this would facilitate an investigation in her favor as she took responsibility for shooting Jack. Her story was that Jack had come to her room, and after several years of divorce had tried to force himself upon her. Her claim was that she shot him in self-defense to avoid being raped by her ex-husband. Many however, believe that Towhead White lured Jack to the room so he could murder him, and then convinced Louise to tell the story of Jack attacking her, while making the plea of self-defense.

Louise was charged in Jack's death, however, in the state of Tennessee at the time, if there were no witnesses to the shooting and no other evidence was available to substantiate the charges, the charges would be dropped.

After a short inquiry, Louise was free of all charges, but friends and family say she never got over Jack's death, that at times she would be seen crying about the matter. They believe that she was manipulated by White in his plan to take over the Hathcock estate. Some close to her suggest that she did not know what White had planned to do until Jack was already dead.

It has been suggested by many and documented in White's FBI file that Louise and Towhead were indeed romantically involved. One such FBI document indicates that this relationship was a ploy of White's to gain full control of the state line properties, warning that they feared he would eventually kill Louise as well, as soon as he had control of the state line. Regardless, with Jack being dead and out of the picture, the state line was now being run by Louise Hathcock and her employee and probable lover, Towhead White.

It would be still be another four months before Buford Pusser will become Sheriff of McNairy County and only one Hathcock is left at the state line.

As you can easily see, the real story is nothing like the fable that Buford told and was made famous in mostly fictional movies and books where writers, even today, simply accepted Buford's tall tales without properly vetting them. In many instances, these people simply ignored the real story as the truth got in the way of their own agendas of creating a tale that would make them money by making movies and writing mostly fictional novels about Buford.

Make no mistake, The Hathcocks were not angels. They did break laws. They sold bootlegged liquor shipped in from out of state, they sold drinks to minors, and the "razzle game" was played at the Shamrock. Yes, the crowds there could be rough and there were often fights that got out of hand, but the record shows that their story was highly embellished to make movies and books exciting. All of this was done for the benefit and promotion of the money making "Pusser Legend".

Pauline Pusser's death drew the attention of W.R. Morris who wrote "The Twelfth of August." This novel had many inaccuracies and omissions and its main source of information, Buford Pusser, was poorly vetted before the book was published. As such, the book embellished the Hathcock's story to be far more than it ever was. "The Twelfth of August" then became the launch pad for the movie WALKING TALL, which was even far more inaccurate and embellished than Morris' book, on which it was based.

The movie production company which made "WALKING TALL" must have understood that much of their information was bogus as they changed locations and most of the names for the movie. They had the "Lucky Spot" (Plantation Club) open and operating while Buford was Sheriff. The Shamrock, which was actually a restaurant and motel was shown in the movie as a nightclub called the "Pine Ridge." W.O. Hathcock was called "Buell Jaggers" while Louise became "Callie Hacker." There was no real life "Lutie McVeigh" or "John Witter" and the real Towhead White was not even portrayed in the movie. Many of the scenes in the movie hardly represented real events. Many of the scenes depicted in the movie never actually happened to Buford, but rather to other law enforcement officers in the area.

All these changes, names, locations, and such suggests that the production company was aware of just how inaccurate and slanderous the movie was, and the changes helped them avoid lawsuits.

The movie company said their story was "inspired by certain events" in Buford's life, while movie trailers and countless magazine articles called it a "true story," thus deceiving viewers and readers regarding this version of this tall tale. All of this creative scripting turned Buford's story into something far bigger than it ever really was.

The problem here, is that while Buford's reputation was enhanced by all of this, the Hathcock families already tainted reputation was trashed even more.

Locals in both McNairy, Alcorn, and surrounding counties for that matter, knew who "Buell Jaggers" was in real life..., W.O. Hathcock, just as it was easy to figure out that the "Callie Hacker" character represented Louise Hathcock. Unfortunately, many movie goers, not knowing or understanding the real story, believed much of it to be true.

The Hathcocks were not the only ones whose family members have suffered from the false telling of the story. The Smith family, the Andersons as well as the Bivins family and others have suffered as well as people can be so judgmental.

The bottom line is that there are no winners in this story. The "Good Guy," Buford, wasn't nearly as good as everyone thought, just as the "Bad Guys" weren't nearly as bad as they were portrayed either.

Chapter 6
The Day Jack Died

We all know what the state line was all about..., selling illegal alcohol and a little gambling every now and then, mostly the "razzle game". This is something the Hathcocks had been doing for years. It wasn't all that unusual as this kind of activity took place in a lot of other counties and in a lot of other states as well.

Of course, the Hathcock's story has been told, embellished, and retold again, and again, with each story growing bigger than the one before. Jack Hathcock had a reputation, some it deserved, while much of it was made of distortions and lies.

One writer would tell of the Hathcocks murdering people and dumping their bodies into the Tennessee River. Of course, there is no documentation to be found to support this outlandish claim.

As you now know, Jack and Louise divorced in 1957 before the construction of the Shamrock was completed. Even though they were divorced, Jack and Louise continued to work together to a great degree with Louise running the Shamrock for the most part, but Jack was always there.

As already mentioned, Jack had hired Towhead White years before to work at the State Line Club and later the 45 Grill. This gave Towhead an inside look at the money that could be made in such an establishment, and he of course had his own ideas about how to improve the earning potential of such a place.

Now, just a few years later, and with Jack and Louise, being divorced, Towhead saw his opportunity to establish himself at the Shamrock. Things seemed to go well at first as Louise allowed Towhead to slowly take over managing the Shamrock. However, once he had entrenched himself there, he began to make his own decisions regarding the Shamrock, doing things that Jack and Louise did not necessarily approve of.

Towhead would make overtures to Louise and she mistakenly let him in her heart. With Louise now under his influence, Towhead decided that Jack had become an impediment to his plans and Jack needed to go.

It is the night of May 22, 1964. Louise as usual had a number of her family members staying at the Shamrock. Louise occupies room #1 as it is closest to the office. Bobby Anderson and Susan, Louise's adopted daughter share room #2 which has twin beds. Sandra, Barbara's mother, and Barbara have room #3.

Towhead has instructed Bobby Floyd to find Jack and borrow his gun so Jack will be unarmed for the event that is about to take place… his assassination.

Louise and Towhead are in room #1. The room has an enjoining door to room #2. Jack, having been told that Louise needed to speak with him, enters Louise's room with no idea of what is about to happen. There is a discussion going on between Louise, Jack, and Towhead when Bobby Anderson, Louise and Jack's nephew, attempts to enter the room through the adjoining door between rooms one and two.

Knowing what is about to happen, Towhead pushes young Bobby back into room #2 as he closed and locked the door to keep is little friend out of the room and

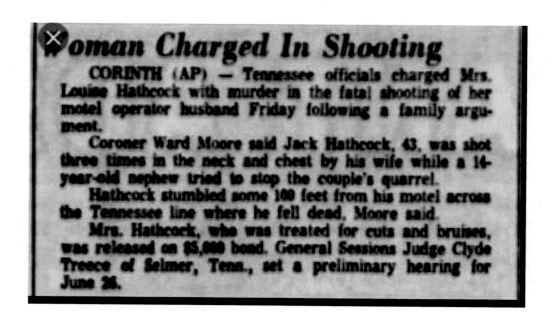

Woman Charged In Shooting

CORINTH (AP) — Tennessee officials charged Mrs. Louise Hathcock with murder in the fatal shooting of her motel operator husband Friday following a family argument.

Coroner Ward Moore said Jack Hathcock, 43, was shot three times in the neck and chest by his wife while a 14-year-old nephew tried to stop the couple's quarrel.

Hathcock stumbled some 100 feet from his motel across the Tennessee line where he fell dead, Moore said.

Mrs. Hathcock, who was treated for cuts and bruises, was released on $5,000 bond. General Sessions Judge Clyde Treece of Selmer, Tenn., set a preliminary hearing for June 26.

Notice in the second paragraph of this newspaper clipping, it mentions that a fourteen-year old boy was present. This boy was Bobby Anderson. Why was he not interviewed about the shooting?

spare him the sight of his uncle being murdered. Newspaper accounts would even state that a fourteen- year-old boy was present. Bobby Anderson could have placed Towhead in the room as Jack was being murdered.

Several gunshots would be heard. Those shots would strike Jack in the chest and neck, but they would fail to bring the big man down. Somehow, while dying, Jack Hathcock managed to walk out of the room, travel approximately one hundred feet before collapsing onto the paved driveway between the motel and the restaurant.

It is difficult to say what was probably going through his mind as he took his last few steps. He probably knew he was dying and maybe was even thinking about who had shot him and possibly why.

McNairy County Sheriff James Dickey points to the spot

where Jack Hathcock collapsed and died after being shot.

Authorities would of course be called to the scene bringing McNairy County Sheriff James Dickey from the Tennessee side of the state line as well as Alcorn County Sheriff Cleeton Wilbanks from the Mississippi side as the two states border lay directly between the motel and the restaurant. These two sheriffs apparently agreed that the shooting death occurred in McNairy County where Dickey had jurisdiction.

There would be an investigation into Jack's death and Louise Hathcock would claim that it was she who fired the shots which took Jack's life. Louise would be charged with murder, however, charges would be dismissed by Judge Clyde Treece when she made the claim that she fired the shots in self-defense saying Jack had come to her room wanting sex as he assaulted and attempted to rape her. With no witnesses to counter her claim, Judge Treece had little choice but to release her from the charges.

No witnesses? What about Towhead, who Bobby knew was there. Did Sheriff Dickey even ask questions of the people who were in rooms closest to the shooting, those who obviously heard the shots? Did the sheriff interview Bobby, who was there just seconds before shots were fired? Even if Sheriff Dickey did interview Bobby, did the young man answer his questions honestly, or knowing what Towhead was capable of, was Bobby afraid to speak up? A better question might be, did Sheriff Dickey even care about the truth?

Yet another possibility exists that Sheriff Dickey was told exactly what happened, however, being on the payroll of Louise and Towhead, he simply ignored what he was told or at least suspected and accepted Louise's claim of self-defense as it was so convenient for all involved. We will never know.

As far as I know, no autopsy was performed on Jack which could have provided valuable information regarding the trajectory of the gunshots fired.

Towhead stood at six foot three inches, making him significantly taller than Louise, who stood at only five foot, four inches tall. Louise would probably have fired from a much lower position than Towhead, in an upward trajectory. Had an autopsy been performed, it might have suggested who the actual shooter might have been.

Louise and Towhead were said to have been lovers and Towhead's FBI report would indeed later classify Louise as Tow's "common law wife." Others will say Louise, having divorced Jack years earlier (1957), had indeed married Towhead, although no proof of such a marriage has been found.

Was the reason for Towhead's show of affection forLouise just a means of being able to eliminate Jack from the picture and taking Towhead closer to gaining control of the state line?

So many questions..., was the plan to kill Jack and remove him as an obstacle in the Shamrock's operation Towhead's idea or was it a collaborative effort of both Towhead and Louise? Did Towhead make the plan and shoot Jack without Louise's prior knowledge and then convince Louise to lie and say she had killed Jack in self-defense? Did Towhead then beat Louise to make it appear that Jack had indeed assaulted her as she fought him off, as FBI reports suggest?

With so many people knowing that Towhead was at the Shamrock when the shooting occurred, why was he, especially with his reputation, not considered a suspect in Jack's Death? Did Sheriff Dickey even consider how Jack's death could benefit Towhead... or was the "fix" in as H.M. Ray's letter to his superiors in the department of Justice suggests?

Looking at these things with critical thinking, I would suggest that Towhead had so much to gain from Jack's death while Louise already had everything she needed.

With Bobby placing Towhead at the scene and Towhead pushing Bobby back into room #2, it suggests that the shooting was premeditated and Towhead, in my opinion, was the one who fired shots which took Jack's life, comfortable in the knowledge that Sheriff Dickey would give him a "get out of jail free" card.

I'm told that Jack's death really took an emotional toll on Louise as family members say she would often be found crying about his early demise. Family members say that this particular event really changed Louise, as she became more violent, more volatile than they had ever seen her. They suggest that Towhead was at the root of her behavioral changes.

Of course, Towhead would go to prison in September of 1965 for his involvement in his "Three State Moonshine Operation." During this time was when Louise would contact attorneys, looking for one who would appeal Towhead's conviction or at least get his sentence reduced. All of these efforts failed.

Five months later, Louise would be killed by McNairy County Sheriff Buford Pusser in yet another very questionable shooting in room #1 at the Shamrock Motel.

Prison officials would allow Towhead to return to West Point Mississippi to attend Louise's funeral. This is something that usually happens only when a couple is legally married, leading to the question, were Louise and Towhead married or was it simply a ruse that worked to Towhead's benefit?

Towhead would return to the state line area and walk into the funeral home for Louise's viewing, in handcuffs with a Marshall at his side. Apparently, he had convinced prison officials that he and Louise were indeed married. Many would be surprised to see him there, while others seemed to expect it.

Oddly, Towhead was seen later that night by several people who attended a party at the Shamrock, where he was without his handcuffs and without his prison escort anywhere in sight. Towhead partied with his friends that night and there was lots of drinking. Partying was not the only reason Towhead was at the Shamrock that night however, as at one point he was going to all the places where Louise kept her money hidden. One such place was behind a hidden panel in a vault in the motel office. Another was in the motel office kitchen where a panel in the wall concealed cold cream jars stuffed full of cash.

He also went to a spot located behind the Shamrock Motel where a small bridge crossed over a ditch. Near the bridge, cash was buried in a metal container. There well may have been other such hiding places, but these were the ones that family members knew of.

Towhead recovered all the cash as he was seen breaking cold cream jars in a bathtub at the motel and retrieving bills of various denominations. Unconfirmed stories circulated that he paid his prison escort ten thousand dollars to allow him to walk free for twenty-four hours so he could gather the cash and spend a little time with friends.

There has always been a great deal of speculation that McNairy County Sheriff Buford Pusser shot and killed Louise Hathcock on February 1, 1966 so he could search for this money as the Shamrock was about to be taken by the IRS for nonpayment of back taxes on the Jack Hathcock estate. The state line properties were listed in Jack Hathcock's name and he had failed to pay taxes for quite some time, leaving the IRS to place a lien on the properties.

According to many, including Hathcock family members, Buford would look for the money Louise had stashed away, but he would eventually give up on his search for the treasure. Having failed to locate the money, Buford left it behind for Towhead to find just days later when he returned for Louise's funeral. Towhead would give the money to others whom he could trust to hold for him until he was out of prison.

It has been suggested that Towhead divided up the money giving varying sums to Howard Bunch, Nimbo Price, Bill McPeters, and others including his Alabama associate Dewitt Dawson for safe keeping. Dividing the money up in such a way was kind of like an insurance policy so that no one individual could steal all his cash, besides, these people knew Towhead well and knew better than to cross him by trying to take his money.

Towhead would return to Corinth about two and a half years later and it is not surprising to see that he never seemed to be short of cash.

Towhead had plans for that money as he tired of the criminal life and wanted to go straight, start a jukebox business and among other things, build a house for his mother. He would have blueprints drawn for his mother's new home that was never built as he was killed before construction would start. His untimely death is yet another story in a later chapter.

Chapter 7

Buford Runs for Sheriff

It's early 1964 and Buford is examining his options. He is currently Chief of Police of Adamsville as well as the Constable of McNairy Counties 3rd district..., but he wants more. The time that he has spent with his mentor, Sheriff James Dickey, has given Buford a taste of what law enforcement is like over a larger area than his current jurisdiction(s) provide. McNairy County holds more moonshine stills, more clubs, more bootleggers and much more excitement than the small area of the county where he currently has jurisdiction.

Buford and his father discuss Buford's future, and Carl Pusser, being somewhat politically savvy, sees an opportunity for Buford. Carl, himself having been involved in moonshining as well as law enforcement over the years, was well aware of a sheriff's potential to make money, if he was willing to bend the rules as so many other sheriffs had done.

Sheriffs in southern counties had a tradition of supplementing their meager sheriff's salaries by accepting payoffs from club operators, beer joint owners, moonshiners and bootleggers to "look the other way" as they conducted their business. It was no big secret as a lot of people knew this went on, and most sheriff's didn't get too greedy. The Pussers however, seemed to have bigger plans...much bigger plans.

Buford would have to run against his old friend and mentor James Dickey, and defeating an incumbent sheriff was not a simple task as local citizens knew what they already had as a sheriff and were often reluctant to replace him.

I have been told that it was Carl Pusser who came up with the idea of conducting raids on the state line prior to the election, to draw attention to Buford's candidacy for sheriff. Such raids would bring light, not only to the state line operations, but to the young and energetic lawman who wanted to be sheriff as well. The only problem was that the state line clubs were not in Buford's 3rd district of McNairy County and he had no authority there. Still, the raids went on as planned.

Illegal as the raids were, they caught the attention of the locals who saw Buford as someone willing to stand up to the state line crowd for a change, as Sheriff Dickey had not been so tough on them. Again, most people probably suspected that payoffs were made to Dickey in order to gain his cooperation in overlooking their business practices at the state line. Voters hoped Buford might bring change to this situation.

After the Pussers conducted these raids, made a few arrests and confiscated beer from these joints, all would be forgiven by the courts, the charges against the state liners being dropped and the judge ordering the confiscated beer to be returned to the rightful owners as[1] the raids were out of Buford's jurisdiction and therefore, illegal. Still, those raids got Buford's name in front of the public and the publicity helped his candidacy, just as Carl Pusser had predicted it would. The older Pusser would tell in magazine articles a few years later how the illegal raids were, indeed, calculated to help Buford.

On top of this, Buford had a second opponent in the sheriff's race..., local Selmer businessman George Weatherford. Weatherford was well known and well liked in the area and made for a formidable candidate against both Dickey and Pusser.

Carl and Buford started actively campaigning and it wasn't long before Buford had enough in contributions for campaign signs and cards. Try as hard as he might, Buford knew it would be difficult to defeat Sheriff Dickey in the election. He was concerned about Weatherford as well but he saw Dickey as his chief political adversary.

Many people are not aware however that state officials were investigating the incumbent Sheriff Dickey. They were apparently aware of payoffs and other acts of alleged malfeasance by Dickey and they were ready to act.

In the state of Tennessee, if a sheriff can not perform his duties for any reason, the county coroner will assume the position of sheriff until a new sheriff is either elected or appointed. The state had already contacted County Coroner Ward Moore, telling him quietly, that he needed to prepare himself to step into the sheriff's role.

As with many parts of the Pusser legend, situations can sometimes be less than clear and a little difficult to understand. This is the case with Sheriff Dickey. He has been friends with and allegedly on the payroll of Louise and Towhead for sometime now. Like many others, Louise and Towhead White are aware that their sheriff is being investigated and very well may soon be removed from office, leaving them without the protections Dickey had always provided.

The story I have been told is that Towhead saw the opportunity to help himself and Buford..., after all he and Buford had a relationship that went back to their days in Chicago. Towhead is said to have feared that James Dickey, even if he won the election, would soon be removed from office, leaving him and Louise in uncharted waters. Towhead also feared that should Dickey be prosecuted, he might just roll over on Towhead and Louise in an attempt to gain leniency from the state.

Towhead knew that if Dickey were to be removed before the election, the race would be between Buford and Weatherford and that his best bet would be to help get Buford elected. People suggest that Towhead thought that Dickey was now a liability and had to go.

W.O. Hathcock would be asked in later years, what the worst thing he could recall that happened at the state line? Many, myself included, would anticipate that his answer would be about how he was robbed, assaulted and almost killed by Buford, Wright and King when they [2] came to his Plantation Club that December night in 1959. Instead, his reply was a simple one.The worst thing he could recall was the manner in which Sheriff James Dickey was killed.

According to Hathcock's story, Dickey had become ill the evening before and had spent the night at the Shamrock. Another thing many do not know is that Dickey was said to have cancer and was in poor health.

The next morning, Towhead, Buford and Dickey were all at the Shamrock restaurant. Some of their conversation centered around the loaner car Dickey was driving while his patrol car was in the shop for maintenance.

Towhead White is said to have used this to his advantage as he began to question who was driving the faster car that day..., Buford or Dickey? I'm told that Towhead kept goading Dickey, until he agreed to race Buford north on highway 45 as they both left the state line and headed back to Selmer.

It's said that they left the Shamrock, engines roaring, as they headed down the two lane highway toward the county seat. Seconds later and about a mile north of the Shamrock, Sheriff Dickey's car careened from the roadway and down an embankment, finally crashing into a large oak tree. Dickey was ejected from the vehicle and was pronounced dead approximately 30 minutes later.

While no one seems to know the exact cause of this accident as there were allegedly no witnesses, many however, would have their suspicions.

Of course WALKING TALL would show a very different version of all of this as they would show Sheriff Al Thurman as Buford's political enemy. They would show him chasing after Buford in an attempt to arrest him for reckless driving after Buford had sped away from Willie Ray's after he and Thurman had a confrontation inside the club. Thurman's patrol car would be shown going off the road as he neared a bridge, trying to run Buford over, inexplicably exploding before it hit the water below.

In the real story, with Sheriff Dickey, now dead and out of the picture, the state's investigation into his activities evaporates, leaving the Sheriff's race a two man event..., Pusser vs Weatherford.

County Coroner Ward Moore told me that he had prepared himself to step in as interim sheriff of McNairy County as required by law, but he expected it to be because of Sheriff Dickey's arrest by state officials.., not his death.

Moore went on to say during our interview that on his first morning, as he arrived at the Sheriff's office, he received a phone call from Louise Hathcock. She mentioned the election, saying her "horse had died midstream and she needed to buy another one", instructing rather than asking Moore, to send both George Weatherford and Buford Pusser to the Shamrock to speak with her. Moore told me that only one of the men accepted her instructions, but he wouldn't say which man made the trip to see her at the state line.

Of course books and movies would show when the election took place, Buford narrowly defeated a now dead sheriff in the race for this high office. This close election between Dickey and Pusser, according to the movie, was due to the state line syndicate pumping so much money into the election to support their now dead candidate. It would be laughable now, except so many people believe the movie version and the writings of W.R. Morris to be true. Morris would write that when the election was over, Buford was a little more than three hundred votes ahead of James Dickey.

What is the truth?

Buford, running on the Republican ticket received a total of 3288 votes, defeating George Weatherford on the Democrat ticket by 248 votes with Weatherford garnering a total of 3040 votes. Our now dead incumbent Sheriff James Dickey received a total of only 307 votes.

The factual election results show that Buford had carried a number of the outlying rural districts along with Adamsville, while Weatherford captured more votes in Selmer, Ramer, Bethel Springs and a few small outlying precincts. In the end, even carrying the majority of votes in the more populated precincts, it wasn't enough to make Weatherford the next sheriff of McNairy County.

This serves to show us how myths and legends are often made by writers and movie makers as again, most people, except for the locals, don't even know that George Weatherford even existed, let alone ran for sheriff against Buford.

With Sheriff Dickey dead and unable to complete his term, a decision was made by officials to allow Buford to take office early. Buford was sworn in as Sheriff of McNairy County on September 1st, 1964.

There was a new sheriff in town and things would soon change..., but not necessarily in a way people expected.

Chapter 8
Payoffs..., a good reason to be sheriff

There are two chapters in this book that I had difficulty writing, not because of a lack of knowledge, but by having gained too much knowledge. This is the first of those two chapters.

I have a background in law enforcement, and I can tell you that for many in this profession, it is a true brotherhood. When you are faced with a call that results in a serious threat, you have your partner's back, and they have yours. You depend on them and they depend on you. It's a matter of survival and these people become like family to you.

That being said, I will tell you that after seeing *Walking Tall* for the first time, I held Sheriff Buford Hayes Pusser in the highest regard as he was a member of this brotherhood. As years went by and I researched his story, I was amazed to find that so little of what we had been told was a true story was actually far from it.

I find no pleasure in writing this chapter, as for me, it destroys the legend I once thought to be real. It is difficult for me to speak so poorly of someone in the brotherhood.

Barbara Bivins, who penned "Tommy *and Me,*" told me that one of the first things that Buford did after becoming sheriff was to head to the state line to see Louise Hathcock and get the payoffs started. Her story was eerily similar to the one McNairy County Corner Ward Moore had told me about Louise needing to "buy a new sheriff" after James Dickey had been killed just before the election.

I know many who read this will have their doubts about what I say here as I have no documentation to prove that Buford accepted payoffs from those he was actually protecting instead of arresting. However, as Barbara Bivins once told me, and others have echoed, Buford didn't give receipts when he accepted payoffs as that would leave a paper trail.

What I have done is interview many people who claim to have paid Buford in order to operate illegally. Some were club owners, while others were moonshiners and bootleggers.

Something that is important for everyone to understand, is that these people were most often competitors, not business partners..., they were not in a syndicate as we were led to believe by *Walking Tall*, whose sworn enemy was Buford Pusser. As it turns out, Buford Pusser appears to have been part of the problem in McNairy County, not part of the solution.

Each of these people were trying to gain a market share of the business they were in. According to many, including Bill McPeters, a well known and well respected citizen of Corinth, competition was so intense that most club and beer joint owners maintained a personal residence at the establishments they operated, as they feared some of their competition might attempt to burn them out if no one was there to protect the premises.

If there was a state line mob during Pusser's tenure as Sheriff, which so many want to believe, understand this. During Buford's era as Sheriff of McNairy County, there was only a seventeen month period where such a "mob" existed, and that mob consisted of Louise Hathcock and Towhead White. Everyone else was their competitor.

Consider this for a moment. Buford took office on September 1, 1964. Towhead White went to prison after being arrested for moonshining in Tishomingo County Mississippi a year later in 1965. Buford would shoot and kill Louise Hathcock just a few months later on February1, 1966. All of this took place in only seventeen months, yet many people believe Buford was fighting a mob the entire time that he was sheriff. There wasn't much left at the state line the last four plus years that Buford was in office as the "state line mob" no longer existed after February 1, 1966.

Louise and Towhead were alleged to have had Buford on their payroll during that seventeen months according to Hathcock and Anderson family members. Stories vary on what Louise and Towhead paid him each month as he allegedly got $500 a month in the beginning. There are stories that Buford kept raising that figure over time to $1500 a month. Are these stories true? All I can say is that many others I have interviewed claim that they too had to pay Buford. It isn't as if people at the state line were the only ones who paid Buford.

Skeets Adkins.... Catherine's Club
Selmer Tennessee

I interviewed Skeets Adkins, whose wife operated Catherine's Club in Selmer. Skeets said Catherine paid $150 a month to Buford. That was a great deal of money in the mid 1960's economy. For this, Pusser would overlook the fact that she was selling hard liquor which she had to keep out of public view. Skeets hated Buford with a passion as he felt it was cowardly for Buford to take her money when Catherine was doing all the work and taking all the risks.

In an on camera interview, Skeets told me that Buford would never accept the payoffs from him, that payments had to come directly from Catherine.

Buford didn't like Skeets, as Adkins would keep Buford's father Carl supplied with drink. Yes, Skeets and Carl Pusser were friends. He said that Buford confronted him several times about this matter. Skeets went on to tell me that things became so tense, that one night while he and Catherine were sleeping, a car drove past the house and gunfire erupted with bullets striking the wall just above their heads. Skeets went on to say that when the gunfire ceased, he jumped from the bed and ran to the window just in time to see Buford's car pulling away. He said that there were two other people in the car with Buford, but in the semi darkness he could not identify them.

W.R. Morris would write about Buford and Skeets Adkins final confrontation at the Moose Lodge in Selmer. Buford had served three consecutive terms as sheriff and had to step down due to Tennessee's term limits law. Skeets stated that he was in the lodge one day when the former sheriff came in. After a few minutes Skeets thought he might have a little fun and embarrass Pusser by rather loudly attempting to offer Buford his last payoff from Catherine's Club.

Buford tried to ignore Skeets, which only made Skeets speak even louder so as to draw more attention to their conversation.

According to Morris, Buford finally had had enough, hitting Skeets so hard that fecal matter ran down Skeets pant leg and onto his boots. Skeets on the other hand said Morris lied about this just to fluff up his book. His version of the same story had a different ending.

In Skeets version, Pusser having had enough, angrily invited Skeets to step outside to settle the matter. Skeets, of course, knew that in a fight, he didn't stand a chance against the much larger Pusser. What he told me next is something I didn't expect. Skeets said he was immediately off his bar stool and heading for the door, with Buford right behind him. Skeets said he had a .38 caliber handgun in the pocket of the windbreaker he was wearing. His plan..., as soon as they cleared the entrance door and were outside, Skeets would turn around quickly, pull his weapon and "gut shoot" Pusser. Skeets went on to explain that as soon as they cleared the door, Buford hit him in the back of the head so hard it rendered him unconscious.

In a change of subjects, I asked Skeets about other clubs and joints in the area. He knew the places I spoke of, but when I would ask about the owners or operators, he didn't have much information to share, like most, saying they were competitors.

Skeets Adkins in 1981   Skeets when I interviewed him in 2009

Betty Sparks... The Anchor Club
Rural McNairy County

Betty Sparks operated The Anchor Club on the west side of the county, and it was one of the busiest in McNairy County, yet few people outside of the area don't know about the club as writers and movie makers were all caught up in the embellished state line story.

In an interview several years ago, Betty told me that she too paid Buford, mentioning an amount of $500 dollars a month. She stated that she and Buford were friends and that $500 a month was a business investment and the best money she ever spent. She said she was allowed to stay open past the time clubs and beer joints were supposed to close at night. Her club, unlike others, was open on Sunday and she could sell hard liquor in McNairy County where it was legal to sell only beer. Of course, one of the important benefits was that she would be informed if there were any impending raids planned.

She went on to say that her sister in law ran a beer joint in Selmer and that she too paid Buford. I was told it cost the sister in law $100 a month to operate without a beer permit.

Paul Moore.... Moore's Place
Highway 57 Michie Tennessee

I visited at length with Paul on one trip to McNairy County. It was a well known fact that he and Buford were good friends. Paul took me and others through his old club that had not been in operation for years. The bar was still there as was a rather low platform where a band could play. The platform had to be low as the building's rafters were only about eight foot from the floor, giving the building a very closed in feeling for a club.

Although one end of the building was being used for storage of some of Paul's farm equipment, there were still some tables and chairs scattered around the other end and to a great degree, it still looked much as it does in a video I have of Eddie Bond playing at the club back in the 70's when he was making films about Buford.

I asked Paul if he had ever thought about opening the club up again, to which he replied that if he did, he would probably wouldn't get much business as people in the area would now rather spend their money on meth rather than beer.

I inquired with Paul about Buford visiting his club and he told me that Buford spent a lot of time there. He told me how Buford would often bring trouble upon himself when he was there. For instance, if people got too loud, Buford would tell them to quiet down. If they didn't, he wasn't so polite with his second request with Paul saying Buford never wore a uniform and some people had no idea that he was the sheriff. Paul felt that a lot of trouble could have been avoided had Buford only identified himself as the McNairy County Sheriff when he talked to people the first time, suggesting that Buford was sometimes just looking for a fight.

I questioned Paul about serving hard liquor at the club and he readily admitted that it was a quite widespread practice at his and other places. When I asked if he had to pay Buford for the privilege, he led me to believe he paid even though he wouldn't discuss details. Paul made it clear that Buford knew that he was selling more than just beer eventually admitting he wasn't allowed to sell anything larger than a fifth. Half pints were the best to sell as they were small and concealable.

Paul Moore and myself when I interviewed him at Moore's Place on Hwy 57 in Michie TN. Paul was a friend of Buford's, however, like so many others, he would point out the mistakes and embellishments that are part of the "Pusser Legend."

Willie B's Place
Guys Tennessee

Willie B's was a club that catered to the black community of McNairy County. I interviewed a man who claimed to be a former McNairy County Deputy, who asked not to be named, because of his dealings with Buford. He referred to himself as one of Buford's "dirty deputies." He claimed that part of his job was to collect payoffs from certain people. He stated that all the payments came in sealed envelopes and that when he delivered them to Buford, the sheriff would give him some of the proceeds, admitting that he never knew how much money was in each envelope.

He said that one day he made his usual stop at Willie B's and was given a wad of cash which was not in a sealed envelope as he expected it to be.

He went on to say that when he met with Buford and handed him the cash, Buford became extremely angry as his "dirty deputy" now knew how much Buford was getting, at least from Willie B's, and just how little he was getting for picking up the pay off.

I have absolutely no idea if this story is true as there wasn't much I could do to vet the story properly. Lots of people make claims about knowing Buford, working for him and so on. Many of these claims can be verified, however, some can't as it has just been too many years that have gone by.

As an example of such "storytelling," I once had a man contact me and rather convincingly tell me that he had once seen Buford with his shirt off. He described Buford's chest, saying the scars looked like "railroad tracks," referring to the carving up Buford allegedly took at the Plantation Club.

Willie B's was a club on Guys Rd that catered to the Black population in the area.

I emailed this man three photos of a shirtless Buford Pusser asking him to identify the scars in the photos as I could not see them.... I never received a reply.

The story about the "dirty deputy" picking up payoff's for Buford..., you will simply have to decide for yourself if it is true or not. I don't know. I am sure some of these stories are true while others are not. That's the way it all too often is with such legends.

Junior and Shirley Smith..., The Old Hickory Grill
Guys Tennessee

This club was on Guys Road off Highway 45 a ways north of the state line. Operated by Junior and Shirley Smith, this club had the reputation as a hangout for bikers as well as many locals. Like most clubs of the time, the interior of the building was rather small, with low ceilings.

Outdoors, on the back side of the building itself, was an open air venue with picnic tables and such. Buford spent a lot of time at the Old Hickory as he and the Smiths were friends. Buford is said to have preferred the outside venue of the club when weather permitted. It's also well rumored that Buford was a silent partner in the club with Junior and Shirley.

It was one evening, outside this club, that Barbara Bivins and Shirley Smith overheard an angry Pauline Pusser confront Buford about seeing Pearl Wade. Pearl was a beautiful light skinned black girl that had drawn the interest of both Buford and allegedly Towhead White. It should be noted that Pearl was the niece of Willie Wade, who ran Willie B's, the black club that operated near the Old Hickory Grill.

With Towhead serving time at a Federal minimum security prison in Alabama, Buford had Pearl all to himself.

On the night in question, prior to the August 12th ambush, Bivins and Smith, while out of the Pusser's line of sight near the parking area, overheard the Pussers arguing. Pauline, having grown tired of Buford's philandering threatened to call the TBI and inform them of Buford's corruption. Buford was quick to respond that if she did, it would be the last thing she would ever do, as she wouldn't live to see the light of day. Bivins and Smith took this as a serious threat against Pauline. Just hours after this, the alleged ambush took place, resulting in Pauline's death.

Whether out of fear of Buford, or blind loyalty to him, the Smiths would stay close to Buford, publicly at least. Barbara Bivins on the other hand was not so gracious as she clearly felt that Buford had killed, or at the very least, had an accomplice kill Pauline as she would later outline in her own Book, *"Tommy and Me."* More on the ambush later.

The Old Hickory Grill on Guys Road North of the state Line

Hollis Jourdan....... Jourdan's
Old Highway 45..., north of the state line

Jourdan's was a beer tavern on what is now old highway 45. Ironically, it is just a few hundred yards from the location where McNairy County Sheriff James Dickey was killed in 1964. The B&R currently sits on the same basic lot, although it is slightly northof the site Jourdan's once occupied. Many people erroneously believe that the B&R is the old Jourdan's, which indeed it is not.

From highway 45, the building had the appearance of being a one story structure with a sign on top that simply said "Jourdan's." However, as you got closer to this tavern you would have seen a lower level, dug out of a hillside. While the top floor was a bar, the lower level had pool tables and such. Jourdan's was another hang out of Buford's as he and Hollis were friends.

In full disclosure, I have absolutely no information regarding Hollis Jourdan paying Buford to operate. I can only say they were very close friends.

It's difficult to get good information regarding Hollis as he was killed by his own wife and son. Hollis has been physically abusing his wife Alice for years. Alice apparently couldn't take this treatment any longer and the son stood up for his mother as well as both fired the shots that killed Hollis.

Unverified stories abound about time that Buford spent at Jourdan's with Hollis before the beer joint operator was killed.

One story tells of Buford being at Jourdan's one day when he saw a very physical looking black man at the bar. It's told that Buford couldn't resist wanting to fight this fellow just to see who was the toughest. Proving himself to be physical superior over others seems to have been important to Buford.

Allegedly, this man wanted no part of Buford's invitation to fight, but Buford kept insisting, finally giving his sidearm to Hollis as a show of good faith to his opponent.

The story goes that Buford had misjudged this fellow, as he was soon losing the fight. The story continues that Buford was so distraught over taking a beating that he did not expect that he tried to retrieve his firearm from Hollis so he could shoot the man. Hollis refused to give Buford his gun until the black man was far away from the premises.

Another story associated with Jourdan's that I and an associate of mine were told, goes to the morning of the alleged August 12th ambush.

The gentleman telling us his story asked that his name be withheld. He said that early on the morning of August 12th, he and a few friends were still at Hollis Jourdan's place into the wee hours of the morning. He claimed that Buford came in, bleeding from a wound to his face.

He said that Hollis grabbed a towel to place on the wound as he escorted Buford to a back room and out of sight of those in the bar, only to return in a matter of seconds and usher everyone out of the building, abruptly closing the establishment for the night.

As he was leaving and walking across the darkened parking lot, this gentleman claimed he observed Pusser's car from a distance. He said Pauline was in the front seat and appeared to be asleep. He didn't think much more about this until the next day when he heard about the alleged ambush. When he saw Pauline just hours before, was she already dead, he questioned to himself? Did Pusser next leave Jourdan's and stage the ambush? Was Hollis otherwise involved with this?

Are these two stories true? Unfortunately, all too often, that is the way it is with the Pusser Legend as many stories are difficult or impossible to fully vet. I am afraid we will never know if they are true or not. Each of us must individually decide for ourselves if they hold any weight as I have been unsuccessful in vetting either of them.

There were others who could create additional revenue streams for Buford as clubs and beer joints were only the beginning.

Ronnie Flanagan..., Bootlegger
McNairy County

Ronnie would tell me a story of how he had been injured and was unable to hold steady employment. He claimed that he went to work for Junior Smith hauling untaxed liquor from Caruthersville Missouri back into Tennessee and specifically to the Old Hickory Grill. This, of course, meant that not only was the liquor untaxed in the state of Tennessee, but that it was being sold at the Old Hickory and in violation to McNairy County laws where only beer was permitted for sale.

Ronnie told me that he was driving a rented U-Haul with a load of out of state booze when he had engine trouble just after entering McNairy County. With the vehicle's engine dying, he managed to stop on the roadside.

Knowing what was in the back of the truck and fearing that law enforcement might make a safety check on the stalled vehicle, he called Junior Smith to inform him about his precarious situation. Junior told him to stay with the vehicle as he would send help at once without explaining what type of help might be.

Flanagan insisted it wasn't long before a vehicle pulled up. Unable to see for the glare of the vehicle's headlights, he didn't know who it was until Buford stepped into view wearing a McNairy County Sheriff's uniform. Ronnie thought it was strange as he had never seen Pusser in a uniform before.

Buford explained that he was there to run interference until the U-Haul could be moved, should a state trooper roll by. This was enough to convince Flanagan that Buford was somehow connected to the Old Hickory and Junior Smith. Ronnie's story was verified by friends and relatives.

Ronnie Flanigan would share information about how he ran bootlegged liquor from Caruthersville Missouri to the Old Hickory Grill for Junior Smith and how Buford Pusser was complicate with the operation as he provided "protection" when needed.

Dewitt Dawson... bootlegger
Florence Alabama

Dawson was a well known criminal from Northern Alabama. He was into everything, bank robberies, bootlegging etc. He was also a friend of Towhead White.

The story goes that Buford stopped one of Dewitt's vehicles loaded with untaxed liquor, presumably going from Caruthersville Missouri and on its way to Dawson's home turf in Alabama. Sheriff Pusser impounded the vehicle along with the liquor.

Allegedly, Dawson paid Buford a visit, where Buford charged Dawson approximately seven hundred dollars for the return of his vehicle and the liquor.

Many Pusser advocates will claim this gave Dawson cause to want Sheriff Pusser dead, and thus suggest he was behind the August twelfth ambush. There is however, no evidence to even remotely connect Dawson to the alleged Pusser hit. I believe it goes without saying that it is unlikely that Dawson would risk a charge of capital murder of a law enforcement officer over just seven hundred dollars.

Willie "Dewitt" Dawson was an infamous criminal and associate of Towhead White. He allegedly paid Buford Pusser $700.00 for the return of his truck and its load of bootleg whiskey being transported from Caruthersville Missouri to Florence Alabama.

Carl Hathcock..., Bootlegger
McNairy County

Another story that is well documented in newspaper clipping is one where two associates of Carl Hathcock were attempting to sell Junior Smith a load of illegal liquor at the Old Hickory Grill.

Suggesting that he was calling to make payment arrangements for the load, Junior Smith called Buford instead and reported the two men. Buford showed up and arrested the two bootleggers that day and confiscated their load of booze in a trailer which was registered to a Carl Hathcock of Texas who was not at the scene. This leaves the question, was Carl Hathcock actually a bootlegger or did he simply loan or rent his trailer to the two people who were?

It should be noted that Carl Hathcock was not related to the Hathcock's of state line fame, although some Pusser advocates and novel writers will, of course, disagree without offering proof of such a relationship. If such a relationship did exist, it must be very distant in both the bloodline and proximity to the state line as Carl Hathcock was a resident of the state of Texas. This is the only time in the Pusser legend that Carl Hathcock is mentioned. It seems to Pusser advocates and some novel writers, all Hathcocks must be of the same bloodline.

Buford with a load of bootleg liquor confiscated at the Old Hickory Grill

Yet another revenue stream for Buford came from moonshiners. This incident is the only time I can find that Carl Hathcock had any dealings in McNairy County.

Paul David English... self-professed moonshiner
Michie Tennessee

I have been told by several sources that Buford would collect from moonshiners, just like he did from club owners, beer joint operators and bootleggers.

I found Paul David English who claims to have paid Sheriff Pusser for the privilege of making moonshine. According to English and other players, moonshiners were treated no differently by Buford..., if you didn't pay, you didn't play.

In *"WALKING TALL PART TWO,"* English was morphed into the role of one Pinky Dobson. If you saw this movie, you would know that Dobson worked for the also fictitious John Witter. Witter was the imagined and very fictitious mob boss in McNairy County and Dobson was a big-time moonshiner who thus, answered to Witter. In one of the movie scenes Dobson escaped from a hospital while under guard. In a pursuit scene, Buford shoots into the back of Dobson's car, with one projectile entering Dobson's back, partially paralyzing him.

This is one of those "certain events" on which the movie was based. In real life, Paul David English was being held in the McNairy County Jail where he had earned the position of trustee. A trustee pretty much has run of the jail complex, doing odd jobs such as cleaning, taking meals to prisoners, etc.

According to English, his wife would often bring him meals she had cooked at home. The jailer would of course check her and the food for contraband items. Having never found any such contraband items, these inspections soon stopped. It was then that English convinced his wife to smuggle a rope into him. She did so, hiding it under her clothing.

Once English had this rope, he went out on the roof where he was allowed to smoke. Much like in the movie, he used the rope to scale down the wall to the ground, escaping and heading to Corinth. Once there he stole his father's car.

Buford, suspecting English might go to his father's place, headed there as well with Corinth Police Chief Art Murphy. A car chase followed, leading Buford to shoot through the car's trunk and hitting English in the spine.

English claimed that sometime after this, when he was free again, he ran into Buford at Paul Moore's Place in Michie. He told Buford that he had heard that Buford would allow you to make moonshine if you paid him. He reminded Buford that since he had been shot and partially paralyzed, that he could not find work, asking Buford to allow him to make moonshine.

English claimed that Buford asked where he would set up a still, to which English gave a location. Buford rejected the idea, telling English he would set it up on his father's land, also telling him where he would get the worm (cooper coil) for the still, where he would buy the sugar required to make the brew, how much moonshine he could make each month, who he could sell it to as well as how much he could charge per gallon.

Paul David English was the model used as the fictional character
"Pinky Dobson" in WALKING TALL II

English laughed a little as he told me this, saying he quickly understood that Buford was management and he was labor. He went on to say even with these restrictions, he had never made so much money in his life, adding that Buford would send Deputy Peatie Plunk down on a regular basis to make sure he was following Buford's rules.

English indicated that he didn't make moonshine for long as he ran into other "legal entanglements" at that time.

English would laugh about the "Pinky Dobson" character that was modeled after him, joking that he never realized that he had worked for a state line crime syndicate or had ever plotted to kill Pusser until he saw "*Walking Tall II.*"

Again, I was able to vet much of his story, but unfortunately, not all. Many parts of his tale are indeed true while others are still in question as I have not been able to completely substantiate them to my satisfaction. Having said this, keep in mind that Paul David English was only one of many moonshiners who claims to have paid the sheriff.

The bottom line is that it appears that Buford was probably making more money through these various revenue streams than any one criminal in the county, while he hid behind the badge of a sheriff.

Chapter 9
Towhead White

Carl Douglas "Towhead" White

This story would not be complete without Towhead White. White, in my opinion, was the only person in the Pusser Legend who truly earned his reputation.

White was a native of Mississippi, having been born on December 31, 1936, in the small town of Eupora in Webster County to Weldon and Elizabeth White.

White's life is a tale of swindles, robberies, fraud, moonshining, bootlegging, prison escapes, and many suspect him as committing murder on multiple occasions. Even with all of this in his criminal resume, it is the alleged ambush of Buford and Pauline Pusser of August 12, 1967 which seems to have brought him so much attention and fame.

Towhead aspired to be the "Al Capone of the South" and his criminal record had him headed squarely in that direction. Some of the events in White's past have been difficult to verify, as like with so many situations in the Pusser Legend, it becomes a matter of connecting dots. One of these is his alleged connections with Carlos Marcello of the New Orleans crime syndicate, where he is said to have been employed as a driver for the infamous crime boss.

I have found nothing to corroborate this information, except that White was also acquainted with R.D. Mathews, who ran the Dallas operation for Carlos Marcello. While in Texas, White did manage to make that state's "Ten Most Wanted List" for the crimes he committed there. Many will often claim he was on the FBI's ten most wanted list, which is incorrect, as it was actually the Texas ten most wanted list.

We know that he came to the state line from the area in the mid 1950's along with his friend Junior Smith. Both went to work for Jack Hathcock at that time.

We do know that White left the state line and Hathcock's employ for a period of time and headed for the bright lights of Chicago. This was the same period in which Buford lived in Chicago and is said to have worked at a bar that Towhead allegedly managed at the time.

As has already been discussed, Jack Hathcock and his wife Louise were divorced in 1957. While Jack retained ownership of the state line businesses in the divorce settlement, it was Louise who continued to manage them with Towhead's assistance once he returned home to Mississippi. It was at this point that White would attempt to launch his own criminal empire. It was also in this time period that he had a run in with his friend Tommy Bivins, which almost sent Towhead to prison for attempted murder.

June 24th, 1964 was a big story concerning White. Early that morning, sometime around 3:30 am, White was at the Shamrock Restaurant. Most of the local establishments had closed down for the night and the restaurant was a gathering place for a lot of late night people as it offered twenty four hour service. W.O. and Larece Hathcock were at the Shamrock during the early hours of that day as was Tommy Bivins and many others.

Towhead had been drinking, when someone, seeing Tommy Bivins in the restaurant, and wanting to create a little excitement, remarked to White about just how tough Bivins could be, not that Tommy had been involved in anything to indicate that he had a mean streak.

It wasn't just Tommy's size and build, six foot three and 225 pounds that impressed people, so much as the fact that he worked twelve hour shifts on a pipeline, a very physical job that had toned his muscle structure. Tommy simply looked to be a man that could handle himself in just about any situation and people seemed to respect that.

Now you have to understand that Towhead and Tommy were friends, however, Towhead wouldn't allow mere friendship to stand in the way of his reputation as he wanted everyone to know that he was the toughest man at the state line. Being somewhat intoxicated, Towhead decided to prove that point to everyone in the restaurant.

Tommy was sitting in a booth minding his own business, just visiting with W.O. and Larece, who were sitting nearby, when Towhead approached Tommy, wanting to fight. White thought it was time to show everyone just how tough he could be and fighting Bivins, he thought, was the way to make his point clear to everyone.

Tommy told Towhead that he wasn't looking for trouble and attempted to dismiss him, pointing out that Towhead was drunk. This only served to fuel Towhead's anger as he reached for

Harry K "Tommy" Bivins

Tommy, hitting Bivins in the face and bringing first blood. That was all it took for Bivins to come out of the booth where he had been seated.

Tommy stood up to defend himself, grabbing Towhead by the shirt with his left hand as he pounded Towhead to the floor with his powerful right fist. Not yet satisfied however, Towhead is said to have come at Tommy again only to receive a second and equal pounding from Bivins, even as Louise tried to separate the two men. Once the two were separated, Louise took a bleeding Towhead away to tend to his wounds.

I am told that W.O. and Larece, knowing what Towhead was capable of, used this opportunity to try to get Tommy to leave the restaurant with them before Towhead returned. Tommy, being a proud man, didn't want to give Towhead the satisfaction of thinking he had chased him from the restaurant.

Even as the Hathcocks were trying to convince Bivins it was time to leave, Towhead returned with Louise's .38 caliber Smith &Wesson handgun, the same gun that would soon be used to snuff out the life of Jack Hathcock. Towhead stuck in Tommy's face, and pulled the trigger.

The gun went off with a deafening sound. The bullet penetrated Tommy's left cheek near the nose and blood began to gush from the wound.

Although wounded, Tommy had to again defend himself as the fight now continued with Tommy beating Towhead to a pulp. Both men ended up at the hospital that night. Tommy was in serious condition from the gunshot wound and was transferred from the Corinth hospital to the hospital in Memphis for the extensive treatment and care Tommy would require.

Towhead drove himself to the hospital in Corinth to have his wounds cared for, including one to his buttocks. Towhead would claim his wounds were from an auto accident he had been in as he drove himself to the hospital.

Others however, would tell that Tommy, after being shot and attacked for a third time, had the wherewithal to grab a butter knife from a table and stab Towhead in his backside. Having been attacked twice, shot in the face, and then attacked a third time and still being able to subdue your opponent would certainly suggest that Tommy Bivins was indeed the much tougher man of the two.

Towhead would sober up and visit Tommy in the hospital, trying as best he could to make amends, telling Tommy he was drunk and out of his head at the time of their fight and was now looking for Tommy's forgiveness. What Towhead was really looking for and so desperately needed however was a way to avoid prison on a charge of attempted murder...., not Tommy's forgiveness.

Corinth Police Chief Art Murphy and D.A. Neal Biggers would also make their visits to see Tommy as well, asking Tommy about the attack which almost took his life. The two men finally convinced Tommy that it was in his best interest to give a formal statement so a warrant could be issued for Towhead's arrest. After a certain amount of consternation, Tommy finally agreed and signed the necessary documents to make Towhead's arrest possible.

Towhead was arrested however, when it came time for him to appear in court, Tommy recanted his statement about White, saying he wasn't sure who had attacked him, thus allowing Towhead to go free. People say that Tommy was too kind to Towhead, letting an old friend off the hook, even under such serious circumstances.

Events like this were entered into White's FBI file and were also noted by the local federal prosecutor who recognized White as a criminal menace. Towhead's FBI rap sheet would show that over the years, Towhead had been charged with everything from minor acts such as public drunkenness and hitchhiking to robberies, flight to avoid prosecution and much more. Other FBI documents found in his file clearly show that White was managing the Shamrock Motel and Restaurant as well as the White Iris in 1964.

A letter, written later in the year, from Federal Prosecutor H.M. Ray to his superiors at the Department of Justice clearly expresses Ray's concerns with Towhead's enterprises at the state line. In that letter, the Federal Prosecutor also mentioned Sheriff Dickey's demise and that he suspected that White had already made arrangements with the newly elected McNairy County Sheriff (Pusser), to continue the deals that Dickey had made with Towhead.

When you start connecting all of these dots, the picture becomes a little clearer. White and Pusser knew each other before Buford was sheriff. They were in Chicago at the same time. Sheriff Dickey had become a liability to White as Dickey was being investigated for his ties to the state line as well as the local moonshing industry. White knew that Dickey could easily roll over on him in a bid for leniency from the court. This had made Dickey a dangerous man to have around as far as Towhead was concerned.

W.O. Hathcock would place White and Pusser at the state line the very morning that Sheriff Dickey was killed in an alleged auto accident and expressed his concerns about the happenings of that day. W.O. saw it as something more than an "accident".

After Dickey's death, Interim County Sheriff Ward Moore said that Louise Hathcock called, asking him to send both sheriff candidates to the state to see her as she needed to "buy another sheriff." We also have another dot that we can connect and that is author Barbara Bivins research showing Buford did indeed make contact with White and Hathcock as one of his first acts as sheriff.

A recording exists where Buford would admit that Louise first offered him three hundred dollars a month in payoffs to look the other way as the Shamrock practiced their illegal activities. He said that when he refused, the offer went to five hundred a month, then to a thousand dollars a month.

Of course, Buford denied ever having accepted Hathcock's money even though his lifestyle on a meager sheriff's salary would suggest otherwise.

While some may say that all of this is improbable, you have to consider that you have people from both sides of the story, W.O. Hathcock and Barbara Bivins on the state line side, giving similar information that seems to be shored up and supported by H.M. Ray and Ward Moore on the law enforcement side of the story.

When Buford was elected sheriff, a certain calm overcame things at the state line, or so it seemed. Things rocked along well for Buford and Towhead at first. The Shamrock and White Iris were making good money as was Buford, according to many.

Make no mistake, as time went on the relationship between White and Pusser began to sour. This often happens when you put two "type A" personalities together.

One situation that allegedly led to some contention between the two however, was Pearl Wade, the young and beautiful light skinned black girl who was Willie Wade's niece. Both Pusser and Towhead were said to have had an interest in Pearl. This would allegedly spill over into their business dealings. Both allegedly admired admired and wanted Pearl. In interviews with White's family, however, I am told that Towhead had no interest in Pearl and the version Morris presented in his writings were pure fiction.

Regardless, White and Pusser both seemed to be in a competition about who was in charge at the state line.

White, along with Louise Hathcock, was paying Pusser for what I would call "protective services" and White thought he could do anything he wanted in McNairy County. The way he saw things is that Buford worked for him.

Pusser on the other hand was the high Sheriff of McNairy County and felt he was in control of what White would be allowed to do on his turf. A hatred been the two men began to build, things began to come to a head on January 14, 1965 when Pusser received an anonymous tip of a moonshine still near the state line area.

While Pusser and Deputy Tommy Brown were in the woods searching for the reported moonshine still, Towhead alledgedly had someone set Pusser's car on fire, totaling the vehicle and causing the loss of five hundred dollars worth of Pusser's personal equipment. White of course, had an alibi as he was at the White Iris at the time of the fire, however, Buford suspected that White was behind the arson, according to White's FBI file.

Still, they apparently put their personal quarrels aside and continued to do business with a new venture... "The Three State Moonshine Operation" that was to be set up in McNairy County.

During the planning of this new venture, Towhead must have been going through some other issues at the time as his attitude, according to those around him, seemed to spiral out of control and he became more violent.

FBI records show that he had assaulted Louise Hathcock on January 12th. She was injured badly enough that she was treated at the hospital in Corinth but was not held there overnight.

Shortly thereafter, on March 25, 1965, Towhead and a group of men robbed the Red Carpet Inn in Biloxi, Mississippi. The Inn was a Casino located on the popular beach strip. White's plan was a simple one. Towhead would be playing poker, acting as a guest of the Inn. This gave him the advantage of knowing who had any real money at the Casino. Later, the rest of the gang came in, guns drawn. Guests, including White, would be lined up against a wall and all their cash and valuables taken from them. Ironically, a good friend of Towhead's would be in the casino that night as Bill McPeters and his companion from Corinth would be at the Inn as well.

I had an opportunity to ask McPeters about this incident. Bill said that when he saw that this gang intended to take the belongings of every individual there, he told his companion to remove her rings, which were of some value, and place them in her mouth.

Towhead, still acting as a member of the crowd, was lined up on the wall near McPeters. As the gang collected everyone's valuables, they approached McPeters. Towhead was overheard telling the gang to skip McPeters and the lady who was with him ..., and they passed the couple by continuing down the line gathering cash, watches, rings, anything of value from all others there. It was then, McPeters told me, that he knew that Towhead was involved in the heist. Why else would they have skipped us, McPeters said, they were following Towhead's instructions. Keep in mind that Towhead considered McPeters as a friend.

Others who were lined up on the wall noticed that the gang didn't frisk White for his valuables in the same manner as they had everyone else, making them suspicious of White.

The source stated that [   ] of Columbus, Miss., was seen there by [   ] knows him and that he is a gambler.

The source stated that [   ] heard from some of the people hanging around the state line, but not from LOUISE HATHCOCK, that 48% of the business is owned by the Gold Coast Syndicate, that is by some gamblers from around the Gold Coast of Mississippi.

The source said if [   ] WHITE would end up by killing LOUISE HATHCOCK. She claimed she could give no further information concerning the allegation concerning the Gold Coast Syndicate.

On 1/19/65, [   ] of the Little Rock Office, advised SA [   ] that CARL WHITE, who is also known as "TOWHEAD", manages the Shamrock Motel, Corinth, Miss., and had moved his fencing activities to the White Iris Restaurant at Selmer, Tenn., where WHITE has a "fix" with local law enforcement officers.

This source reported that as of 1/13/65 the following individuals were hanging out at the restaurant and believed to be staying at Selmer, Tenn.

[   ]
pounds, [   ] place of [   ] unknown, reportedly resides in a motel, name unknown, at Selmer, Tenn. It was stated that he recently was hospitalized for gunshot wounds, place unknown. He is supposed to have been shot with a .38 calibre through the left thumb and right shoulder with one bullet. The source described [   ] as a safe man and a gambler and said he was driving a 1965 Bonneville Pontiac convertible with Tennessee license, number unknown.

COVER PAGE

FBI report suggests that Towhead had a "FIX" I with Local law enforcement

The gang left with all their goods, but Towhead, still acting as a guest, as well as a victim of the robbery, stayed and was seated at a blackjack table when police arrived a short while later to arrest him, however, Louise Hathcock made the necessary arrangements to bail Towhead out of jail.

In one of my visits with Bill McPeters, he would share with me, information not only about the Red Carpet robbery, but also some inside knowledge about White and Pusser. According to Bill, White hated Pusser, but was more than willing to use the sheriff to build his empire. McPeters would indicate that their relationship did indeed seem strained.

A couple of months later, on May 22, 1964, is when Jack Hathcock was gunned down at the Shamrock. While Louise took the blame for the death of her former husband, many well connected people believe it was Towhead who pulled the trigger sending five .38 caliber rounds in Hathcock's neck and chest.

Towhead's next criminal act was to set up his "Three State Moonshine Operation" in McNairy County. His still was said to be a 1,500 gallon beast and stories boast that it could produce 4000 gallonsof shine every five days. This was a big time operation that put most, if not all, other stills in the region to shame.

Towhead must have had quite a customer base as he would complain about having difficulties keeping up with demand for his product. With McNairy County having only about 18,000 total population at that time, one can only surmise that much of the brew was going elsewhere. I have been told that much of it was going to Chicago.

To make a long story short about his moonshine operation, Towhead gained information that state authorities had received word about his still operating in McNairy County and they were making plans to take it down. It's unknown exactly how White obtained this information, but several fingers pointed in Buford's direction. This is particularly interesting when you realize that the state Alcohol Beverage Control (ABC) bureau stopped sharing information with Buford and failed to invited him on raids they performed in his county.

Flashback to Towhead's friend Tommy Bivins. White quickly hired Tommy Bivins, yes, the man he had shot in the face at the Shamrock Restaurant, to move one hundred fifty metal drums, each of fifty five gallon capacity, from McNairy County to a new site he had set up in Tishomingo County Mississippi. In late March and early April Bivins, using a truck owned by White, made several trips to move these drums to the new site.

Now, I find it a little more than strange that Sheriff Pusser could never seem to find and destroy the still while it was set up in McNairy County, let alone ever arresting White on any kind of charge.

Towhead had the operation moved from McNairy County and had it set up just a few days later in Tishomingo County. It was never fully operational at the new site as it was there only four days later, on April 6th, when County Sheriff James Bishop and three Federal agents raided the still, arresting Tommy Bivins, Ray Troxell, Jack Newton, Bobby Gene Vandiver and Donald Dawson at the site. White was arrested a short time later in Corinth.

White and his moonshine crew appeared in Federal Court on September 15th, 1965 where they all pleaded guilty of the alcohol related charges filed against them. White received a three year sentence and was immediately transported to a Federal minimum security facility at Maxwell Air Force Base in Montgomery Alabama to serve out his term.

A month later, on October 16th of that same year, White would again be sentenced to a two year prison term, having pleaded guilty to charges of being an accessory to armed robbery in the Red Carpet Inn heist, which was to run concurrently with his sentence in the moonshine case.

As for the others, Jack Newton would get a three year sentence for his part in the moonshine operation. Bobby Gene Vandiver was hit with 2 years to be served. Donald Dawson was given 18 months in federal prison. Ray Troxell was lucky and got 18 months' probation.

Tommy Bivins also got off lightly with 18 months' probation as he had no prior criminal history. How Bivins allowed Towhead to talk him into helping with the operation in the first place, we will probably never know. Bivins obviously made good money working on the pipeline and didn't need the extra income.

One of the things that probably helped Bivins get off easy was his demeanor and the fact that he was well liked by the people in his community. When people would later ask him about the arrest, he would just laugh it off saying, "I thought we were out there making jelly."

White would be in prison serving time for the moonshine and robbery charges on the morning that Buford Pusser would shoot and kill Louise Hathcock at the Shamrock Motel. This is where the real story makes an interesting twist.

Towhead White, Howard Carroll, and John Henry Fowlkes at the state line.

Chapter 10
The Death of Louise Hathcock

Laura Louise Anderson Hathcock

Sheriff Buford Pusser, Jim Moffett and Peatie Plunk, armed with two search warrants, pull their car into the parking area of the Shamrock Motel.

February 1st, 1966 is a cold winter's day in the area, one of the coldest in over a hundred years, or so the local newspapers would say. Even so, Sheriff Pusser is oddly dressed for such a frigid day as while his deputies are outfitted in their sheriff's department uniforms and wearing heavy coats, Buford is dressed in business attire, as if he is ready for a photo opportunity.

Pulling into the parking area, Buford spots a young couple waiting near a pay phone. He steps from his car and has a short visit with George and Dorothy Vogel, the couple who had contacted the Sheriff's Office about the alleged theft of Mrs. Vogel's Purse.

George Vogel explained that they were traveling through the area and were on their way back home to Illinois. Mr. Vogel told Sheriff Pusser that they were returning from a trip to the gulf coast, but with the weather getting bad the night before, and with the onset of darkness, they had decided to get a motel room for the night rather than drive on. It is unclear why they passed through Corinth without seeking a room there, however, when they reached the state line, they saw the Shamrock Motel and Restaurant. The facility appeared to be rather new with all the modern conveniences, so the Vogels checked in for the night.

They visited the restaurant for a meal before they retired to their room for the evening, they explained to Sheriff Pusser. When they awoke the next morning however, Dorothy Vogel noticed that her purse was missing. When asked, she described the purse and told the sheriff that it held about one hundred twenty-five dollars in cash, a rosary, and a few other personal items.

They went on to tell Sheriff Pusser that upon discovering that the purse was missing from their room this morning, they went to the motel office to report it. Louise Hathcock told the couple that she knew nothing about the purse. They described Louise to the sheriff as being both drunk and threatening. That is when they called the Sheriff's Office for assistance.

Stories seem to vary about Buford's trip down from Selmer to the Shamrock as some will say it was Peatie Plunk who told Buford he should strap on his gun, while others will claim it was Chief Deputy Jim Moffett who made the suggestion. The fact is, we do not know if this happened at all.

Buford instructed Deputy Plunk to wait outside with the Vogels as he and Jim Moffett stepped inside the motel's small lobby to speak with Louise. According to Pusser and Moffett, Louise was indeed intoxicated just as the Vogel's had described. She was described as being belligerent toward Pusser and Moffett as they asked her about the missing purse.

Buford informed Hathcock that he had two search warrants, one for stolen property, the other for intoxicating liquors. Louise and the sheriff exchange a few words as Moffett listens. Realizing that Pusser was serious about the search warrants, Louise allegedly tells him that if he would step into her private living quarters, she will give him the low down on what is going on with the state line operation... at least that was Pusser's story.

One has to wonder why she would tell Buford such a thing as she, for all intents and purposes, was "the state line". Jack was dead, Towhead was in prison and W.O. had shut down the Plantation Club almost two years earlier when Alcorn County refused to renew his liquor permits. Louise is now all that is left of the state line operation. This brings Pusser's statement under scrutiny.

According to Sheriff Pusser, he followed her into her room as she had asked, which was attached to the motel office by a hallway behind the registration desk. Pusser would claim that Louise said she was going to kill him as she pulled out a .38 caliber Smith and Wesson handgun, took aim at him and pulled the trigger. Pusser would tell that he fell back on her bed as the projectile whizzed past his ear, and went through the windowpane, lodging itself in an awning support post in front of the motel.

According to Pusser, Louise stepped in front of him as he lay sprawled across the bed, again took aim, and pulled the trigger. His story was that the gun failed to fire as the hammer smashed onto the chambered round. He would describe Louise as having a strange look on her face when she realized the gun failed to fire.

Buford then claimed this gave him the opportunity to draw his weapon, a .41 magnum, and return fire, his first shot nipping her shoulder near the neck. He would go on to claim that she started to raise her weapon to fire once more, forcing him to shoot her again, this shot striking her torso. Buford would erroneously later tell that this shot "blew her heart out." Buford never seemed to want to speak much about the third shot he fired that day, one to her head as she lay on the floor.

Jim Moffett was in the hallway, just outside the room as the shooting took place. His view was blocked as the door was almost completely closed as the shots rang out. Some dry-cleaning left hanging on the doorknob had prevented the door, which hinged on his left, from being completely closed. His view was blocked. Deputy Plunk is said to have rushed into the office, gun drawn, when he heard the gun play.

After shots were fired, Buford heard a noise coming from a room in the back of the office and instructed Plunk to see who was there. Two people of the were found there, one being Howard Carroll, the other, a local man whose name I cannot reveal as he is still living and doesn't wish to have his name disclosed.

Carroll had of course heard the shots and upon seeing Sheriff Pusser, said, "she's dead, ain't she?" Carroll's recollections of what he heard that morning would however be far different than what Buford claimed to have happened. The other man, like Carroll, disagrees with Pusser's version of the shooting.

The TBI was informed of the officer involved shooting and Investigator Warren Jones would make his way to the motel hours later. McNairy County Coroner Ward Moore would be called to the scene as well.

They would find Louise lying on the floor, her handgun still in her right hand and her drinking glass still in her left hand. There was also a large roll of cash laying on her cleavage. Her pants were wet almost to her knees, as having been shot, she had lost control of her bodily functions and had urinated on herself.

District Attorney Will Terry Abernathy and Harry Peeler, McNairy Counties Medical Examiner would concur on the need for an autopsy to be performed on Hathcock. Once the scene had been investigated, her body was transported to the State Medical Examiner's office in Memphis.

Three people would be involved in performing the autopsy..., Tennessee State Medical Examiner Dr Jerry Francisco would be there, along with Dr. Sprunt taking the lead in the autopsy with Richmond assisting.

Howard Carroll would tell friends that
he heard Buford's gun fire first

Their findings would not support the shooting scenario as Buford had described it. Their report wound show that the shot to the neck and shoulder area, the first shot as Buford described it, would enter the back of the neck and shoulder area, indicating that Louise was facing away from the sheriff as the shot was fired.

The shot to the torso entered to the left and a little below the left shoulder blade, exiting under Hathcock's right breast. Again, Pusser would have us believe that he was facing Hathcock during the shootout, however, the autopsy report shows otherwise.

The third shot was to her head. This projectile entered the left jawline and exited the back of the skull, taking some teeth and leaving them embedded in the carpet as they exited the back of the skull. Such a trajectory would be consistent only with Hathcock being shot as she lay, already dying, on the floor as Buford stood near her feet.

Howard Carroll who was with a second individual in a living room/kitchen area in the back of the motel office, would tell that he heard the loud report of Pusser's .41 magnum before he heard the single "pop" from Hathcock's .38 Smith and Wesson.

Now if you examine the photos that are available of the scene, you will indeed see dry cleaning hanging on the doorknob of the door separating the office hallway from Hathcock's living quarters. This is said to have kept the door from being completely closed.

Chief Deputy Jim Moffett was said to be in the hallway, not in the room as the shooting took place, therefore his view obscured by the partially closed door.

There is a photo of Buford standing in the room near Hathcock's body. As you look at this photo you see the back of County Coroner Ward Moore as he stands over Hathcock's body, which is completely out of sight, as she had collapsed in the open area between the closet and the bathroom. This means that even if the door to the hallway had been wide open, Moffett probably would not have had a view of Hathcock as shots were fired. In short, he would not have been able to see if Louise was actually facing Buford as the Sheriff would have you to believe, or if her back was to him as he fired his weapon as the autopsy would indicate.

Next look at the photo of the bullet hole in the window, the one made by the bullet which Buford claimed whizzed past his ear.

I have a brick from the Shamrock, one with mortar still attached. If you examine a photo taken from outside of the same room, count the rows of bricks beneath the window and take into consideration the height of a brick with the mortar, you will see that the shot Buford says Hathcock fired went through the window pane at approximately forty six inches above the floor. Buford was six feet six inches tall. That is 78 inches in height, leading me to further question Buford's account of the shooting with the bullet whizzing past his ear.

That bullet continued an upward trajectory before lodging itself in an awning support post, just outside the room, in front of the motel office at almost eight feet above ground level. What does all of this mean? Based on the findings of the autopsy report, the information the photos provide, especially the one indicating the location of Hathcock's body, the statement made by Howard Carroll, in addition to the measurements showing the angle and height of the bullet hole in the window pane, it indicates that the shooting did not happen as Sheriff Pusser described.

These factors suggest that Pusser fired first, into Hathcock's posterior side, possibly as she tried to flee the room as she understood what was about to happen. The available trajectory evidence suggests that Sheriff Pusser then knelled down beside Hathcock's lifeless body, picked up her .38 and from a kneeling position, fired a shot through the window in an attempt to make it appear that Hathcock had fired on him. The projectile's angle from the window to the awning support post does not fit with Buford's story as the shot should have struck the post much lower. Buford most likely then placed the .38 in Hathcock's right hand.

Studies show that a good percentage of the time when people are shot, especially when they are killed, they lose control of the body and often drop whatever is in their hands, including a gun. Why was Louise an exception to this common action?

Three factors would come into play here that turns Pusser's story upside down. First, what Howard Carroll said regarding the order of the gunshots fired and secondly, the findings of the autopsy report that did not support Pusser's version of the shooting. Thirdly, the trajectory of the shot Hathcock allegedly fired at Buford.

When you consider the evidence, it appears that Buford very well may have actually committed a murder.

There is a difference between murder and homicide. Homicide is the taking of one's life. Homicide is often justifiable, such as in a case of self-defense. Murder, on the other hand, is the intentional and wrongful act of taking of one's life.

Buford is now faced with a real problem...., how to overcome the evidence against him which indicates that Hathcock's death was a case of murder. But first, we need to understand what Buford's motive would be for killing Louise Hathcock.

Buford had been taking payoffs from Louise for about a year and a half.
Buford wasn't the only one getting payoff as other law enforcement officers were as well, but Buford received far more than anyone and the amount of the payoffs seemed to escalate. One family member recalls one month in particular when Buford received in excess of twenty-five hundred dollars from Louise.

Those big paydays were coming to an end however, and Buford knew it. Buford was aware that Jack Hathcock, before his death, had failed to pay the IRS as he should have, and they had filed a lien on the Shamrock and other properties for back taxes owed. Louise was about to lose the Shamrock, and as such, Buford's big paydays at the Shamrock were coming to an end. Buford also knew that Louise kept large sums of money hidden at the Shamrock. All he needed was an opportunity to search for it.

One of the factors that is said to have led authorities into looking at Sheriff James Dickey was his bank account that had more money than a person of his known income should have. Louise was certainly smart enough not to make that mistake, thus she kept a lot of money hidden away at the Shamrock rather than in a bank where prying eyes could cause trouble.

The Vogel's report of the stolen purse provided Buford with the opportunity he needed. With Louise dead, Buford would have an opportunity to search for Hathcock's hidden money. With Louise dead, all Buford had to now was convince a grand jury that he was forced to shoot Hathcock in self-defense. But what about all the evidence which suggested otherwise? Howard Carroll wasn't going to be much of a problem, after all, he was known to almost everyone who knew him as a drunk. Who would believe him or trust what he might say? Howard's friend that was in the backroom that day wasn't going to talk then and still doesn't wish to be connected to this story even today.

Next was the findings of Hathcock's autopsy report. It would pose a different problem altogether as the evidence in the report was very damning.

Then there was of course the dynamics of the room itself where measurements and trajectories could be calculated. Buford needed help with these situations.

As it turns out, the district attorney would call only two people to testify before the grand jury. Buford's Chief Deputy Jim Moffett and TBI investigator Warren Jones. Howard Carroll, nor anyone else from the motel or restaurant who were present when the shooting occurred, including the Vogels, would be called as witnesses. Moffett had little he could testify to as he did not see the shooting. Who knows what questions the District attorney asked TBI investigator Jones during the proceedings? Were they tough questions or more the softball variety? We will probably never know.

Regardless, what we do know is that the autopsy report, probably the most damning piece of evidence against Buford, was never presented to the grand jury investigating Hathcock's death. Instead, they were presented with close up photos of Hathcock's wounds.

I spoke with one of the people who sat in on the grand jury proceedings. James Opal Gray, who would later become McNairy County Sheriff. Even after all the years that have passed, Gray would still honor the rules of the grand jury, refusing to say what was discussed or shown to them.

However, when I asked about the autopsy report, he seemed a little stunned. He did reveal that it was never presented to them and that he did not know that an autopsy had even been performed. It seems Buford may have found a friend in the prosecutor.

Without the evidence provided by the autopsy report, the grand jury returned a "No True Bill" against Buford in the taking of Hathcock's life, making him unaccountable for her death. This leaves us to wonder if the outcome would have been different had more witnesses have been called to testify and all the evidence against Pusser, especially the autopsy report, had been submitted as it should have been.

As it turned out, Dorothy Vogel's wallet, not a purse, would be found by young Bobby Anderson in a booth at the restaurant next door to the motel. The very restaurant where the Vogel's had dined the night before.

As for Buford, try as he might, he would never find the money Louise had hidden at the Shamrock. Family members tell of his destruction of Hathcock's living quarters and office as soon as the investigation was completed by the TBI.

Where was the money hidden and who got it? That's in the next chapter.

Chapter 11
What Became of Louise's Money?

Many people knew that Louise kept a great deal of money hidden at the Shamrock. Members of her family who often stayed at the motel knew she kept money there, as did Buford and Towhead White.

What many people don't know is that Louise and Towhead were alleged to have been married sometime after Jack was killed. FBI files indicate that Louise was White's "common law" wife. Others, however, would claim they were legally married, however, neither I nor the

Hathcock or Anderson families have found any documents which show they were legally

. What I did find was that Louise was making every effort to get Towhead's sentence

overturned or at the very least, shortened, while making it appear that they were married.

Louise would file for a Social Security card using the name Louise White. Card number 587-24-8161 was issuewd to Louise. The first three digits of the card number tells us that the card was related to a filing in the state of Mississippi.

Social Security Card showing the last name "White"

Previously, Louise had used a Social Security card issued in the state of Ohio. That card number was 268-30-0487 where her name appears as Laura Louise Hathcock. Was this her first step in making it appear that she and Towhead were married?

Hathcock's original Social Security card showing
the name Laura Louise Hathcock

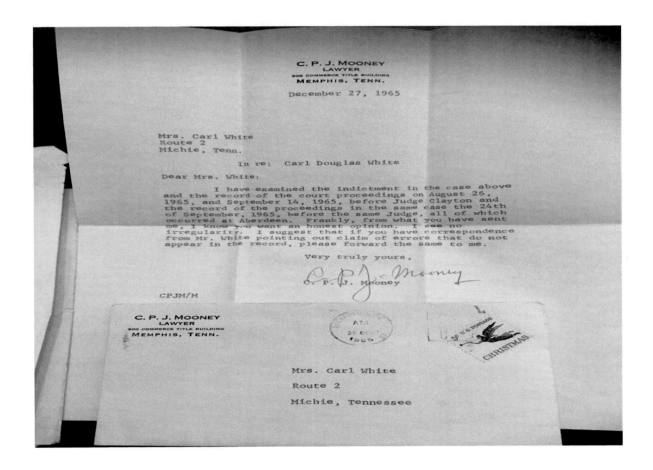

In correspondence with C.P.J. Mooney, a Memphis attorney, Louise was seeking legal assistance in getting Towhead's prison sentence reduced or overturned. Mooney would respond that he saw no errors in the case that he could contest. In this letter, Lawyer Mooney addresses his response to "Mrs. Carl White."

Louise contacted another attorney, a Mr. Taylor, on Towhead's behalf, asking for his aid in getting Towhead's sentenced reduced. In this letter dated 12/22/1965, Louise states that she is a "close personal friend" of Towheads. This correspondence obviously failed to achieve the results Louise hoped for as well.

December 22nd, 19

Mr. Taylor-   Re: Carl D. White

In regards to our nice telephone conversation last week, I am enclosing the information that you so kindly ask me to do.

Carl Douglas White, an inmate at Texarkana, Arkansas, is serving a 3-year term for conspiracy to operate a whiskey still.

The sentence was imposed by the United States District Court for the Northern District of Mississippi, Eastern Division, Judge Claude Clayton presiding. There was some five or six parties involved in this and all of them entered a plea of guilty.

No doubt, he was technically guilty, but was not one of the principles. The still was to be operated by other parties. The still was captured and destroyed before operation began.

One of the principles who was to operate the still I believe received a three-year sentence; one either a year or fifteen months, and all the other suspended sentences.

I would like very much to see White's sentence cut to a minimum time.

Mr. Taylor, if I am out of order in asking this, I feel sure that you would inform me so, but if you can be of any help in getting this sentence reduced, I will greatly appreciate same.

Carl is a close, personal friend of mine and if I didn't have confidence in him, I certainly would not try to seek this favor at the present time.

I plan to be in Santa Fe the latter part of February next year and will certainly drop in to see you nice people. I wish for you and your family a nice 1966 and that we all may have peace and contentment. (God knows we all need it).

Will personal regards, I am

Sincerely,

Letter from Louise to Attorney Taylor where she uses the name Hathcock instead of White.

To add to this confusion, on her last driver's license, issued on November 15, 1965, her name appeared as Louise A. White. Her two previous licenses issued, one issued on November 17, 1958 and the other renewed on September 30, 1963, her name appeared as Laura Louise Hathcock.

The question is, prior to her death, was Louise a "friend" as she claimed in one letter, or was she Towhead's wife as her last Social Security card and drivers license suggests?

Why would Louise be using the name "White" after Towhead was in prison? It was possibly done so she could handle Towhead's business affairs while he was away. It could also be that by portraying herself to be Towhead's wife as she believed it might help in her efforts to get Towhead's prison sentence reduced. Then again, the possibility does exist that they were indeed married.

The use of White's last name, however, came into play for Towhead after Louise was killed by Sheriff Pusser.

Relatives of Louise were shocked as Towhead was escorted into the funeral home in handcuffs for her visitation service. He was the last person many of them expected to see.

For a federal prisoner to be allowed to attend a funeral is rare and usually occurs only when two people are closely related. Did White beat the system after Louise took his last name?

After being at the funeral home and under guard, Towhead showed up later that evening at the Shamrock Motel without his law enforcement escort. According to some who may know, Towhead allegedly paid his prison escort ten thousand dollars for the privilege of being released for twenty for hours without their supervision.

A gathering of sorts was held at the Shamrock that night during which Towhead got to see his friends as they partied. Towhead however, had more important plans while he was there..., to collect the money Louise had hidden on the premises.

According to Hathcock and Anderson family members, Sheriff Pusser had torn room #1 apart looking for Louise's stash of cash. He is said to have taken some personal items from Hathcock's room but failed to find her money.

However, during his visit to the Shamrock, Towhead was able to recover the money which was hidden behind a secret panel in the vault located in the motel office. Louise kept the money in cold creme jars. While it is said that Pusser looked in the vault itself, he never spotted the secret panel behind which the jars, full of cash, were hidden.

Immediately behind the motel office was a hallway which, to the right, led to room #1, Hathcock's onsite living quarters where Pusser had done an extensive search and found nothing. The hallway also gave access to a small kitchen and living room area immediately behind the motel registration desk. Towhead recovered more jars of money from a hidden compartment in the kitchen wall, a place where Buford had failed to look.

White then went outside to a location behind the motel, crossing a small bridge over an open ditch, to get to a pasture area where horses were kept. There, he dug up a metal box containing even more cash that was buried in the ground.

Family members don't know if these were all the places where Louise kept money, but they suspect there may have been others. Towhead would have been aware of other such places where money was hidden as he and Louise had managed the Shamrock together.

Towhead was said to have gone to the bathroom in room #1 where he broke the cold creme jars in the bathtub, recovering the cash they held. The amount recovered by Towhead is unknown, but some family member place it between one hundred thousand and possibly as much as two hundred fifty thousand dollars.

Of course, Towhead couldn't take this money back to prison with him, so he is said to have divided it up between certain friends for safe keeping while he was without his prison escort. The next day he attended Louise's funeral and was escorted back to prison.

When you look at his circle of friends that Towhead might have trusted, a few names come to mind. His protege Nimbo Price. Nimbo admired Towhead and wanted to be just like him. Howard Bunch also comes to mind. Of course, there is also Bill McPeters who was close friends with Towhead. Another that comes to mind is Dewitt Dawson, a close associate of White.

`With the money recovered and appropriately dispersed, Towhead could returned to prison and serve the remainder of his sentence, confident that his money was safe as his friends knew better than to try and cross Towhead and keep any of his stash of cash.

Chapter 12
Prior to the Alleged Ambush

Many people will question why I use the term "alleged ambush. The reasons are really pretty obvious when one examines not only the ambush, but the many events which occurred prior to the ambush. Each of these events may not seem like much when examined individually, however, when they are laid out in a time line, you have to question if the event which took the life of Pauline Pusser was an actual ambush by parties unknown, or if she died the victim of a marital dispute.

When we follow these events of the hours just prior to the alleged ambush as told by the people who were actually there, it draws a very different picture than anything we have heard before. It is certainly different from what we saw in WALKING TALL.

At the "Old Hickory Grill"

Just hours prior to the ambush, Buford had shown up at one of his favorite places, Junior Smith's "Old Hickory Grill" on Guys Road just north of the state line. It was late in the evening when Shirley Smith and Barbara Bivins were outside the establishment, near the parking area, when Pauline arrived looking for Buford. Buford may have sensed trouble as he walked to the car to meet Pauline.

Not realizing they were in ear shot of Smith and Bivins, Buford and Pauline started to argue. Pauline was questioning Buford about his relationship with Pearl Wade. Wade was a beautiful light skinned black girl, and the niece of Willie Wade, that Buford had been seeing. I guess I should say, one of several women Buford had been seeing as there were several.

Pauline was angry that Buford had been with Pearl again and was demanding that Buford put an end to seeing her.

Barbara Drewry Bivins   Shirley Smith

As words were exchanged, Smith and Bivins made every attempt to remain out of sight, not wanting to be seen by anyone, especially Buford, as they listened to Pussers arguing. Pauline and Buford were separated at this time according to Lavon Plunk, Pauline's best friend, as well as TBI investigator Warren Jones, who was also aware of the Pusser's marital issues and problems. Both Plunk and Jones were aware that Pauline had been residing at a motel in Savannah, a small town near Adamsville.

As tempers continued to flare in the parking lot this night, Pauline foolishly threatened to leave Buford for good and get a divorce, telling him that she would also contact the TBI and expose his corruption of accepting payoffs and other criminal acts.

This angered Buford as he was overheard threatening Pauline, telling her that would be the last thing she would ever do, if she did, she would not live to see the light of day.

Both Smith and Bivins took Buford's words to Pauline as being serious threat on her life. Now, understand this was only the beginning of a chain of events, involving several people, which would cause many of us who have researched the Pusser Legend to rethink Buford's version of the ambush. Remarkably, most of the people involved would not immediately know what others had heard or observed prior to the alleged ambush. It is only when you piece these many puzzle pieces together that you finally get a much clearer picture of what would eventually occur.

Dennis and Johnny

In the first chapter, I made mention of two young men who visited the ambush site shortly after Buford was shot and Pauline was killed. Their story was first revealed to me in an article on the Condo News, written by Jerry Heacock. Heacock's wife was from Corinth and she had always talked about Buford, Towhead and of course the state line. Ironically, Heacock was apparently captivated by the stories he had heard about Towhead White and was planning to write a book about him.

Jerry Heacock   Condo News

Of course, the "Walking Tall" movies had all been released by then and this too captured Heacock's attention and he began to research Pusser's true story as well. While spending some time in the Corinth area, Heacock managed to find and interview a number of people who had known and had interactions with Sheriff Pusser. These were people from both sides of the story.

The article Heacock wrote for the Condo News intrigued me as I had never heard this side of the Pusser Legend. Heacock mentioned events and gave names, one of those being Dennis Hathcock.

Dennis is the son of W.O. Hathcock, the man who owned and operated the Plantation Club where Buford was allegedly robbed, beaten, carved up and left for dead in the rain.

While I was interested in the article, I took no immediate action to learn how true this information was. It was probably two years later that I was on a gun forum, Firing Line, which a lot of law enforcement officers follow. I followed a thread on that forum one evening regarding a .25 caliber semi automatic handgun like the one Pauline Pusser is said to have carried. When the name Pusser was mentioned, all of the officers started talking about what a great man Buford was.

I had done just enough research by that time that I had developed a lot of questions about the legend and I shared this with the group on Firing Line that night. Needless to say, I was immediately chastised by all of these experts on Buford Pusser whose only research had been to watch the WALKING TALL movies. Most had no desire to learn the truth regarding Pusser.

A short time later, I received a text, inquiring as to where I had gained my information about Pusser, saying it was the most accurate account the reader had seen on the great sheriff. The person making the inquiry was Dennis Hathcock, the person I had read about in the Condo News.

I made telephone contact with Dennis as I knew there had to be much more that he could tell about Buford than was covered by the article in the Condo News. Suspicious of Hathcock at first, I wasn't sure if I could trust him. While I thought I knew a lot about the state line and Pusser, didn't realize I was about to be schooled by Hathcock.

Over the next two weeks I spoke with Dennis almost nightly, interviewing him for as much detail as I could glean. Finally I decided Hathcock was the real deal and we made arrangements to meet in Selmer as I not only wanted to meet Hathcock, but to see the places where so many of these events had taken place.

Dennis had told me his story about following Sheriff Pusser in the hours just prior to the alleged ambush, something he and his friend Johnny Harrison had apparently done quite often. The two teenage boys knew where Buford often met one of his girlfriends, a woman I will simply refer to as "Lady A" as she is still living in the area at the time of this writing.

Just hours before the alleged ambush, Dennis and Johnny arrived at a state highway maintenance lot in the small town of Eastview, which lies midway between Selmer and the state line. They hid their motor cycle behind a large pile of chat, then climbed to the top of the pile of road building material as they waited to see if Buford would show up as he so often did.

After a while headlights lit up the maintenance lot as Pusser pulled in and parked his Plymouth Fury. This was followed a short time later by a second car driven by "Lady A". The two talked for a short time, however, the longer they spoke, the louder their conversation became, finally with Buford angrily telling this young girl to "Get the fuck out of here".

Lady A left the lot, as did Buford, however, Buford returned almost immediately and pulled his vehicle onto the lot and parked again, obviously waiting for someone to arrive. Dennis and Johnny continued to conceal themselves from Buford's view as they too waited to see who might show up. Would it be one of Buford's buddies, another girlfriend..., who could the sheriff be expecting?

About this time a white 65 Chevrolet Biscayne pulled onto the lot. The two young detectives noticed the car had Oklahoma tags and proceeded to write the tag number down. Two men occupied the Biscayne, however, only one got out to meet with Pusser.

Pusser and this individual proceeded to the trunk of Pusser's Fury as the two boys atop that pile of chat continued to watch the activities below. Pusser opened the trunk of his car, reached in, and brought out two rifles. These were taken and placed in the trunk of the Chevy Biscayne. Both Pusser and the Chevy Biscayne then left the lot.

Unsure of what they had witnessed, young Dennis and Johnny decided to continue follow Buford this night. As Buford left the maintenance lot, the two boys mounted their motorcycle only to lose contact with the Plymouth Fury as Buford sped away, as usual, at a high rate of speed as he headed back toward Selmer.

Dennis (far left) and Johnny (next to Dennis) at the first ambush
site sharing what they had observed with investigators.

Both Dennis and Johnny suspected they knew where Buford was headed as they set their course for Selmer. They arrived at the location where they thought Buford might be, while exercising caution by taking a position on a hill across the highway from Lady A's home. This is the dwelling where the teen aged Lady A lived with her parents.

To their surprise they spotted Buford a couple of doors down at "Star's" house. Star is the name I will use for Peatie Plunk's girlfriend as this woman is also alive at the time of this writing.

Buford was walking around the outside of the house, trying doors and windows to find a means of entry. He was calling out for Lady A to let him in. Dennis and Johnny thought that the sheriff must be on something, pills, booze, both…,they didn't know which, but they knew Buford was not acting in a normal fashion. Buford continued to circle the house for approximately fifteen minutes before the door opened, allowing Buford inside.

A short time later the door again opened and Lady A came running out with Buford right behind her as she ran for her home just a short distance away.

As she ran across a neighbor's backyard, she ran into a clothes line which caught her about the neck, forcing her to the ground. Buford now had her in his sights and he grabbed for her as she attempted to get up and run again. She somehow managed to escape Buford's grasp and ran to the private entrance of her bedroom and locked the door as she got inside.

Sheriff Pusser lingered outside the door for a short time before he realized she would not be coming back outside again. At this point he returned to his car, squalling his tires as he left the area.

Dennis and Johnny got on their motorcycle once again and continued to follow Buford to a service station a short distance away in down town Selmer. As they continued to observe the sheriff, they watched as he went inside the station and made a phone call. The two boys had no way of knowing who Buford was calling.

At this point Pusser returned to his car and set his course for Adamsville. Thinking that Sheriff Pusser was headed home, the two boys decided that with it being near two am, it was time to call it quits for the night.

After taking Johnny home, Dennis would make the trek back down highway 45 to his grandmothers home where he would spend the night, not knowing that in just a few short hours his adventure would continue.

106

Lavon Plunk

Lavon Plunk would be with Pauline Pusser this same night as they were saying their goodbyes to each other. During my interview with Lavon, she told me she and Pauline had made plans to go out together one last time before Pauline headed out with her three children to Haysi Virginia. They had kept their plans private as Buford did not want Pauline spending time with Lavon. This seemed a little strange to me as Lavon was married to Peatie Plunk, one of Buford's most trusted deputies.

Pauline, now separated from Buford, had been staying at a motel in nearby Savannah. She needed space between herself and Buford as she made decisions about her future. On this night, she was returning to the Pusser residence in Adamsville only to gather a few personal belongings as well as her children who were staying at the Pusser residence.

To be clear, Buford had indeed told people at the barber shop that day about how he and the family were taking a "vacation" to visit Pauline's parents in Virginia. I assume however, that he suspected Pauline would not be returning home with him from this "vacation," just as she had been threatened during their argument at the Old Hickory Grill. Apparently, while considering her options, she had decided to leave Buford behind in Adamsville. It might just be easier that way rather than telling him she was divorcing him while they were at her parents home in Haysi. It was now time for her to get her children, gather a few things, and not look back.

As Lavon pulled up to the Pauline's home, she was invited in while Pauline went about her tasks. Lavon, knowing how Buford felt toward her refused the offer as she was afraid of what Buford might do if he came home while she was there against his wishes. She told Pauline as much and advised her that she would park down the street a ways and when Pauline was ready to leave, she could signal her by flashing the front porch lights on and off.

Lavon told me during our interview that she had pulled her car in a neighbor's driveway, patiently waiting for Pauline's signal when Buford roared by and pulled in his driveway. Lavon told me she became frightened as Buford went in the house. She went on to say that a short time later she heard a single gunshot. Terrified and not knowing what to do, she quickly drove away.

A couple of hours later she would get a call from her husband Peatie telling her that Buford and Pauline had gone on a disturbance call that was apparently a set up to kill Buford. Peatie told his wife that Buford had been wounded in the ambush and that Pauline was dead. She, of course, knew this was a lie and that Peatie was probably covering for Buford.

Lavon told me that she felt totally helpless as she didn't know who she could trust with what she had heard at the Pusser home that night. She obviously felt that even her own husband was getting caught up in something she wanted no part of.

In later times, usually when she had maybe a little too much to drink, Lavon would share her story with friends. Jerry Heacock apparently heard these stories, located and interviewed her for his article in the Condo News. She asked that her name not be disclosed in the article as all of this was still so political in 1981 when the article was published and Heacock complied with her wishes. I learned of Lavon's identity through one of her friends who had heard her tell the story. With Lavon having now passed, I can share her observations of that fateful night.

Beverly Maxwell

I attempted to locate Diane Vance regarding Sheriff Pusser's time in office as well as the death of her mother. I was unsuccessful in locating her as Diane Vance. I did not know to search for her as Diane Mullins, which was her name at the time of her death. Her whereabouts seemed to be a well guarded family secret. It was as if she were being hidden from the general public.

I was however given an a recorded interview made of Beverly Maxwell telling of her conversations with Diane. Maxwell had attended junior college in Jackson Tennessee and was good friends with Diane. Maxwell stated that this was long before WALKING TALL was even dreamed of. She said that one day Diane was really down and depressed and just wanted to talk. Beverly listened as Diane said she was certain that Buford had killed her mother.

Diane had been staying with Buford's sister in Memphis as she couldn't bear being around Buford. Maxwell said she didn't ask questions of Diane, but rather just sat there and listened as Diane told her story. Diane said that her mother had called and insisted that she come home from Memphis, saying that she and Buford were having troubles. Diane agreed to return to Adamsville as her mother had asked.

Diane went on to say that on the night in question, she was awakened by a disturbance in the Pusser home. In full disclosure, Diane did not describe what noise had awakened her or at least on the taped interview Maxwell didn't say what had awakened Diane. According to Maxwell, Diane did say that Buford and Pauline arguing and she was afraid to open her door and look out to see what was happening. The house grew quiet for a while then she heard the front door open. Maxwell never addressed the gunshot that Lavon Plunk had heard.

As Diane looked out a window, she saw Buford carry his wife to his car, placing Pauline in the passenger's front seat. Pauline appeared to be unconscious. Buford walked back toward the house to retrieve the shoes that had fallen from Pauline's feet, placing them on the passenger's side floorboard. Diane watched as Buford pulled away from the house. She would tell Maxwell that she would never see her mother alive again.

Diane would go on to tell Maxwell that prior to this, she had been staying in Memphis with Buford's sister as she had been repeatedly molested by Buford and eventually raped by him as well. Diane did not say if Pauline was aware of this and Maxwell didn't dare ask as Diane spoke about such traumatic events, she just listened and allowed her friend to vent.

Diane would repeat this story a few times, but only to very close friends. I can only assume that this may be the reason why Diane's character was not included in WALKING TALL. Buford would of course say that Diane was a rebel who wanted to stay out late and had even written checks on his checking account and that she was into drug use, although he never offered proof of this. On the other hand Diane had no desire to be in a movie that glorified Buford.

It's important to note that all of these events witnessed by Dennis and Johnny, Lady A, Lavon Plunk and Beverly Maxwell happened independently of each other. It was only through research and some luck that I found these people and started connecting the dots in this incredible story.

Only when you reconstruct these events and examine the time frame in which they occurred does it leads you to wonder about the alleged ambush. Was it real, or was the alleged ambush a desperately planned setup designed to prevent Pauline Pusser from giving information to the authorities that could easily have sent Buford to prison?

It was Jerry Heacock's article in the Condo News that gave me cause to think about the Pusser Legend, although others such as Camilla Wilson and Ellie Grossman also researched the Pusser Legend and found information that the media of that time never reported. This was followed by Barbara Bivins who exposed even more of the Pusser Legend as a hoax. Sadly, so many people have no idea just how much of the Pusser legend is fiction.

If you think all of this seems like a lot to digest, what until you read about the alleged ambush.

Chapter 13
The Alleged Ambush of August 12th

This was one of the more difficult chapters for me to write. Coming from a law enforcement background myself, I can tell you that the profession is a true brotherhood. In times of trouble, you are always covering another officer's back and in turn they are watching out for you. You trust them with your life. As such, to speak out in a negative fashion about another officer is rarely done.

Make no mistake, I defended Buford for a long time when people would tell me that he was actually a corrupt sheriff. It was not until I saw the autopsy report of Louise Hathcock that I began to have my doubts. The next shoe to drop were the photos of the alleged August 12th ambush. While I wanted to believe that Pusser was much like his character in the movies, the evidence told me otherwise.

Buford's Version of the Ambush

As Buford would tell his version of the ambush, his father Carl was working at the jail that night when a call came in about a disturbance in the state line area. Carl would claim that he did not call Buford out for calls after 2:00 am.

The story goes on that, not getting a response by calling the sheriff's office, the caller placed a call to Buford's home. The call was said be about a disturbance at Jourdan's beer joint, about a mile north of the state line on highway 45.

Buford would go on to say that Pauline insisted on going with him on the disturbance call. We are given two different reasons for her going along. The first being that they were going on vacation that very day, traveling to Haysi Virginia to visit Pauline's parents. Pauline wanted to make sure that Buford did not get delayed by this call. The second version was that Pauline feared for Buford's life on calls near the state line and insisted on going with him.

Regardless, Buford and Pauline headed down a convoluted course of unimproved back roads that would take them through the sparsely populated towns of Stantonville and Michie where they would take a short drive on highway 57. From there they would drive down more secluded back roads which would finally intersect with New Hope Road.

Buford then drove past the New Hope Methodist Church. During this trip, Pauline commented to Buford about what a beautiful day it was, as they came upon a small bridge on the narrow county road, just eight tenths of a mile south of the church. Buford would say that the headlights of a dark colored Cadillac would suddenly come on as the vehicle pulled along beside Pusser's Plymouth Fury. Two shots would be fired, one striking Pauline in the head.

Buford would step down hard on the gas pedal and accelerate, hoping to shake the car that was pursing him. He traveled two and one tenth miles from the bridge before stopping approximately fifty feet north of the intersection of New Hope and Davis Yancy Roads. Buford said he thought he had lost his pursuers and stopped to check on Pauline. He stated that he opened his door only to find that the Cadillac had located him again. He said that Pauline had fallen against him making it difficult to reach for his gun.

As the Cadillac pulled closely beside him and came to a stop and with shots being fired, Buford would claim that he reached out and grabbed the barrel of the rifle. Twelve more shots would be fired with another bullet hit striking Pauline again in the head, another striking Buford's chin. He said that he fell to his right and to the floorboard as the Cadillac sped away.

As Buford raised himself up, he looked in the rear view mirror and claimed his chin was hanging down to his chest. Pauline lay dead in the seat beside him.

Buford would go on to say that he drove down New Hope Road to highway 45 and turned north toward Selmer, making it to Eastview where he pulled over at Allen McCoy's store. This is where Selmer Chief of Police Hugh Kirkpatrick would find him as he responded to Buford's garbled radio call.

Buford would initially be transported to the medical facility in Selmer before being transferred to Baptist Hospital in Memphis. Pauline's body would remain in the car until authorities processed the crime scene. No autopsy would be performed on Pauline as District Attorney Will Terry Abernathy and the County Medical Examiner Harry Peeler could not concur on the need for one. According to state law at that time, both had to agree that an autopsy was relevant and needed. Obviously, one of them could not see the need for one.

Chief Deputy Jim Moffett and TBI Investigator Warren Jones would travel to Memphis to try and get more information from Buford. Buford was said to be able to communicate through broken words and hand signals.

Sheriff Pusser would tell investigators that three people were in the Cadillac at the time of the ambush and that the car was a dark color. He initially indicated that he would recognize the shooter if he saw him again, a claim he would almost immediately change.

Later in the investigation Buford would change the location of the disturbance he and Pauline were responding to, saying the disturbance was on New Hope Road. He would also give investigators the impression that the failed assassination attempt was executed by people from the state line.

Sheriff Did Not Recognize Killers, He Tells Lawmen

By DONALD TATE and BILL EVANS
Press-Scimitar Staff Writers

The shooting mystery of McNairy County deepened today as the brother of Sheriff Buford Pusser revealed the sheriff apparently did not recognize the assailants who roared out of pre-dawn darkness Saturday, riddled his car with carbine slugs and killed his wife.

The tough 29-year-old sheriff, an ex-professional wrestler, was in fair condition at Baptist Hospital today, recovering from a wound caused by a bullet which ripped into his jaw.

The brother, John Pusser, 38, of Peoria, Ill., said the sheriff could still only mumble and nod his head to questions. But he said law officers who interviewed the sheriff Sunday said the wounded man was unable to identify either the killers or the make of their car.

"They said he told them it happened too fast," John Pusser said.

CONCLUSIONS

He said the officers, Warren Jones, TBI agent at Jackson, and McNairy County Deputy Sheriff Jim Moffett, determined from the sheriff that the gunmen first roared up with their lights off about 4:45 a.m. on isolated New Hope Road just north of the Mississippi State line. The sheriff was answering a "disturbance" call at a state line beer tavern and was accompanied by his 33-year-old wife, Pauline.

John Pusser said: "The officers told me the first set of 30 caliber shots apparently caught Pauline in the back of the head. She fell over on my brother, grabbing him by the arm. He couldn't get his arm loose to pull his pistol and he stepped on the gas. That car can leave anything. It's a souped-up '67 Plymouth and can do 140.

STOPPED HIS CAR

"He left them, the officers told me, and thought he had lost them. Then he stopped the car and was trying to help his wife. That's when they came up on him again.

"They stopped about five feet away, point blank, and he had his door open a bit and was trying to get out,

Turn to Page 5—WOUNDED

Buford would initially say he would recognize the shooter, but then changed his story.

(Memphis Press Scimitar)

Early that morning, Johnny Harrison called Dennis Hathcock and told him about the ambush. Dennis is the son of W.O. Hathcock who had once operated the Plantation Club, just on the Mississippi side of the state line.

On this day, he was staying at his grandmother's home on highway 45 just as he often did. Dennis got on his motorcycle and headed for the crime scene. Johnny had told Dennis that the ambush had occurred on New Hope Road, however, he did not know the specific location of the attack.

The young Hathcock took a shortcut from highway 45 using a field road he sometimes used to get to New Hope Road. The end of this road would intersect with New Hope just a few hundred feet south of the New Hope Methodist Church. At the intersection, Dennis looks both north and south, not seeing any signs of the ambush that had taken place. At this point, he decides to head south toward the state line.

Traveling south, Dennis arrived at a small and narrow bridge. Only one officer was there. Constable R.C. Matlock would be the first officer on the scene at the bridge. Matlock would find only two shell casings at the first ambush site. These would be of different calibers and appeared to be weathered, as if they had been there some time.

Upon seeing Dennis, Matlock would yell out, "what are you doing here little Hathcock?" Dennis tells the constable that he had heard about the ambush and was there to see what had happened. Constable Matlock would tell Dennis he needed to leave the scene, which Dennis did, somewhat disappointed, continuing to ride south toward the state line.

Along the way, however, two and one tenth mile south of the bridge, he saw shell casings near the intersection of New Hope and Davis Yancy Roads. There was also a lot of broken glass on the freshly resurfaced road. He saw several shell casings on the east shoulder of the highway, with three or four near the middle of the road, with another two other casings in-between. The young Hathcock also spotted a piece of scalp with hair attached on the west side of the road in the freshly grated ditch. The hair was soaked with blood with what appeared to be a piece of skull lying on top.

As Dennis got back on his motorcycle and prepared to head back north to report to Constable Matlock about what he had found, he spotted something else. Approximately one foot from the ditch was a matchbook cover from Hernando's Hideaway in Memphis. Hernando's was a Night Club that the Pussers were known to frequent, but not always as a couple.

Once again at the bridge, Dennis tried to tell Matlock what he had discovered, only to have the constable once again telling Dennis, "you better get your ass out of here as everyone is on their way here." His warning was a little late as law enforcement officials arrived at the scene.

McNairy County Deputy Peatie Plunk started wading through the weeds and brush on the west side of the bridge when he declared that he had found what he thought to be a "snipers nest." After close examination, investigators thought otherwise, considering the projectiles had entered the driver's side of the car rather than the passenger's side.

Photo of Dennis Hathcock (left) and Johnny Harrison (2nd from left)
at the first ambush site with Investigators August 12, 1967.
Photo: Press Scimitar

Investigators had not spoken with Buford yet and had little information about how the ambush had played out. They knew that Pusser's car had more bullet holes in it than this site could account for. This is when Dennis told them of what he had seen at the intersection near the Saint Rest Cemetery.

As investigators arrived at the site it became clear that young Hathcock was right as this was where most of the ambush had occurred. They processed the scene, gathering all the

evidence they could find. This included some of Pauline's brain which appeared to many, including former McNairy County Sheriff Coleman and County Coroner Ward Moore, to have been "stacked" as if had been placed there intentionally after Pauline had been shot.
Bill Way would be there to photograph the scene as would James Reid of the Memphis Press Scimitar.

Later in the day, Dennis and Johnny talked about what they had observed the night before at the road maintenance facility in Eastview. They thought about the 65 Chevy Biscayne and observing a man taking rifles from the trunk of Pusser's car and placing them in the trunk of his Chevy Biscayne. They thought about the license number they had written down and decided to give it to Johnny's father, who inturn was said to have given it to Jim Moffett. They never heard anything about the tag number again.

The FBI would soon come onboard offering the use of their lab services, however, they had no agents working on the investigation itself as the FBI had no jurisdiction in a state investigation. Mississippi would offer their assistance, assigning Rex Armisted and Charlie Goforth to help with the investigation.

McNairy County Chief Deputy Jim Moffett would tell that threats had been made over the past four weeks that Buford "would be stalked and killed," although he never, to my knowledge, indicated how these threats were communicated.

Buford would not be present at Pauline's funeral. He would however return to work eighteen days after the alleged assassination attempt.

It should also be noted that many citizens of the county including several enforcement officers, were skeptical of Buford's story about the ambush. Many would say that Buford had murdered his wife. District Attorney Abernathy would make a press release that these allegations were unfounded, and they were looking at other suspects.

TBI investigator Warren Jones was however aware of Buford's womanizing, just as he was aware that Buford and Pauline's marital problems. Jones, also knew that the couple had separated, and Pauline had been staying at a motel in Savannah.

TBI Investigator John Sloan and State Trooper McClanahan would visit a site where they knew Buford would often target practice and they searched for fired projectiles to see if any would match any of Buford's firearms. They found none with striations that would make such a match with the bullets from the ambush gun.

In the meantime, Armisted and Goforth would check on a Cadillac in Mississippi like the one which Buford had described, one that matched a car that W.O. Hathcock had owned. During their investigation they learned that Hathcock had sold the Cadillac in question two weeks prior to the ambush. Still, they took soil samples from the tires and under carriage, however, these did not match samples taken from the New Hope Road area. It was common knowledge however, that W.O. Hathcock made some of his living, buying cars, especially Cadillac's, refurbishing and then selling them. The lead on the Cadillac was another dead end.

`Upon hearing of the ambush, W.O. Hathcock and his wife Larece suspected that Buford would try to make it appear that W.O. was somehow behind the assassination attempt. As such, they are said to have driven to Nashville to the Tennessee Bureau of Investigation office and voluntarily took polygraph tests, which both passed. They were escorted, for their safety, back to Corinth by TBI agents.

Warren Jones was puzzled by the lack of an autopsy being performed on Pauline. Had an autopsy been performed, it would have given him a lot of valuable information about the shooting, the angle, the distance of shots fired and so on. Without an autopsy report, his job became more difficult. He wonders why the District Attorney and the County Medical Examiner could not agree on the need for an autopsy report.

During my interview with Dr Jerry Francisco, the State Medical Examiner at that time, he said that Jones had asked him to come to McNairy County to assist him in examining the crime scene. Dr. Francisco told Jones that his expertise was examining bodies, that he had no experience with crime scene investigation. Still, he traveled with Jones to look at the ambush site but could contribute nothing to the investigation.

During the investigation, a request went out from the TBI to police agencies requesting any information regarding possible suspects who may have been involved in the ambush. Arkansas State Police sent back information on Kirksey McCord Nix Jr, a member of the Dixie Mafia who had a criminal history in that state.

Since Buford had claimed that he got a good look at the shooter on the day of the ambush, he was shown photos of Nix for identification purposes. Pusser claimed he could not positively identify Nix as the shooter from the photos, suggesting that he would have to see him in person.

The TBI put out another bulletin that they were looking for Nix regarding their investigation. Oklahoma City officials responded that Nix was in their custody, so Warren Jones took Buford there to hopefully make a positive identification of Nix as the shooter.

I understand that when they met in the Oklahoma City holding facility, Pusser and Nix starred at each other without exchanging words. Pusser then told Investigator Jones that he was not positive that Nix was the man he saw in the car that day.

No one was ever arrested in for the murder of Pauline Pusser. In most cases as such, when a spouse is murdered, investigators usually look deeply into the history of the surviving spouse. This is something that investigators seemed to have failed to do with Buford. My question is why? Why would they immediately go chasing after people who were loosely connected with the state line gang instead of investigating Buford more thoroughly?

It had been eighteen months since Louise Hathcock had been shot and killed and the IRS had taken over the properties and sold it to satisfy their lien. Howard Bunch and W.O. Hathcock were the new owners of the state line properties.

The two men had bought the properties as a business investment. Why wouldn't they want this property considering they knew the property was worth more than two hundred thousand dollars and they could pay off the lien for a mere one hundred thousand dollars and make a huge profit when the properties are resold?

Of course, they were going to make Towhead a one third partner in this venture, however, he refused the offer saying he was done with the state line lifestyle according to an FBI informant.

Unanswered questions about Pusser's version of the ambush

1) Why did Carl Pusser, who was on duty at the Sheriff's office when the call came in about a "disturbance" at Jourdan's Beer Joint on highway 45, refuse to call Buford out? Think about it..., what if the call had been real, the Sheriff's Office was called, and no one responded? If someone had been injured or killed, how would Carl explain his actions?

2) Why was there no research to find from where the call was made? If the disturbance were anywhere near the state line area, as Hollis Jourdan's beer joint was, it would have been a long-distance call to the Sheriff's Office in Selmer. This would have made it easy to trace the origin of the call.

3) Why did the caller wait so long to call Buford's home to reach him directly?

4) Why was Pauline at the Pusser residence since she had been staying in a Savannah motel, as she and Buford were separated?

5) Why would she want to go with Buford on a disturbance, especially around four am?

6) Disturbance calls are one of the most dangerous calls that an officer can respond to, so why would Buford allow her to go with him?

7) What good would a one hundred ten-pound woman have been at the disturbance, as you would think if there was real trouble, Buford would have been concerned about protecting her while trying to control the disturbance?

8) Diane was at home that night and was awakened by Buford and Pauline having their own disturbance in the living room. Why did investigators not interview Diane?

9) Why was there no investigation involving the Pusser residence after the ambush to see what might have occurred there?

10) When the Pussers did leave the residence, why did Buford insist on taking a route to Jourdan's beer joint that involved travel on unimproved back roads when traveling down highways 64 and 45 would have been much faster?

11) How would the ambush party know that Buford would take such an odd route and wait behind the New Hope Methodist Church on New Hope Road instead of somewhere along highways 64&45?

12) If Buford drove fast as he was known to usually do, how could the ambush party have left the church and caught up with Buford in only eight tenths of a mile in the darkness of predawn hours without the use of their head lights?

13) The ambush party's car would have had to have been almost side by side at the bridge as all all of the side windows were blown out, otherwise, the car suffered no other damage at this site. Why didn't Buford attempt to run them off the road?

14) Buford said that he thought he had lost his pursuers in the two and one tenth miles between the first and second ambush sites. This was very rural country with no side roads. Exactly how did he think he had lost them in such a short distance, especially considering they now had the use of their headlights?

15) He said that he stopped his Plymouth Fury just yards north of the intersection of New Hope and Yancy Davis Roads. He claimed that he opened his door and started to get out and check on Pauline when his pursuers appeared once again, stopping beside his car, and firing shots into his vehicle from less than five feet away. How did he not see them coming up from behind him on this fairly flat and straight section of road, especially after they had the use of headlights?

16) He next claimed that as the pursuer's car stopped alongside him and again opened fire, he reached out and gabbed the barrel of their rifle as twelve more shots were fired. How did he hold

on to that hot gun barrel?

17) Buford would say that as he fell toward the passenger's floorboard, his attackers drove away. Why would professional killers drive away without first making sure their intended victim was dead?

18) Dennis Hathcock would show investigators the second ambush site, where they would find several shell casings on the opposite shoulder of the road from where Buford's car had stopped. They would also find four or five shell casings in the middle of the road. Buford said the shooter was sitting in the front passenger's seat as shots were fired. Why weren't more shell casings found in the middle of the road? Why were so many found on the east shoulder and behind where the Cadillac would be as shots were fired from only one position? How did the shell casings get on the shoulder of the road instead of being ejected in the back seat of the Cadillac and some being possibly ejected into Buford's car through the already shattered windows?

19) Why was blood all over the outside of the car..., the grill, front bumper, hood outside windshield, top, the sides and even the back of the car if Buford and Pauline were shot while sitting in the car? Buford would tell that neither he nor Pauline exited the vehicle.

20)) And what about the "stack of brain that was found in the ditch? Former McNairy County Sheriff Clifford Coleman and the current County Medical Examiner thought they had been placed there rather than blown there by a gun blast. Why did we hear nothing about this from the investigators?

21) Then there is a match book cover from Hernando's Hideaway in Memphis which was found in the freshly grated ditch. Hernando's was a place where the Pussers sometimes went..., but not always as a couple? What are the odds in a county with only eighteen thousand total residents, that someone else would have disposed that matchbook right where Pauline was killed, especially considering that the ditch has been bladed only a day or so before?

22) After shots were fired, Buford then drove the short distance down to the state line. The story goes that he pulled over at a gas station and spoke briefly with Albert Kiddy, showing him a handful of Pauline's brain with her wedding band placed on top. Why would he have removed the wedding band from Pauline's finger and display it as he did?

23) Why was Kiddy never interviewed about this?

24) Buford left the gas station and proceeded north on highway 45 for a short distance and pulled his car in front of the Kiddy residence. When Buford heard sirens coming from the Mississippi side of the state line, he pulled back on the highway and headed toward Selmer. With the hospital in Corinth be much closer and far better equipped than the Selmer facility, why didn't he turn to Corinth or wait on an ambulance where he was?

Hired Killers at Work?

Sheriff Grabbed, Held Attack Rifle

By ROBERT KOLLAR
Staff Correspondent

SELMER, Tenn. — McNairy County Sheriff Buford Pusser may have been shot by hired killers—who fled after the sheriff grabbed a rifle barrel from an assailant and held it away from himself, reliable sources said here yesterday.

The sources said Pusser came into close combat with his assailant after the sheriff had been wounded in the chin and his wife killed early last Saturday on a lonely road near the Mississippi-Tennessee border.

The sheriff and his wife, Pauline, were on a routine disturbance call at a beer tavern when they were stalked by another vehicle which began following them down a rural road.

PUSSER'S AUTO was fired on two different times with a high-powered rifle. The first volley left his attractive wife dead.

The 29-year-old sheriff is recovering in a Memphis hospital. No details on Pusser's combat with his attacker could be obtained. The sheriff was quoted as saying he did not recognize the attacker.

A long string of circumstances, sources said, has led law officers to believe the sheriff and his wife were the victims of an assassination plot instigated by outside killers.

The sheriff, a former professional wrestler, took office three years ago and did not wear a pistol until about a year ago.

THREE MONTHS ago, Pusser was shot twice in the face when he approached a motorist he had stopped on State 45. Pusser has been quoted as saying he knows the man was a hired killer from Arkansas, but was never able to prove it, so he let the matter drop.

Yesterday, Pusser's father, Carl, said about three weeks ago he received a threatening telephone call while on duty as county jailer. Carl Pusser quoted the anonymous caller as saying:

"I'm going to kill you and

---

your son both, and I have been offered $10,000 for your bodies."

CARL PUSSER further quoted the caller as saying he would receive the money, for displaying his and the sheriff's bodies in a prominent place in Selmer.

In other developments yesterday:

● Sheriff Pusser was moved from the intensive care unit

---

at a Memphis hospital to an undisclosed private room. He is being kept under heavy guard by Memphis city police and Shelby County deputies.

● "Consumer Guide," a weekly publication of the McNairy County Independent, devoted a full-page plea for contributions to a reward fund. William E. Smith of Selmer, treasurer of the fund,

(Turn to Page 15, Column 0)

(Story and additional picture on)

Memphis Sees Light Drink Vote

By JOHN HEMPHILL
Staff Correspondent

MEMPHIS—Faced with predictions of a light turnout, "wets" and "drys" wound up their campaigns for and against liquor by the drink here yesterday, each predicting victory.

Disputing each others' philosophies, facts and propaganda, supporters of legalizing the sale of mixed drinks and their opponents agreed on only one thing—a small percentage of Memphians will vote on the issue today.

A Shelby County election commission spokesman, O. McKinley Parker, reported approximately 1,800 absentee ballots have been received so far. This, he added, indicates light voter interest in the first liquor-by-the-drink vote in Tennessee in this century.

BOTH SIDES estimated that between 60,000 and 80,000 persons will vote today, with a heavier vote favoring the "wets," Brandon Davis, staff chief for the Beverage Control Committee, a Chamber of

Tennessean Today

Page		Page
Amusements	31	Horoscope	33
Anne Adams	32	Lawrence	45
Ask Andy	48	Market	

LBJ Warns Of City Crisis

By ROBERT B. SEMPLE JR.
The New York Times News Service

WASHINGTON — President Johnson warned Congress yesterday that it could no longer afford "business as usual" in meeting the crisis of the nation's cities.

In a letter to Senate Majority Leader Mike Mansfield of Montana, the President said that nothing less than an "all-out commitment" is necessary to prevent recurrence of "the tragic events of this summer."

SPECIALLY he urged the Senate to:

● Restore $425 million cut by the House earlier this year from the Model Cities Program, which the administration regards as its major weapon in the war on urban blight. Johnson had asked for $662 million for the program in the present fiscal year.

● Approve 23 additional measures aimed at improving the conditions of life in urban areas, ranging from a $35 million measure to help fight mental retardation to the

$2.06 billion anti-poverty program.

THE LETTER, which Mansfield read to the Senate, represented the beginning of an "intensive push" for urban-aid legislation now stalled on Capitol Hill.

If there were any doubts as to the seriousness of the administration's intentions, they were dispelled when Mansfield followed the Johnson letter with a carefully prepared statement of his own.

"This eminently responsible and urgent call from the President on behalf of the cities impels a decent, sober and prompt response from the Congress," he declared, calling on his colleagues to "establish an urban environment that is as hostile to riders as it is to rats."

THE PRESIDENT also marked the passing of more than two weeks of violence at the White House the urban dilemma.

(Turn to Page 4, Column 1)

Brooks Promises School to Continue

By BILL KOVACH

Fred Brooks, director of the controversial Liberation School, said last night Metro's decision to deny the school use of public parks is judged legal, he will "abide by the law."

anti-poverty project and evicted from St. Anselm's Episcopal Church, held its first public meeting in Watkins Park yesterday.

Brooks, director of the project and Mrs. Nancy Wood, wife of the rector of St. Anselm's led 10 Negro youth

---

25) Buford traveled approximately four miles to Eastview where he pulled over and parked by Allen McCoy's Store. This is where State Trooper J. Reid and Selmer Police Chief Hugh Kirkpatrick would find he and Pauline. When Buford tried to tell what had happened Kirkpatrick told him to be quiet and say nothing (they were said to be distantly related). Usually when a victim has life threatening injuries, police want to learn as much as they can in case the victim should pass. Why would Kirkpatrick not want Buford to talk?

26) When Buford arrived at the Selmer Hospital, one of his deputies also arrived and went into his room. Not realizing that a nurse was standing on the opposite side of a curtain that partitioned the room, the deputy is alleged to have asked, "Buford, what the fuck have you gotten us into now?" Buford is alleged to have made a statement about how they might get out of the situation. What did the deputy already know if this were the case?

27) Buford, upon arrival at Baptist Hospital in Memphis, was examined by the medical staff. A doctor who wishes to remain anonymous, said he believed the gunshot wound to Buford's chin was self-inflicted. Why would investigators not use this piece of professional observation?

28) After Dennis and Johnny gave the car tag number they had observed the night before in Eastview to Johnny's father, who in turn was said to have passed it along to Jim Moffett, why was no information developed on who the car was registered to?

29) Buford later changed his story to the location of the disturbance he was responding to as a location on New Hope Road, why did this not arouse investigators attention and suspicions about his story? Why did Buford change his story?

30) Oddly, when many residents of the county voiced their suspicions that Buford had killed Pauline, District attorney Will Terry Abernathy was quick to make a press release that indicated there was no basis for this allegation. It was done a short time after the shooting and long before the investigation was in full swing. Why the rush to clear Buford?

31) Why was Buford never subjected to a polygraph examination?

Investigators never developed any real suspects, at least that they could arrest. All kinds of persons of interest were named, Cleo Epps, "Fats" Jerry James, Albert McDonald, Eugene Sparks, Raymond Carmine Gagliardi, George Albert McGann as well as others like W.O. Hathcock, Howard Bunch, Towhead White and of course Kirksey McCord Nix Jr. Leads on these people seemed to lead to dead ends in the investigation.

So, who was behind the alleged ambush? We will probably never know for certain. For me personally, there are too many unanswered questions about Buford Pusser's ever changing version of the ambush. The available evidence points in his direction and investigators were never able to find a better suspect than Buford. I suspect that he killed Pauline or had her killed to keep from going to prison for taking bribes if she reported his dishonesty as she had had threatened to.

Of course, he may have had an accomplice involved. I suspect that his gunshot wound was self-inflicted, just as the doctors did as well. There is a good possibility however, that he may have been shot by Pauline during a struggle. It is also entirely possible that an accomplice may have shot Buford, or Buford may have shot himself, intending to make it appear that the ambush was real. How would it have appeared with Pauline, having been shot twice in the head during an ambush, while Buford, being closest to the shooter, was unscathed? Regardless, when we examine the evidence of the alleged amhush on new Hope Road, Buford's version of the shooting has far more hole in it than his Plymouth Fury did.

This the approximate view the gunman would have had at the second site as he fired twelve shots at Buford. Although Pauline was in the front passengers seat and was partially blocked from view by Buford's much larger frame, she was stuck in the head while Buford was shot in the chin. Buford's door was open as shots were fired. We know this as two projectiles struck the doorpost. How did an alleged professional killer miss his primary target thirteen times out of a total of fourteen shots fired during the alleged ambush that morning? Buford had motive to kill Pauline as she was leaving him that very day and planned to report his corruption according to her best friend, Lavon Plunk.

The New Hope Methodist Church where the ambush party allegedly waited for Buford. This of course, was only a theory presented by the TBI as it was about the only place on New Hope Road where an ambush party could have possibly concealed themselves from Buford's view.

(private collection)

Buford Pusser researcher Edwin Lovell (left) and author Mike Elam at the first ambush site. Both men wonder why so many people place so much emphasis on this site as most of the ambush took place two and one tenth miles south of this location. Only two shots were alleged to have been fired here while twelve were fired at the second site near the intersection of New Hope and Davis Yancy Roads.

There was barely room for two cars to be on the bridge at the same time. As you go across the bridge at the first ambush site, the road curves to the right. How were two cars traveling at high speeds able to go across the bridge, side by side, and make this curve together without having an accident and trading paint? Paint from Buford's Fury found on the alleged Cadillac could have been evidence as would have been damage to the cars themselves.

(Photo from private collection)

This is the straight stretch of road just before the bridge at the first ambush site. The alleged ambush occurred sometime around 4:45 am in the predawn hours of August 12th. Buford claimed that he did not see the car approaching from behind until it was almost beside him and the driver turned the car's headlights on . This leads to the question, if Buford couldn't see the Cadillac approaching him from behind in the darkness, how could the driver of the Cadillac see to negotiate the curves and the roadway at high speeds prior to this straight stretch of road? A reconstruction of this ambush revealed that this a car leaving from behind the church would have failed to catch up with Buford's car at the bridge, even in the daylight hours.

(Photo: Memphis Press Scimitar)

Investigators at the first ambush site at the bridge. They would find only two shell casings here and they were of different calibers. Buford claimed there was only one shooter however. Buford claimed that Pauline was shot in the head once at this location. The ambush vehicle would had to have been basically side by side with Pusser's Plymouth Fury as shots were fired as the bullets entered the drivers side windows, shattering them. The back windscreen of Pusser's Fury was not damaged in the alleged ambush. Several of the investigators are said to have had doubts about Buford's version of how the ambush happened as the dynamics of the attack were difficult to believe. Two separate ambush sites. Buford stopped allowing the Cadillac to catch up with him. Pauline was hit in the head twice, once at each site while shielded by Buford's body. Blood spatter was all over the exterior of the car even though neither exited the vehicle. Buford was only hit in the chin. Pauline's brain matter appeared to have be "stacked" with a piece of her skull laying on top, but what bothered them most was that Pauline allegedly went with Buford on a disturbance call while they were having marital issues and were separated. Investigators were aware of just how dangerous disturbance calls could be and wondered why Buford would take is wife to such a call.

(Photo: Mermphis Press Scimitar)

Investigators at the second ambush site at the intersection of New Hope and Davis Yancy Roads. Buford stopped his car approximately where the car on the far left is shown. Investigators would find several; shell casings at this location. The location of the casings were inconsistent with Buford's story, as he claimed that the shooter was sitting in the front passenger's seat of the Cadillac. Pusser claimed he grabbed the barrel of the rifle indicating the car's were close to each other. Shell casings however were found in three different places. Most were found on the shoulder of the road on the drivers side of the Cadillac. These were in a very confined area. A couple more were on the roadway directly behind where the Cadillac would have stopped, while a few more were in the middle of the road between where the cars would have been. This indicates that the shooter was probably on foot rather than in a car as Buford had stated. Why was the evidence (shell casing locations) inconsistent with Buford's story? Was Buford the shooter who was on foot or was there possibly an accomplice who fired the shots? Obviouslsy, Buford's version of th ambush was inconsistant with the location(s) of the shell casings. Why?

Looking south at the second ambush site. Saint Rest Cemetery is on the right, just past the tree line. Many people mistakenly believe the second part of the ambush took place in front of the cemetery.As you can see from the photo, the road has been recently maintainedand the ditches are bladed out.This made it easy for Dennis to see the shell casings on the road. ASD he examined the area he saw the stack of brain matter and the matchbook coverfrom Hernando's Hideaway laying in the ditch. McNairy County Coroner Ward Moorsewould tell me in an interview that both he and former McNairy County Sheriff Clifford Colemansaw the scene exactly as Dennis Hathcockhad described it to investigators. More stated that neither he nor Colemanbought into Buford's version of the ambush

(Photo: Mermphis Press Scimitar)

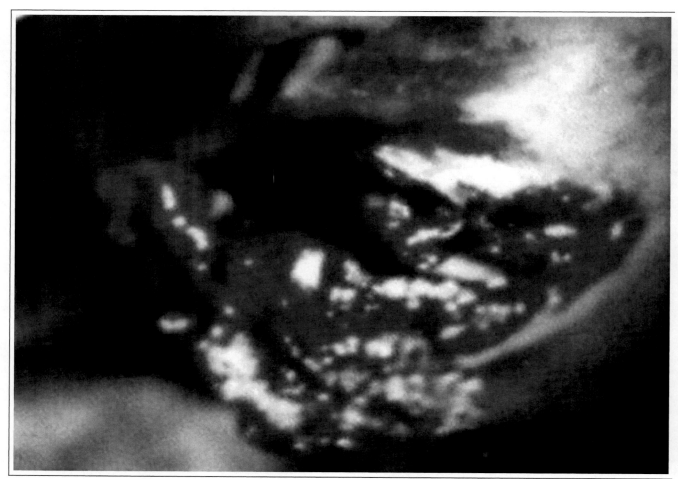

This is said to be a photograph of Pusser's chin wound. As you can easily see, the jaw bone is intact and has not been blown away as the legend tells the story. Buford would return to duty eighteen days after the alleged ambush. The "Pusser Legend" also tells that Buford had sixteen surgeries to repair the damage from the ambush. This is not true as the majority of his surgeries were to repair an eye socket damaged in an unrelated accident. This does not appear to be a wound caused by a high powered .30 caliber rifle as one would expect such a weapon to have done far more damage.

(Photo from the Robert Farish Collection)

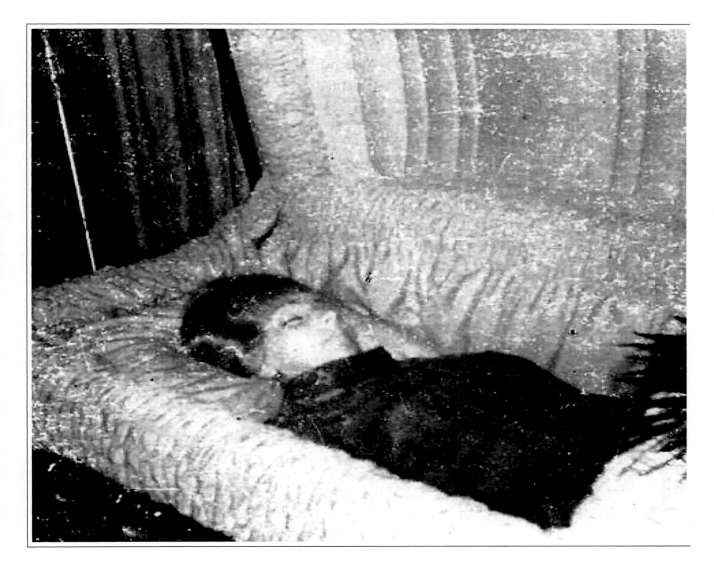

Pauline Pusser in her casket. Ward Moore was not only the McNairy County Coroner, but was also employed at Shackelford Funeral Home. Moore told me during an interview that it took him eight hours to rebuild the top and back of Pauline's head with cotton and plaster of Paris as it had been blown away. He also stated that she had a wound to her neck, something I had never heard before. She was laid to rest in clothing with a high neck collar which conceals her neck and any wound that was possibly there.

Rumor At Selmer Is 'Unfounded'

SELMER, Tenn. — A widespread rumor here that McNairy County Sheriff Buford Pusser has been arrested in connection with the shooting death of his wife in mid-August "has absolutely no foundation," the district attorney general's office reported this morning.

A car occupied by Sheriff Pusser and his wife was fired on in pre-dawn hours Aug. 12 while the officer was reportedly on the way to investigate complaints of a disturbance at a nightspot near the Mississippi state line.

A spokesman at the office of Dist. Atty. Gen. Will Terry Abernathy said the rumor was being circulated "this morning" but is without basis.

He said "several leads are being checked out" in connection with the case and investigation is continuing.

This article states that there was a "widespread rumor" that McNairy County Sheriff Buford had been arrested in connection with the death of his wife Pauline. District Attorney General Will Terry Abernathy would say that the story "has absolutely no foundation".

The newspaper report also says Buford was responding to "complaints of a disturbance at a nightspot near the Mississippi state line." Why did Buford change his story to the disturbance on New Hope Road?

True enough, Buford had not been arrested for Pauline's murder, but I do find it interesting that such a rumor spread so quickly. It makes one wonder just how many people knew of the Pusser's marital problems that so many would so easily believe such a rumor.

Also, this article indicates that "several leads are being checked out." Where did these leads come from and why did they take investigators nowhere?

McNairy Sheriff Blames 'Syndicate'

SELMER, Tenn. (AP) —Sheriff Buford Pusser linked today the killing of his wife last month to an "organized crime syndicate in the United States."

The 29-year-old sheriff was wounded seriously and his wife shot to death as they rode along a lonely country road Aug. 12.

Pusser said bootlegging, gambling and confidence games had "flourished for 10 or 15 years" along the Tennessee-Mississippi line until he became sheriff.

"I cracked down on them and put them out of business," he said. "They've been closed down for 18 months and they don't like it and are trying to get back in."

He said operators of the crime rings "came here from all over the United States.

"It was a big operation they were running. They grossed about $1 million a year. I've cost them a lot of money by closing them down. But they're still closed and they're going to stay closed."

This newspaper article states that Sheriff Pusser "linked today the killing of his wife last month to an organized crime syndicate in the United States."

In the article he also claimed the operators of the crime rings "came from all over the United States."

Oddly, there is nothing in his or Towhead Whites FBI files to support his claim.

Buford went on to state that "They've been closed down for eighteen months and they don't like it and are trying to get back in." Jack snd Louise were dead and Towhead was in federal prison.

Buford claimed "It was a big operation they were running," referring to the state line and going on to say,"I've cost them a lot of moneyby closing them down." Oddly, no one can name a single major player Pusser sent to prison or a single place he actually closed down.

F B I

Date: 8/14/67

Transmit the following in _____
(Type in plaintext or code)

Via ___ AIRTEL ___
(Priority)

TO: DIRECTOR, FBI

FROM: SAC, MEMPHIS (62-0)

SUBJECT: SHERIFF BUFORD PUSSER,
MC NAIRY COUNTY,
SELMER, TENNESSEE
INFORMATION CONCERNING

b6
b7C

On 8/14/67 at approximately 4:30 a.m., Sheriff
BUFORD PUSSER, McNairy County, Tenn., received a telephone
call at his residence in Adamsville, Tenn., to come to the
New Hope Road near the Mississippi border. Sheriff PUSSER,
accompanied by his wife PAULINE, was ambushed on the New Hope
Road by three unknown assailants driving a 1964 or 1965 gray
Cadillac. PAULINE PUSSER was killed and the sheriff was shot
in the face. He is presently confined to a Memphis hospital
in fair condition.

TBI Agents and local authorities are conducting
investigation to identify unknown assailants. The services
of the Bureau's Laboratory were offered to the TBI. Memphis
is following local investigation and will keep the Bureau fully
advised.

REC-63   62 111758 - 1

MCT-18   AUG 15 1967

Airtel
Telet..
A. ..
A. ..   3 - Bureau
S: 1 - Memphis
r.   WMP/ngm
             (4)

Approved: _____   Sent _____ M
59   Special Agent in Charge

This is the report to the Director of the FBI regarding the alleged ambush. The report goes on to say
the Memphis office was "following" the TBI investigation and had offered the use of the FBI's
laboratory services. The FBI had no agents working this case, something Loyd Tatum, Buford's
friend and personal attorney confirmed as well when I interviewed him. Notice the report has an
incorrect date for the ambush.

Dennis Hathcock (left) and author Mike Elam at the second ambush site. Hathcock's recollections regarding the events of the ambush were confirmed by McNairy County Coroner Ward Moore, State Medical Examiner Dr Jerry Francisco, Pauline Pusser's best friend Lavon Plunk and Buford's attorney Loyd Tatum.

Chapter 14
Susan

Jeanette Susan Anderson Hathcock Jones

Many of the stories told about the state line and the people there are either wrong, incomplete, or almost totally fabricated versions spun by people with little knowledge of the real events.

The life of Jeanette Susan Anderson Hathcock Jones is one of those stories. Most people don't recognize her name or her connection to the state line even though she was far more relevant to the story than most would realize, as she would one day, own most of the properties at the state line.

Some writers have concocted outrageous stories and lies suggesting that W.O. Hathcock and Howard Bunch had Susan and her husband Raymond murdered by a rogue investigator from the Mississippi Bureau of Investigation so they could take control of the state line properties. This upsets Susans's cousin Barbara Anderson greatly. Why? Because Barbara was there that day, she lives everyday with the tragic loss of Susan.

She has stated for a fact that there was no one else in the house that day. That day will forever be in her heart and mind.

This a story which I feel was relayed most accurately by Susan's first cousin and best friend Barbara Anderson. The following are Barbara's own words describing events concerning the life and times of Jeanette Susan Anderson Hathcock Jones. No one else knows the true account and facts as Barbara does as she was there when Susan was murdered.

****

A statement from Barbara Anderson before she tells her story

****

Karen Susan's daughter was 3 years old and had a lifetime ahead of her. She and I were hurt deeper by Susan's death than anyone will ever know. The saddest part about all of this is I didn't see what was coming and couldn't stop it. I'm sure many others who knew Susan and Raymond feel the same way. My hope is that one day people will let my family rest. It matters not who you refer to Susan, Louise, Jack, W. O., Buford, or Towhead..., they all left friends and family behind in these tragic events. Each of their family members had to suffer not only the memories but the gossip and lies as well. I am amazed as I flip through the books that have been written at how many direct quotes are in them. When actually, no one was present to hear what was said.

What happened? How did we come to this? I was present for one of the many tragedies in my family so I can only speak for one. So many have made false accusations and I feel it necessary to tell my personal account of what happened that day in December when Susan and Raymond lost their lives. It's not my intent to hurt anyone, only to clarify some of the misgivings around their deaths. They were loved by many and this tragedy has caused grief for many years. When their lives began together, Susan and Raymond loved each other, however because of circumstances in life, Susan's feelings changed while Raymond's did not. He loved her to death, literally and figuratively. The following is my personal account of what happened the day we lost Susan and Raymond. It is time for people to hear the truth as I lived it that horrifying day.

The True Story of
Jeanette Susan Anderson Hathcock Jones
As Told by Barbara Anderson

****

Susan, as she was known to family and friends, was born on the first day of November in 1948 to William "Bill" and Mae Swindle Anderson. Susan's life got off to a rough start as her mother passed away at her birth, due to hemorrhaging, leaving Bill with a small baby, which he soon realized he was ill prepared to adequately care for. Louise, being Bill's sister stepped up, not only taking Susan into she and Jack's home, but adopting her as well. While Louise took care of Susan and provided for all of her needs, it was Jack that Susan grew so close to as he would indulge his adopted daughter with lots of love and attention. Jack always took time to be with her. He was a big kid himself. Needless to say, when Louise and Jack built the Shamrock and moved in there, Susan was moved in also and spent a lot of time there as did her cousins who were near her age. There was Jean, who was the daughter of Dorothy, Louise's sister and Bobby and Barbara Ann, who were Bob's children, Louise's brother's children.

While Louise had the reputation of being a hardened soul to many, she took care of those kids as if they were her own, making sure that each received a good education as she wanted them to have a better life. Life was good to the kids as they grew up. They were loved and well cared for. Many may find this maybe a bit strange to hear that these kids were loved, but the Hathcocks were a family, much like any other family, even though their lifestyle might seem a bit out of the ordinary to some.

Jack and Louise had been having marital problems for a while and they were divorced in 1957 before construction of the Shamrock was completed. Although their marriage was over, their business venture at the Shamrock continued as they worked hand in hand. Their divorce was not revealed to the children of the families for several years.

When the Shamrock was completed, it was a beautiful place, rated AAA and the kids could traverse any area of the grounds, whether it be in the restaurant, the motel office, out by the pool, just about anywhere on the grounds. They even had horses in the back pasture for their riding pleasure. The kids also had their chores in helping to make the place run smoothly. They could often be found working there. Whether it be serving food in the restaurant or cleaning the motel rooms and pool.

The restaurant soon opened what they often referred to as the back room located behind the restaurant. This area when operating was off limits to children. This area was known to serve liquor and beer and this was where much of it was stored. People gathered nightly to dance, drink and sometimes engage in a little gambling with dice and cards. Keep in mind that the gambling was nothing like what the movie "WALKING TALL" and books would suggest, as this backroom never had a casino look to it. The kids were not allowed to be in this backroom unless it was closed. The back room only operated in the evening.

Carl Douglas "Towhead" White found his way to the state line, and hearing that the Hathcock's were divorced, saw an opportunity for himself and it wasn't long before he had fully entrenched himself and connected with Louise and the operations at the State Line. Even his FBI report recognized him as the person managing the Shamrock.

At that time, newspapers were saying the Shamrock was bringing in between seven to nine thousand dollars a week, as did Towhead's FBI report. While that may not seem like much, it would be the equivalent of approximately fifty-eight thousand to seventy-four thousand a week in today's economy. That's about three and a half million dollars a year in today's money.

Louise was a strong-willed woman, someone who was always in total control of her surroundings. Even while married to Jack, she called the shots. Now, with Towhead spending more time at the state line and pushing the envelope with his illegal enterprises, Louise was losing control.

Towhead spent little time with us kids, yet he was always ready to share his contagious smile and a few kind words with us. Maybe he did this to stay on the good side of Louise, maybe it was because of the way that Jack cared for the kids, or maybe it was simply his way. He treated his own niece with much respect so it could have been "his way."

As the kids grew older and a little wiser, they all became aware and understood what was happening at the state line. We knew that much of what went on there was illegal, yet it was a normal way of life. They also knew that many who frequented the establishments there were troublemakers and often criminals, however, each of them developed our own way of dealing with the environment.

It's no secret that a lot went on at the state line, things that were indeed illegal. Liquor was sold out of the motel office. At any time, day or night, cars would pull up to the door, blow the horn and Howard Carol would go out and take their order, run inside, and retrieve it, then deliver it back to the cars. The backroom offered the sale of liquor, beer, food, and the "razzle game." None of the Hathcock family members deny this, however it was vastly different to what the movie and many books say it was.

Jack and Louise took care of their family and they wanted for nothing. However, try as she might, Louise simply lacked a mother's touch.

Susan, at the age of fifteen, started dating twenty-year-old Raymond Jones. Being young and immature, Susan was in love with Raymond and as so often happens with young love, hormones took over and they found themselves expecting a child. While this unexpected event would cause a rift in Jack and Louise's lives, Susan and Raymond arranged to get married. Louise, however, made it difficult for Susan to get out sometimes.

Susan and Raymond wanted to be together, so they decided to slip off and get married. Since Louise could make it hard for them to be together, they decided to get married by proxy, then Louise couldn't stop them from being together. They arranged for a relative whose name I choose not to disclose to stand in for her at wedding ceremony in McNairy County, Tennessee. After the ceremony, Raymond came to pick Susan up and Louise refused to let her go anywhere. That's when Raymond and Susan produced the marriage license and told her she couldn't stop them as they were now married. Louise and Jack were livid.

To further convince her parents to let her leave with Raymond, Susan also told them she was pregnant. After learning this, Louise and Jack reluctantly agreed to them being married. Aunt Louise and Uncle Jack made the decision to accept the marriage but also to have the proxy marriage annulled so as to do it right with another ceremony. She and Jack made arrangements for a traditional marriage and set up housekeeping for Susan and Raymond. They moved into the little yellow house across Highway 45 from the Shamrock. Susan and Raymond seemed so happy. By this time, their beautiful daughter Karen was born, and life seemed at its best. Louise and Jack felt better about the situation with Susan was just across the road.

Susan and Raymond's first home across from the highway from Shamrock

Susan and Raymond came to West Point to get me to come and stay the summer. We had some great times at the little yellow house. Karen was the joy of their lives. I returned home in West Point to attend school, only to learn that Raymond had received a job offer and Susan, Raymond, and Karen were making plans to move to Memphis. They didn't stay long in Memphis and returned to Corinth into the house on Proper Street house. Life was being good to them. School was out for the summer and I soon found myself back to Corinth and we continued our carefree lifestyle. We would have a few school friends over and stayed up late talking and having an enjoyable time. No, we did not drink or do drugs. These things were never an issue for any of us. We had good times without that, for we had witnessed the sadness and consequences it could cause.

I enjoyed the summer and returned to West Point to finish high school. While I was gone that summer, I had no idea Susan and Raymond had decided to purchase the home off Farmington Road. Little did anyone know what tragedy their lives held in that home. This was a new subdivision development and there were only three houses built in it at the time. Their home was sandwiched between two other two houses, yet it seemed secluded because there were so many trees around.

Susan loved horses and they soon rented the pasture in front of their house and Susan purchased her Tennessee Walking horses and kept them there. There was little traffic up there except us and the Box family, who lived behind us on a dead end dive. With all this, Susan still became more dissatid=sfied in her marriage.

June of 1967 Susan, Raymond, and Karen showed up at my house in West Point to visit. We ate lunch, laughed, and talked all day. Things seemed normal between them. We were so happy when just being together. Unbeknownst to me, Raymond had approached my Mom and asked her to let me move back to Corinth with them. Years later, Mom told me what Raymond had told her. He told her that Susan was going out almost every night and not coming home until late. He told her that he hoped if I came back up there, she might stop going out or at least stay home more.

It was Raymond that first asked if I could come back to Corinth and stay with them. I personally had no idea at this time that they had bought the house at Farmington and no idea they were having marital problems. I'm still not sure to this day why Raymond thought my presence would change the situation.

I had just graduated high school and wasn't sure what the next chapter in my life would hold. I had started attending Vaughn's Beauty School of Cosmetology in Aberdeen on Saturday's while I was in high school. After much discussion, Mom agreed to let me move to Corinth as long as I continued my education as a Cosmetologist. Susan joined in the conversation and told Mom, "if you will let her come, I'll enroll and go with her." We did just that. Susan and I enrolled in Cosmetology in Selmer, Tennessee. At first, we went every day. Then things began change, we started missing class and soon quit going at all. Life began to spiral.

Susan started telling me the things that were going on in her life and how unhappy she was. She also told me how Raymond had been complaining that someone was coming to the house and asking him if he knew where his wife was while she was out at nights. According to Raymond, this had been going on for a while. This did concern me. I couldn't imagine why this would be happening. Raymond and Susan stayed to themselves and I couldn't imagine them having any enemies.

Susan and I talked several times about Raymond's accusations and Susan was convinced no one was coming to the house, that he was making that up in hopes that she would stay home. Since no one ever came while we were there, we never really put any belief in his story. We very seldom had any company and the road wasn't traveled leading up to the house. Needless to say, Raymond continued with his story about someone coming to the house. Raymond then asked Susan to get him a gun and she finally gave in. We went to the pawn shop in Corinth and they bought a small handgun.

Raymond came from a very faith believing family and this lifestyle was messing with his head I believe. He loved Susan and was not going to give her up without a fight. I feel he loved her so much he couldn't dare let her go.

With all the problems and unhappiness at home, Susan decided we should just leave. Susan, Karen, and I (and another, I decline to name) got into her car and went to a motel in Pickwick and got a room. We spent the night and early the next morning, we were sitting on the bed talking and trying to decide what to do next. Both she and I knew we wouldn't be staying in the motel forever. After discussing the options, I well remember Susan looking at me and saying, "We're going home. That's my damn house, I paid for it, and he can leave, not me." We loaded up in the car and headed back to Corinth.

When we got home, everybody was noticeably quiet. Susan and Raymond did very little talking, and we went about our day as normal. That evening, just about dark, we got in the car and drove down to Fraley's and visited with friends. Susan left with a friend and told me she would be back shortly. After a while, Karen, and I both were tired, so we went back home and of course, when we got there Raymond asked where Susan was. I told him I didn't know. He was pacing the floor and said to me "I'll be back" and he got in his car and left to search for Susan.

He stayed gone for quite some time, then Susan came home, and I told her Raymond was out looking for her. She said she thought she saw him go by, but he didn't see her. It wasn't long and Raymond returned home. By this time, he was terribly upset. I had put Karen to bed and shortly after Raymond came in, I went to bed myself. In the early morning hours, I heard someone in the house and thought maybe someone had broken in on us. I raised my head from my pillow and saw it was Raymond coming down the hall. I lay back down and went back to sleep.

When I woke back up around 7 a. m., Raymond and Susan were in the den. I could hear them talking, they didn't sound like they were fussing. I got up and went to the kitchen and I heard Raymond telling Susan that he was tired of this, she never cooked and did things around the house like a wife should do. Raymond's mother was a stay at home mom, and he was used to home cooked meals, a clean house and a mom that was always there for her children. Susan's lifestyle was completely the opposite. She never had to cook or do laundry as this was always done for her by the employees.

Shortly, Susan came into the kitchen and said, "come on we're going to the grocery store." Susan, Karen, and I went to Big Star (I believe was the name of the store) in Corinth and bought chicken, potatoes, English peas, and a pack of brown and serve rolls. Upon returning home we went straight to the kitchen and started frying chicken and boiling potatoes. We finished preparing dinner when a friend brought their baby over to the house for us to watch. After the friend left, the five of us sat down to dinner.

There wasn't any conversation except for Karen and I, with small talk. Susan and Raymond started talking. I have blocked from my mind what he said to her. I just know that we had eaten most of our dinner and when Raymond said something that Susan took exception with. Susan was smoking a cigarette and she threw it down toward her plate and it bounced off her plate onto the dinner table. She slid her chair back real fast, got up and headed to the bedroom. I picked the cigarette up and put it out just as Raymond got up and headed to the bedroom too. The way the house was built, there was a step down to the hallway which led to the bedrooms. I thought they were about to really have words.

I got up and went to sit in the den where I watched Raymond take his final walk down the hallway. When he reached their bedroom door, one of Karen's little dresses was laying on the floor in the doorway. Raymond kicked it out of the doorway into the hall and went into the bedroom. I heard the door click as he locked it and almost immediately, I heard a gunshot. I sat there for a few seconds then what sounded like a couple of footsteps and then another gunshot. I was in disbelief.

I called out to Susan a couple of times and she never answered. I knew this wasn't good as Susan always answered me. I grabbed Karen and the baby I was watching and for some reason ran out the front door of the house. Now mind you, we never used the front door. Why I used it that day is beyond me. I was carrying the baby and Karen in my arms.

As I ran down the hill to the house next door, totally scared to death at this time, I had to set Karen down and told her to run with me. She was only 3 years old, so we didn't move too fast. As we reached the house, which was the first one coming into the subdivision at that time, we found that no one was home. We ran back up the hill through the trees behind our house to the only other house in the neighborhood. As I said, I don't know why I went out the front door, because if I gone out the carport door as we always did, the second house I ran to would have been much closer to get to.

If I recall correctly, the "Box" family lived there. I banged on the door and Mr. Box came to the door half dressed. I asked him "can you come over to my house to see what happened as I thought Raymond had shot Susan or Susan had shot Raymond, I wasn't sure, but I heard gun shots." At that point, I didn't know who had done what. Mr. Box told me to "wait here while I get dressed and I will." He came out and returned to the house with me.

This entire time I kept my eyes peeled on our house. I still wasn't sure what had happened or if they would come for me or Karen next. Mr. Box and I went back to our house and he asked me "What is their name? Where are they?" Sadly, he didn't even know them, and they lived just feet from his back door. I told him "Raymond and Susan" and we both started calling their names and no one would answer. I knew something was wrong when Susan didn't answer me. She always answered me when I called and so did Raymond.

Mr. Box and I walked toward the hallway as he and I both continued calling their names. Still, no response. He was in front of me and reached their bedroom door first. As he tried to open it, he turned to me and said it's locked. I said, "I know it's locked, Raymond locked it when he went in there." He asked if I had a key and I told him I did in my bedroom. He asked me to get it. I went into my bedroom which was directly across the hall from their bedroom and retrieved the key. I handed Mr. Box the key and he unlocked the door.

As we entered the room, Raymond was laying just inside the door with his feet closest to the door. Mr. Box saw the gun, reached down, picked it up and placed it on the foot of their bed. We could hear Raymond struggling to breath. Susan hadn't moved. Mr. Box asked where the phone was, and I pointed to the other side of the bed.

He stepped over Raymond to get to the phone. When he picked up the receiver, he turned to me and said, "it's dead, is there another one"? I told him yes, in the den, so we both went back up the hall to call authorities. That phone was also dead. Mr. Box pulled the cord to the phone and found it to be cut. It was later determined that Raymond must have cut the phone cords while we were at the grocery store.

Since both phone wires were cut and we couldn't use the phone, we went back to Mr. Box house and called the proper authorities. We then returned to the house to wait on the law. In a matter of minutes, that hill was covered with police cars and people from the area. After the law arrived, investigators determined that the coil wire was also removed from the car in the carport. When the police and ambulance arrived and they told me, "He (Raymond) is still alive, but Susan is gone."

I remember seeing blood and substance fall from the stretcher as they came down the hall with Raymond. I can still hear his breathing. It was a sound like I had never heard before. He was trying hard to get his breath. They proceeded to load Raymond onto the ambulance and headed to the hospital. After they left with Raymond, the Coroner had arrived and picked up Susan.

The officers were asking me all sorts of questions. A couple of floral sprays had caught their attention. In preparation for Christmas, we had earlier gone to the florist to buy two large spray stands of flowers. Each had a ribbon with the words "Mother" on one and "Daddy" on the other. One of their questions was about the flowers. I know they asked me why these flowers, with the banners Mother and Daddy, were sitting in the den. I had to explain that we had bought them for Aunt Louise and Uncle Jack's graves. They said they had thought perhaps this was premeditated and one of them had purchased them in connection with their own death. I assured them they were for Aunt Louise and Uncle Jack.

They wanted to know what all we had been doing and what all was said leading up to the shooting. I couldn't tell them then; I can't tell you now what Susan's and Raymond's conversation was about just before they left the dinner table. I believe my inability to remember is due to this being such a traumatic experience for me, their conversation is blocked from my mind. After things settled down and they were finished questioning me, I told the officer I just want to go home (meaning to West Point). He told me I could not leave, that I had to stay in Corinth until in the morning and after the coroner's inquest was complete.

By this time, my Mom and Aunt Dot (Louise and my Dad's sister) had arrived. The Jones family had taken Karen and the baby to their house. Towhead's mother and sister, Pat White had graciously offered to let me stay at their house until I could leave Corinth. Mom, Aunt Dot, and I went to Ms. White's house and spent the night.

The next morning, I had to go back to the Farmington house for the inquest. The Coroner made the determination that this was indeed a murder/suicide. Raymond had shot Susan and then shot himself. There absolutely at no time any mention of someone else being in our house and doing this. As soon as the inquest was over, I left Corinth, Mississippi.

I went back at Christmas to Chewalla to take Karen her Christmas gifts and visit with her, then never to return until probably 30 years later when Karen contacted me. Mrs. Jones had told her if she wanted to know more about what happened to her parents, to call Barbara Ann. Karen called me just about dark one evening and we talked. I sent her a tape recording of just what I have said here. I then sent her a ring that belonged to her mom. Susan was wearing my letter sweater from basketball and I was wearing a dinner ring of hers on the day she died. I kept that ring with full intention of passing it to Karen when she was older.

Susan was buried in West Point with the Anderson family and Raymond was buried in Chewalla. Later, Karen saw fit to have her mother moved to Chewalla where they are both laid to rest now.

May Susan, Aunt Louise, and Uncle Jack all Rest in Peace.

LAST WILL AND TESTAMENT OF JACK RAYMOND HATHCOCK

I, Jack Raymond Hathcock, a resident citizen of Alcorn County, Mississippi, being of sound and disposing mind and memory and over twenty-one years of age, do make, publish and declare this to be my last Will and Testament, hereby revoking all former Wills and Codicils made by me.

FIRST: I direct that my hereinafter named Executrix pay and discharge all my just debts and expenses of my last illness and funeral; and she is authorized, within her discretion, to pay any or all of said debts and expenses without the same being probated and registered according to law.

SECOND: I hereby give, devise and bequeath all my property of every kind and nature, wheresoever situated or located, to Louise Hathcock and my adopted daughter, Susan Anderson Hathcock, jointly, and share and share alike, if they both survive me. If either Louise Hathcock or my adopted daughter should predecease me, then I give, devise and bequeath unto the survivor of them all my property of every kind and nature, wheresoever situated or located.

THIRD: If my adopted daughter has not attained the age of twenty-one years at the time of my death, then her share of the aforesaid property is to be held in trust for her by Louise Hathcock, as trustee, until such time as my said adopted daughter attains the age of twenty-one years, at which time Louise Hathcock, as trustee of this trust, shall transfer to my adopted daughter, Susan Anderson Hathcock, the residue or remaining balance in the said trust. In administering said trust funds, Louise Hathcock, as trustee, shall

- 1 -

Jack Raymond Hathcock's Last Will and Testament (Page 1)

not be required to report or account to any Court or person, nor make any inventory or appraisal, but shall administer said trust for the benefit of my said adopted daughter in any manner or fashion she sees fit, in her sole and absolute discretion.

FOURTH: My executrix and trustee in the administration of both my estate and the trust established hereunder for the benefit of my adopted daughter, Susan Anderson Hathcock, (if such trust comes into being under the terms of this Will) shall be authorized to do and perform any act deemed by her to be for the best interest of the estate, without any limitation whatsoever. This provision shall be given the widest possible construction and it shall, without limiting the generality thereof, include the power to borrow money, to pledge assets, to vote stock and participate in reorganizations, to sell or exchange property, to invest funds and retain securities without any limitation prescribed by law for investments by fiduciaries.

FIFTH: I hereby appoint Louise Hathcock as Executrix of this my last Will and Testament and relieve her from making bond to serve as such, from making any annual or final account to any court, or from making or causing to be made any inventory or appraisement of my estate; or from obtaining any order of any court in connection with the administration of my estate, giving her full authority to administer and wind up my estate in accordance with the terms of this Will.

IN WITNESS WHEREOF, I have hereunto signed my name to this instrument, my Last Will and Testament on this the _____ day of May, 1961.

Jack Raymond Hathcock
T E S T A T O R

- 2 -

Jack Raymond Hathcock's Last Will and Testament (page2)

147

The foregoing instrument, consisting of two pages and this attestation clause on the third page, was signed, published and declared by the Testator, Jack Raymond Hathcock, as and for his last Will and Testament, in the presence of each of us, and we, at his special instance and request and in his presence, and in the presence of each other, have hereunto signed our names as attesting witnesses on this the _11th_ day of May, 1961.

Thomas H. Lilly

Gary Butler

WITNESSES

Jack Raymond Hathcock's Last Will and Testament (page3)

Jack Hathcock just prior to his murder

Louise Hathcock

Jack and Louise in happier times

Louise with her adopted daughter Susan

Mae Anderson, Susan's biological mother
died of hemorrhaging during to childbirth.

Susan and Raymond Jones

Man, Wife Shot to Death

CORNITH, Miss. (AP) — A man and his wife were dead here today, apparently after a murder-suicide.

Susan Jones, 19, died instantly Monday in her home six miles from Corinth. Her husband, Raymond Lee Jones, 24, died three hours later in a Corinth hospital.

The sheriff's office said Jones apparently shot his wife with a pistol and then shot himself.

Chapter 15
The Easy Times

Most people live with the impression that every day of his six years as Sheriff of McNairy County was a life and death struggle for Buford. In all reality, most of Buford's story takes place in the first seventeen months of his first term as sheriff, and even these events are somewhat questionable. Buford actually had a lot of "easy times." While seventeen months out of his seventy-two months as sheriff, were busy months for Buford, his last two terms were relatively quiet.

Think about this for a moment..., Buford lied about seeing Louise Hathcock beating a sailor to death with a ball-peen hammer , as Kenneth Wayne McCoy died in 2012, not at the White Iris in 1956. Buford's story about being attacked, cut up, robbed and left for dead at the Plantation club in February of 1957 doesn't appear to be true as there are no official documents of this ever happening, just as photos taken of him in that time frame show no scar tissue from the attack and there are no witnesses to confirm that it ever happened. He admitted to reporter Ellie Grossman that he lied about him robbing the Plantation Club and the assault on W.O. Hathcock. He misinformed us about the death of Louise Hathcock as her autopsy and thestatement from Howard Carroll do not support Buford's story about her death.

Next when you examine the eight times he was shot. The legend leads some people to believe he was in eight separated shootings, when the truth is he was involved in only three shootings having a combined total of eight wounds between those three events. When you examine these events closely, you notice that there were no witnesses to any of these shootings. I for one, must wonder if any of these events really happened as Buford has already proved himself wound to his chin were all superficial, leading many to wonder if they were self-inflicted or if he was always attacked by assassins who were inept and couldn't shoot straight even at close range. as a person who did not always telling the truth. All his wounds, except for the alleged ambush

Then there are his knife wounds, seven in total. These seven wounds came in two alleged attacks. There were no witnesses to the first attack where a hitchhiker allegedly stabbed Buford several times in the chest. Oddly, much like his gunshot wounds, these knife wounds were all superficial as well.

There was one witness to the second alleged knife attack on Buford, McNairy County Coroner Ward Moore. Moore said, yes, a bootlegger did try to run over Buford with his car, but the stabbing part of the story never happened. So, what are we to make of Buford's veracity? How can we possibly be expected to believe in the "Pusser Legend"?

The truth is, the state line basically died when Towhead went to prison for his "Three State Moonshine Operation" and Louise Hathcock was killed. Sure, W.O. Hathcock and Howard Bunch bought the state line properties after Louise was killed but FBI reports show no illegal activity there under the new ownership.

About the only thing that happened at the Shamrock after Louise was killed was a little shootout between W.O. Hathcock and Junior Smith when Junior and his friends continued to break the locks off a gate on the Shamrock property so they could gain access to some property behind the motel.

W.O had a wound to his ankle; Junior had a minor gunshot wound to the ear and one of Juniors associates had the worst of it as he had several buckshot wounds to his side and back. All were arrested and each was released on bonds of five hundred dollars each. There isn't much left to tell about this except that the county road supervisor said that the county had never maintained the road in question, thus indicating it was indeed a private drive at the Shamrock.

Of course, there was the alleged August 12th ambush, where there are so man unanswered questions about the event. People with open minds however ask who was left at the state line that wanted Buford dead? They keep in mind that this happened while Buford and Pauline were separated, and Pauline had threatened to inform the TBI of Buford's illegal activities of accepting pay offs. They understand that Buford had motive, means and he apparently made the opportunity to kill his wife. He had been overheard just hours before the alleged ambush threatening to kill Pauline. People with open minds understand that had Pauline succeeded in reporting Buford's activities, he may well have served prison time.

There was one big bootlegging bust during Buford's second term as sheriff when Carl Hathcock, no known relation to the Hathcock family in this story, attempted to sell Junior Smith a trailer load of untaxed liquor at the Old Hickory Grill. Junior told the bootlegger he would make a call and get the money for the load but called Buford instead.

The last big event during Buford's tenure as sheriff took place on Christmas day 1968 when Buford shot and killed Russ Hamilton in yet another questionable shooting. People who can put the legend aside and think logically, want to know why Buford was involved in a situation inside Selmer city limits? Why didn't Selmer Police handle this call? Of course, this is another event where Buford was allegedly fired upon several times and sustained yet another superficial wound that didn't require medical treatment. This was also one of those events where no witnesseswere present. Now with the truth exposed of Buford's propensity to lie or embellish his stories, thinking people have reasonable doubts about Hamilton's death.

There you have it, seventeen months of action during his first term as sheriff followed by seven months of routine law enforcement duties. His second term was fairly quiet, except for the two alleged assassination attempts that many think holds no merit due to Buford's personal circumstances, (marital separation) during those times.

His last term as sheriff, was equally quiet as there was not any big events except for Buford's killing of Russell Hamilton in another questionable shooting.

I often ask myself why we as a people, are so willing to accept what we are told by novel writers and movie makers as being the truth? What makes them the experts when novel writers give direct quotes from some of these real live players, as if they were sitting in the room with these people as they made plans to eliminate people who were in their way of making illegal money?

What does it tell us when writers give direct quotes from people like W.O. Hathcock, Howard Bunch and many others when logic tells us these writers never met these people and were never there to hear such conversations?

What does it tell us when a movie production company has to change the names of people in the movie? In WALKING TALL, people like the real life Louise Hathcock became Callie Hacker and W.O Hathcock was morphed into Buel Jaggers. The real Willie Wade was portrayed as Willie Rea Lockman while Towhead White, a major figure in the real story was completely left out of the movie.

In WALKING TALL II, moonshiner and hired assassin Pinky Dobson's character was modeled after a real Paul David English. Ray Henry represented real life Russ Hamilton, while John Witter was a composite character which represented a state official from Nashville, a mob lieutenant, and to a small degree, Towhead White. Final Chapter continued with this trend. Why?

This was most likely done as the movie writers and producers realized that their script had little to do with the real story. I suspect they feared the possibility of lawsuits that might come their way if they used the real names of people who were still living while knowingly giving an almost totally false narrative in the movie.

I suspect, they changed Chief Deputy Jim Moffett's name, calling his character Grady Coker so they could portray his character in any way they wished and didn't have to pay him for his story.

It's amazing to think about how we as readers and movie goers can be so easily sucked in to believing a story is true simply because of some review we read in a newspaper or magazine or some movie trailer we saw which suggested it was a "true story". Sadly, I must admit that I was once one of those people. After researching the story, I believe I have a better understanding of what actually happened in McNairy County back in the sixties and early seventies.

If you believe as I do, that Buford staged both the January 67 ambush as well as the August 12th ambush, you understand that Buford'd last two terms were actually fairly quiet.

Famed Southern Sheriff Retraces Years Of Wounds, Death, Gunplay

SELMER, Tenn. (UPI) — A jagged river of scar tissue circles Buford Pusser's face, hiding torment felt by the ex-lawman who won fame across the South by busting up a notorious gang on the nearby Tennessee-Mississippi border.

If half Pusser's face had not been blasted away by two 30-calibre carbine slugs, the lines of anguish over the Aug. 12, 1967 murder of his pretty wife would be greater.

As it is, there is only a trace of bitterness in the whisper-soft drawl of the former McNairy County sheriff. Fourteen plastic surgery operations have given him a new appearance.

Moviegoers now munch popcorn as they view a wide screen and see an actor using Pusser's name get shot eight times, stabbed seven and kill two people.

The audience squirms as it watches a replay of the chilling ambush that took the life of Pauline Pusser on a narrow blacktop road next to a patch of fluffy cotton. "Walking Tall" is the name of the movie.

Circling the McNairy County Courthouse once, Pusser pointed his new milk-white Thunderbird south toward the Mississippi-Tennessee line. Slightly sunk in the deep pile black carpet were three pistols—a 9mm, a 357 magnum and a .38 special.

"I guess with the movie coming out some people are going to be rubbed the wrong way," remarked Pusser who served the maximum of three two-year terms as this rural county's top lawman.

In the 1950s, some of the honky tonks that straddled the state line received a transfusion of bad blood when the territory became

a refuge for thugs, many of whom Pusser said were chased out of Phenix City, Ala. by the National Guard.

Until Pusser became one of Tennessee's youngest sheriffs at age 26, illegal gambling, prostitution and liquor flourished. The young sheriff claimed he was offered $1,000 a month to keep his 6-6, 250-pound frame away from state line business.

Traveling at speeds of 85 miles per hour down roads he used to haunt as sheriff, Pusser, now 34, talked about the movie and his run-ins with the state line crowd. He is currently a consultant to the movie.

"You know, I think the movie is pretty accurate," he said, pulling a publicity picture from the fold in the car's sunvisor. "This fellow, Joe Don Baker, does a good job playing me.

"Yeah, they talked to a bunch of big name actors before coming up with Joe Don Baker," he continued. "The people are going to see a story and not a Clint Eastwood or a John Wayne.

"They didn't choose a sex symbol to play my wife because my wife was a sex symbol."

The car had left the Selmer city limits, the town where the lawman killed Charles Hamilton in 1969. After being shot in the stomach, Pusser put a hole to the left of Hamilton's right eye.

For the record, Hamilton stood accused of killing five people in his lifetime, including his wife and a deputy sheriff. He had served 30 years behind bars.

At the state line, Pusser turned the car around in the parking area of the Shamrock Motel, a faded green building in which Louise Hathcock met death Feb. 1, 1966. Mrs. Hathcock, operator

of the Shamrock, fired one shot at Pusser before her gun jammed.

The young sheriff, who had a warrant for her arrest on a robbery charge, put a bullet in her arm which traveled through to her heart.

Backtracking, the sheriff turned off U. S. 45 down winding New Hope Road, breezing past cotton fields and pasture land until he came to a small concrete bridge.

It was nearly dawn Aug. 12, 1967 and Pusser had just returned home from patrolling the county when an anonymous phone caller said there was "serious trouble brewing on the state line."

Pusser had been increasingly active in shutting down the nightspots that operated outside the law and Pauline feared for his life. She insisted on going with him to the stateline.

"This is where the first volley came from," he said, his patchwork face showing little emotion. "This is where they blew half of Pauline's head off.

"We found out later their car had been hiding behind the Methodist Church up the road. They were just waiting for us to come by."

William S. White

Senate Democrats Can't Trap Nixon

WASHINGTON — Of the current Democratic Senate it may later be said that never had ▬▬▬ ▬glected

Slowly, Pusser drove the shiny Thunderbird another two miles down the road and stopped at an intersecting dirt road. "I thought they had stopped chasing us and I stopped here.

"I pulled Pauline over to me and tried to help her. I could tell she was dying. She was gasping for breath. I opened the door and looked back and about that time they were on us again.

"I caught two soft-nose slugs in the face. I tried to call for help on the radio but I couldn't. I pulled the rearview mirror down to see what was wrong and my chin was almost to my lap.

"Blood was spurting everywhere. Later they found my jaw about 20 feet over in that field," Pusser said, pointing in the direction of pasture land enclosed by barbed-wire.

Today, Pusser's jaw is constructed of wire mesh. He has no feeling in part of his face and in cold weather his mouth freezes.

He has lost a wife, the mother of three children. He has vowed to find her killers, but the man he believes put out the contract has since been killed in a shootout over a woman.

Pusser is considered a legend in law enforcement at the age of 34.

slogans, such as that the Senate is "sipping political Geritol." Idle and empty words right out of television land are all right for

Newspapers and magazineswere more than willing to publish stories about sSheriff Pusser without fact checking or doing much investigative work to be certain the stories about the sheriff were true.This helped to build the "Pusser Legend" that people are so willing to believe in today.

156

Chapter 16
Killing Russ Hamilton

It's Christmas day, Wednesday, December 25, 1968. Buford is in his office at the McNairy County Courthouse when the telephone rings. The caller is Don Pipkins. Pipkins tells the sheriff that his tenant, Charles Russell Hamilton, has threatened to kill both he and his wife after recklessly firing several shots in the air with a handgun at his Hamilton's apartment at 559 Peach Street in Selmer. According to Pipkin, Hamilton is intoxicated.

Russ Hamilton is indeed an evil man, one who is very capable of following through on his threat without hesitation. Hamilton is ruthless as he has killed before, taking the life of John York, a McNairy County Deputy, shooting York in the back as the deputy was filling out a warrant for Hamilton. Hamilton served only a short prison term for this 1940 murder.

Hamilton is no stranger to murder as he had also killed his wife in September of 1940. She was last seen on September 5th of that year in the company of Hamilton, according to friends and relatives. Newspaper reports tell that her decaying body was found in a swamp in the Chewalla area on September 30th of that year.

In 1946 Hamilton would again take a life, killing his mother, beating her to death with a flashlight.

You would assume that these murders would be enough to put Hamilton behind bars for life or possibly get him the death penalty, but this would not be the case as on October 16, 1960, he would kill yet again.

John Grossheim, fifty three, of Lauderdale Alabama would be found in his bedroom sitting on the floor, leaning against a bed in a pool of his own blood. Grossheim had been stabbed multiple times in the chest and stomach.

Grossheim had been employed for several years at Wright's Gin Mill where he met and befriended Hamilton. A man with no feeling for others, Hamilton would take an innocent life when he killed his co-worker, once again serving little prison time for his crime.

It should also be noted that Hamilton was suspected of other murders including that of his first wife Annie, who simply "disappeared". Now, Don Pipkins and his wife could be Hamilton's next victims.

While Hamilton was no doubt a very dangerous individual, I have to wonder why Buford was the one to respond to Pipkins' call for help that day. Normally a call from inside the city limits would be answered by an officer from the cities Police Department. Of course there have been stories that officers there were afraid of the fifty nine year old Hamilton and refused to respond, causing Pipkins to call the Sheriff's Office for help. To me, this sounds like another legend building story.

Selmer Chief of Police Hugh Kirkpatrick would tell that he had words with Hamilton on more than one occasion, saying "It just happened that I never had to shoot him." Apparently, Chief Kirkpatrick was not afraid of Hamilton.

Regardless of the circumstances, Buford responded to the call, arriving at Hamilton's apartment in just minutes. The sheriff was armed, later telling that he had a gun with him as Towhead White been released from prison and had made it clear, at least according to Pusser, that Towhead had sworn to kill the sheriff.

Pusser would tell others that he had talked with Hamilton the week before and that he seemed fine. Not waiting for backup, Pusser knocked on Hamilton's door and the old man told him to "come in." According to the sheriff, Hamilton immediately opened fire with a .25 caliber handgun as the killer lay on the couch.

Hamilton's first shot struck the grip of Pusser's revolver and Buford would claim that the shot then "tore a hole in his stomach the size of a walnut." Two other shots missed the sheriff as he drew his revolver and dropped to the floor as he returned fire.

Buford's aim was apparently accurate as he shot the fifty nine year old ex-convict almost directly between the eyes, killing him instantly.

This is where the story gets a little strange as Buford would leave the scene of the shooting and travel a short distance to the home of his girlfriend, "Lady Ann." I'm told that Buford stepped to the hallway of Lady Ann's home and telephoned District Attorney General Will Terry Abernathy to report the shooting.

Being Christmas day, "Lady Ann" had company in her home as some family members were there. Her family didn't care much for Buford and they were a little upset that Buford would come to her house immediately after the shooting, especially on such a holiday. To them, it was as if Buford was there to put on a show in hopes of gaining Lady Ann's sympathy and attention.

Lady Ann, showing concern for Buford, approached him in the hallway as he was making his call to D.A. Abernathy, lifting his shirt to check on his wound. To her surprise, all she could find was a red mark, not an open, bleeding hole in the sheriff's abdomen. Somewhat miffed by her actions, Buford pushed his shirt down to keep her from seeing what really wasn't there.

District Attorney Abernathy would later call for a grand jury to be impaneled to investigate Hamilton's death, and much like with the shooting death of Louise Hathcock, the grand jury would return a "no true bill", exonerating Buford of any wrong doing.

Understandably, if a man ever needed killing, that man would be Russ Hamilton. Still, questions linger in the minds of many. When we examine Buford's own history of violence, you see a reputation of questionable behavior on the part of the sheriff in shooting situations.

Again, why was Buford responding top a call in the cities jurisdiction rather than allowing Selmer officers to handle the call?

Why did Hamilton allegedly open fire on Buford, especially while he was lying on his couch?

Once again, Buford narrowly escaped death, according to his version of the story, while receiving a very superficial wound, in fact it was so superficial that he required no medical attention. Much like other similar incidents, there are no witnesses to the shooting.

One thing I find interesting is that Hamilton died from a single gunshot to the head. A "head shot" seems to have been the signature of every Pusser involved shooting except for one.

* Louise Hathcock suffered a head wound when she was killed in February 1, 1966 when no witnesses were in the room.

* Buford was shot in the left cheek during the January 2, 1967 ambush when no witnesses were present. Many people believe the wound to be self inflicted to throw attention to Towhead who had escaped from prison. Towhead was a man that Buford is said to have feared.

* Pauline Pusser would be shot in the head twice in the alleged August 12, 1967 ambush. Again, when there were no witnesses to the shooting.

* Buford would also he shot in the chin during the same August 12, 1967 ambush, where he was allegedly the intended target, while his wife would be killed.

* Now, December 25, 1968 Russ Hamilton would be shot between the eyes with no one present to give an individual accounting of the shooting.

In fact, the only Pusser involved shooting where no one was shot anywhere about the head was when Buford shot Paul David English. Ironically this was the only time a witness was present as Corinth Police Chief Art Murphy was with Buford when English was shot in the spine, partially paralyzing him during a car chase.

A total of six shootings with five involving a shot to the head…., what are the odds of this happening?

Questions

* Why did Pusser take the disturbance call at the Hamilton residence?

* Why did he not wait for backup since a gun was involved?

* Why did Buford shoot Hamilton in the head rather than shooting at his body mass?

* Why did he claim to have a wound the size of a walnut to his stomach, yet needed no medical attention?

* Why did he leave the crime scene without protecting potential evidence?

159

* Why did he go to his girlfriends house to place a call notifying the District Attorney of the shooting?

If Buford's version of the Hamilton shooting is correct, I would agree that he had every right to dispatch Hamilton to the hereafter. There are, however, so many suspicious actions and unanswered questions regarding the shooting. Therein lies the rub..., all of the shootings Pusser was involved in, with the exception of the one involving Paul David English, have so many unanswered questions.

Russ Hamilton being placed under arrest for the murder of John Grossheim

Charles Hamilton

SELMER—Services for Charles Russell Hamilton, 59, will be at 11 p.m. Saturday at the Shackelford Funeral Home in Selmer with the Rev. Foy Huckabee officiating. Burial will be in Oak Grove Cemetery.

Hamilton was killed in a shoot-out with McNairy County Sheriff Buford Pusser about 8:30 p. m. Tuesday night.

Hamilton's apartment was the small attached dwelling on the left side of the larger building.

The question is, did Buford take justice in his own hands and become Hamilton's judge, jury and executioner? Buford's actions of the day were unusual. Why was he at the jail rather than at home with his children? This was the second consecutive Christmas since Pauline's death that he had not spent much time with Diane, Mike and Dwana. The previous year he had picked Paul David English at the jail where he was incarcerated and taken him to see his mother.

Buford had a two way radio in his car. Why didn't he use it to call for backup before confronting Hamilton, who he knew was a natural born killer who was armed with a handgun.

I have always been curious about his actions after the shooting as well. Why did Pusser leave the scene of the shooting and go to his girlfriend's house rather than drive the short distance back to his office at the courthouse to call District Attorney Abernathy?

In view of how the District Attorney Abernathy had allegedly handled the evidence in the shooting of Louise Hathcock, I have to wonder if he was more straight forward in presenting evidence to the grand jury looking into Hamilton's death?

I look back at other McNairy County Sheriffs and I have to wonder why they were never involved in so much gun play? Clifford Coleman served terms as sheriff both before and after Buford was in office. Hugh Kirkpatrick also served as McNairy County Sheriff before the Pusser era as sheriff and was Selmer's Chief of Police while Buford was in office.

Then there was Buford's mentor, James Dickey who was sheriff, and running for re-election against Buford when he was killed in an auto accident. And lets not forget Sheriff James Opal Gray and Paul Ervin, both of whom, like Clifford Coleman, served as sheriff after Buford left office. To my knowledge, none of these men had to shoot and kill anyone.

Some believers of the Pusser Legend and point to the state line as an example of how difficult Buford's job was. So I ask, why only Buford? Other sheriffs on both sides of the state line had the same problems when each of them served as sheriff.

I think we have established that Buford actually did very little, if anything, to clean up the state line as it appears that he was in their employ and making good money giving them his "protective services."

The death of Russ Hamilton was one of those "certain events" in Pusser's life which was used in WALKING TALL II. Of course, the movie production company changed Hamilton's name to "Ray Henry" and made his character into the fictitious Pinky Dobson's accomplice as they tried and tried again to kill Pusser at the behest of the also fictional of John Witter.

Did Pusser really have to kill Russ Hamilton? We may never know, but at least you now probably know more about the circumstances surrounding the shooting that day than you once did.

With this information, maybe you can come to your own conclusion as even for me, it is not clear. Did Hamilton actually pose as a threat to Pusser? Did Hamilton lose his life so that Buford could seek the attention and sympathy of his girlfriend? Of course it could be that Hamilton was indeed a threat and deserved to be shot, after which Buford went to his girlfriends home instead of his office to contact D.A. Abernathy, using the event to garner the attention he always seemed to seek.

This information regarding the events of December 25, 1965 has always been out there. Unfortunately, so few people have actually researched the story, while some who have, especially writers and authors, choose to ignore the details as it tells a story that is not flattering of Sheriff Pusser and does not conform to their agenda.

It is truly unfortunate that so many events in the real story have been treated with the same disregard, thus, we have the "Pusser Legend."

Chapter 17
Killing Towhead

Carl Douglas "Towhead" White

It is December 11th of 1966. Towhead has tired of being held at the minimum-security prison at Maxwell Air Force Base in Montgomery Alabama. Escape would be an easy task from this facility. He would basically walk away from prison with another inmate, Oliver French. Weeks after his escape, on January 2nd of 1967, Sheriff Buford Pusser was shot when he stopped a car near the state line. Towhead White would become a suspect in this shooting. This alleged shooting is, however, questionable on many levels.

Pusser was shot in the left cheek and one bullet grazed his arm. The firearm used was a .25 caliber semiautomatic handgun. There were no witnesses to this event and the sheriff could provide almost no information regarding the car he had stopped or its occupants. This lack of any usable and relevant information was a trademark of each time Buford was ever stabbed or shot.

Pusser was aware that Towhead had escaped prison and suspected that Towhead might be out to kill him in an act of revenge for Buford having killed Louise just months earlier. Buford knew just how dangerous Towhead could be as he was the one man that Buford feared.
People logically question if this shooting was a real event or a staged one. When you look at the shooting itself, you have to question why anyone trying to kill a man the size of Pusser would use a .25 caliber gun.

Sheriff Pusser was shot one in his left cheek, his left arm was grazed by another bullet and he had a superficial gunshot wound to his abdomen. None of these wounds were life threatening and Pusser was admitted to the hospital one night for observation.

People, including myself, question if Pusser's gunshot wounds may have been self-inflicted for the purpose of building a fire under local and federal law enforcement officers to capture Towhead before he could get to Pusser. I would suggest that had the gunman been Towhead, he would have used something more deadly than a .25 caliber handgun and he would have made sure Buford was dead before he left the scene.

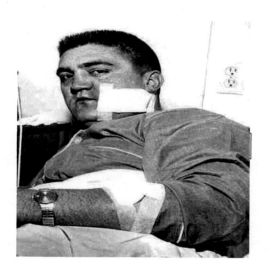

Buford after being shot in January 1967. Were his wounds self-inflicted
in a desperate act to urge law enforcement to find Towhead?

Shortly after this shooting, Towhead surrendered himself to authorities and was returned to prison. He refused to say where he had been or what he had been doing after his escape. It may very well be that hearing that Buford had been shot, he knew that he would be a suspect in the shooting and that authorities might not be so kind to him during an arrest.

After returning to prison, Howard Bunch and W.O Hathcock contacted White to see if he was interested in going in with them to purchase the properties of the Jack Hathcock estate which included the lucrative Shamrock properties as well as the White Iris. Amazingly, Towhead refused the offer. His FBI file shows that an informant said that Towhead wanted out of this lifestyle.

You don't hear much about Towhead after he was released from prison in January 1969. I'm told he spent some time reconnecting with his family and was trying to go straight. He went into a juke box business, partnering with Clarksdale Chief of Police Ben Collins. When city officials learned of this partnership, however, they fired Collins due to his association with Towhead, who of course, was a well known criminal. City officials didn't like the optics of Collins close relationship with Towhead or the fact that Collins was seen as using his influence as Chief of Police while pressuring local businessmen into taking his juke boxes into their establishments.

When you look at at all of this logically, Towhead gave all of the outward appearances of a man trying to change his life. Many people thought that he was trying to start a new chapter in his life, one that would be far removed from that of his past. Others believe that White was still living the same lifestyle that had sent him to prison. Regardless, Towhead had never shared much about his real life with his own family. They to still looking for answers about him and his history.

I might point out that once out of prison, Towhead bought his sister Rachel a new 1969 Chrysler. He is said to have loved his family dearly and was trying to express this to them in any way he could. He was trying to take care of his mother, having plans drawn for a new home he intended to have built for her. It appears however, that he was living a conflicted life, as he had not fully separated himself from his criminal lifestyle. Once out of prison he initially connected with some of his criminal alias and had joined them in a crime spree which was spread over several states. Towhead was aware that Rex Armisted was now holding two warrants for his arrest in connection with these crimes.

Towhead and Bobby Anderson were living in a motel in Clarksdale at this time. Then came the night of April 3, 1969…, the night that Towhead was killed. This is the date of yet another chapter of the "Pusser Legend."

On this Thursday morning, Towhead was going to see his friend Dewitt Dawson in nearby Alabama. Towhead was driving the car he had purchased for his sister as he didn't want to draw attention to himself while he was in Corinth. Towhead always drove a Cadillac, however, he felt that driving a different car on this day might make his presence in Corinth less conspicuous.

Towhead and Bobby Anderson had checked into the El-Ray Motel which was operated by his old friend Junior Smith. Before leaving Corinth and making the short drive to see his friend Dewitt Dawson, Towhead ran into Shirley Smith. He as aware that she and Junior were having marital problems and had been separated for a couple of weeks. There was even talk of a divorce in their future.

Towhead told Shirley that he was going to see his friend and associate who lived near Muscle Shoals Alabama, and asked if she wanted to ride along with him on the trip. Shirley agreed to go. Some people however, suggest that Shirley was part of much bigger plan, a setup to end Towhead's life as others were also aware of the new warrants for Towhead's arrest and they feared that Towhead might roll over on them and provide states evidence against them in order to stay out of prison himself or at least, get a reduced sentence.

Towhead also ran into Ronnie Flanagan that morning and asked Ronnie if he wanted to accompany them as well. Flanagan would tell me he turned down White's offer as he already had plans for the day. Ronnie would also tell me that he was glad he didn't tag along as the night would end tragically for Towhead and he would have been in the car as gunfire would take Towhead's life. Ronnie could only imagine what might have happened to himself as he would have been caught up in the gunfire. He realized that had he gone with Towhead and Shirley that day, he could have easily ended up just like Towhead.

Dewitt Dawson was an associate of Towhead White

Towhead and Shirley made the trip to see Dawson. The purpose of the trip was apparently to recover some of Towhead's money that he had left with his friend. This money was allegedly buried on Dawson's property, in a metal box which was wrapped in aluminum foil to help protect its contents from the elements. According to sources, Towhead allegedly had between five hundred thousand to a million dollars in this box, some of it which he had previously recovered from the Shamrock. I have no way to confirm the actual amount of cash allegedly in the box.

When Towhead returned to the El Ray Motel, he parked his car in front of room #3, where he was staying. Details of the shooting are sketchy at best, as no one seems to know exactly how the shooting took place. Junior Smith would claim that Towhead, upon seeing him, cursed him before he opened fire on Smith as Junior stood near the motel office. After the first shot was fired, Smith ran inside the motel office, got his 30-30 rifle. and stepped back outside to confront Towhead.

According to Smith's account, Towhead fired a second round at him, but missed again. Junior said he returned fire, firing approximately six shots into the Chrysler. Shirley Smith would narrowly escape the car as shots were fired. Towhead would die however, sitting in the

driver's seat, from a gunshot wound to the head. The head shot was not the only wound Towhead would suffer as he also had wounds to his chest and arm as well, the head shot however was the fatal one.

Some would wrongfully claim however, that Buford Pusser was on the roof of the motel that night and fired the fatal shot. I am not suggesting that Buford was or was not somehow

involved, but if he was, he was not on the roof that night as some would claim.

I have been told by multiple sources that the man who fired the fatal shot that night was Glen Alexander, also known as "Blue Tick." While Blue Tick would credit Junior with the kill shot, it is said to be Alexander who actually took Towhead's life. He was not on the roof as has been previously reported, but rather inside Towhead's room. As Towhead pulled his car to a stop in front of room number three, Blue Tick opened the door and fired a shot into White's forehead.

When you look at the angle from the roof to the car below, Towhead would have had to leaned forward over the steering wheel to have been shot in the head from the roof. The trajectory angle from inside Towhead's room was perfect however. Once the shooting is done and Towhead is dead, Blue Tick allegedly gets into a car driven by a woman, and leaves the area. He sticks to the plan and allows Junior to take full credit for killing White.

Sheriff James Bishop of Tishomingo County would also tell that it was Blue tick who fired the shot which took Towhead's life. Sheriff Bishop was a friend of Buford's. What Bishop did not tell us, and possibly did not know, is that it was Buford Pusser who commissioned the contract on White, and that Pusser and a female friend were close by that night to witness White's death.

Junior apparently was under pressure from Buford to kill Towhead as if White made a deal and turned states evidence in order to stay out of prison, it is said he would have taken down Pusser, Smith and several others for their own illegal activities …, and Pusser was not going to allow this to happen.

As shots were fired that night, people nearby began to gather at the El-Ray Motel. Most were friends and relatives of Smith as the Nitefall Motel and Theresa's Truck Stop were in the same area. The same held true for Drewry's Steak House which was directly behind the El-Ray Motel. This was where Barbara Bivins lived at that time.

Towhead was already dead before anyone arrived. He was still sitting in the car, a gaping hole in his forehead. Blood and brain matter covered the inside of the Chrysler. Towhead had a gun in his left hand, with two spent rounds in it's cylinder. Towhead was right handed, leading to questions regarding why he would be shooting at Junior with his left hand.

Towhead had also been "walking around naked" according to many close to him. This description simply means he was unarmed as he was on parole and didn't want to be found with a gun in his possession…, a violation of his parole which could send him back to prison.

Questions that were never answered were, why would Towhead be shooting at his friend Junior and why would he be shooting left handed? Many believe Junior fired two shots into the wall near the office and then mistakenly placed the gun in Towhead's left hand after he was dead. While there was no clear motive for Towhead to be shooting at his friend Junior…, there was motive for Pusser and Junior not just wanting, but needing White dead.

When authorities got the call regarding the shooting, Chief Deputy Hobart Bingham responded, first picking up his brother, Sheriff Grady Bingham at his home. They are said to have arrived at the El-Ray about a half hour after the shooting.

Some of Towhead's friends who came to the El-Ray included Bobby Anderson, Towhead's young protege, who was with Towhead in Corinth. Anderson would search the car for the coins that Towhead had collected from his juke box business, but none were to be found. He also checked Towhead's room, #3, for a shoe box which held an undisclosed sum of money, but it was also missing.

After the car had been processed by law enforcement officials and returned to Towhead's relatives, I'm told that they checked the trunk for the metal box that Towhead had retrieved from Dewitt Dawson's property, and it too was missing. Only the aluminum foil that the box had been wrapped in was there, partially covered in dirt.

Also, in the trunk, were post hole diggers, possibly used to dig the box up. The last object in the trunk was a yellow rug which was covered in blood. This led some of those close to Towhead to believe that he was already dead and in the trunk of the car when he arrived at the El- Ray and that his death scene was staged. Others insist that Towhead was alive when he arrived at the motel and the scene was staged immediately after he was shot.

Alcorn County Sheriff Grady Bingham sided with Towhead's family, believing Towhead was already dead when he arrived at Smith's EL- Ray Motel. Why else would there be a bloody rug in the trunk of the car?

One can only assume that Towhead's family must have known the real purpose of Towhead's trip to Alabama that day was to possibly recover his money. Why else would they have been expecting to find a box in the trunk?

To this day, no one seems to know how the metal box with all the cash disappeared. Did Junior or one of his relatives or friends take it, or was it retrieved by law enforcement officials? No one seems to have an answer for that question.

Also, Towhead was a man accustomed to carrying large amounts of cash on his person, often thousands of dollars. On this night however, he had only five one dollar bills on him, suggesting that someone had rifled his pockets for cash, leaving just enough to make it appear that he still had some cash on him.

When authorities arrived at the crime scene, I'm told there really was not much of an investigation. The atmosphere that night seemed to suggest that as far as they were concerned, one bad guy had killed another bad guy. For them, the world seemed to be a better place with one less bad guy..., in this case, Towhead.

This night would not be the only night that someone had attempted to take Towhead's life as a couple of months after he had been paroled from Leavenworth Federal Penitentiary, the mobile home where he was living was machine gunned. Towhead had survived that attack unscathed. Many have suggested that this was done by Buford Pusser, but I learned that he was eliminated as a suspect as the striations from projectiles recovered from Towhead's residence did not match those made by Buford's AR-15.

In yet another unrelated event that occurred shortly before Towhead was killed at the El-Ray Motel, he would learn that his old friend Howard Carroll had been found dead and floating in Elam Creekin Corinth. Towhead had always had a soft spot for Carroll and wanted to make sure he had a decent burial. Towhead had made arrangements for Carroll's funeral and burial with Bill McPeters, telling Bill that he would cover all of the expenses. What McPeters never expected was that just hours later, he would be also be handling Towhead's funeral and burial as well. With Towhead gone, Bill is said to have covered to cost for both men's funerals. Bill, I am told, had Towhead buried in the most expensive casket he had at the funeral home.

Towhead's funeral would be held at the National Funeral Home in Clarksdale on Friday, April 4, 1969 with Reverend Leroy Tubbs officiating. During the service Reverend Tubbs told the crowd how Towhead had recently come to him recently and had found the Lord Jesus Christ as his savior. He would be buried in Clarksdale Memorial Gardens.

Think about that for a moment, a man who had lived a life of crime, while he is in prison, decides to turn down a seemingly lucrative business opportunity with Howard Bunch and W.O. Hathcock involving the purchase of the Shamrock Motel and Restaurant, the White Iris, and other properties. Also, while in prison, Towhead, according to an FBI informant, had also decided to turn his life around, get away from his life of crime, go straight and spend more time with family. According the minister at his funeral, Towhead had indeed found God.

Was Buford Pusser in any way involved in Towhead's death? We will probably never know, but you must keep in mind that Junior and Shirley Smith were good friends and associates of Buford. Suggestions have been made that Junior shot Towhead at Buford's behest, but honestly, we will never know if this were the case as Buford, Junior and Shirley have all passed on.

Carl Douglas "Towhead" White, the man who once wanted to be known as "the Al Capone of the South," was only thirty-two years old when he died.

How much of this story is true? You will have to decide for yourself, but it came from several different sources, each who lived their own part in this story. Some of it can be validated through documentation, however, this is another one of those stories that is difficult to properly vet as so many of the principal players are now gone, after all, it has been more than fifty years since Towhead was killed.

I would have liked to given the names of the people who provided me with information and shared their stories, however, a few of these people are still living have asked that they not be identified as they are trying, even after all of these years, to move on with their lives. They just wanted the real story to be told.

Photo of a young Towhead White

The Shamrock…., where Towhead once wanted to launch his criminal empire.

Towhead (left), Howard Carroll (center) John Henry Fowlkes (Right). Fowlkes would be charged with manslaughter in the shooting death of Ed George at the 45 Grill in October 1954. Fowlkes was cleared of the charge by claiming self-defense.

Chapter 18
Death of a Legend

Buford Hayes Pusser

It is 11:50 pm on a Tuesday night and Buford is driving his Corvette down highway 64 on his way home from the county fair in Selmer. He is thinking about his day and how busy he had been, having driven earlier in the day to Memphis to meet with executives of Bing Crosby Productions. Buford was going to be in the movies, playing himself in a sequel to "Walking Tall" which had starred Joe Don Baker as Buford Pusser. The sequel, in which the former sheriff is to play himself, is to be called "Buford," a continuation of his story where the original, mostly fabricated story had left off.

I can only imagine how Buford reflects on the last ten or twelve years, thinking about just how far he had come in a relatively brief time. The movie "Walking Tall" had elevated his status from being a local sheriff to that of a national hero, a living legend as the media would often call him. Little did he know that the status of "living legend" was coming to an abrupt end.

Buford has been drinking heavily most of the evening as he is in a celebratory mood, having signed a contract to play himself in the new movie..., it would make him a millionaire, he thought. The former sheriff is driving fast, just as he usually does, as he approaches a location where highway 64 meets Lawton Rd. He is only a few short miles from home.

Suddenly his car veers slightly to the right and the passenger side wheels drop to the shoulder of the road. Buford over corrects as he tries to bring the fast-moving Corvette back on the roadway. Attempting to regain control, he instinctively hits his brakes throwing the powerful but light weight car into a dangerous skid. The Corvette has radial tires which Goodyear has recalled. The radial tires make his attempts to control the skid more difficult. The car crosses the painted center line on the highway, into the oncoming lane leaving black skid marks on the gray pavement. As Buford tries to steer the Corvette, it abruptly leaves the roadway completely, speeding onto a gravel area in front of an old Shell Station where braking at such a high speed on the gravel is impossible. The car continues across Lawton Road hitting an embankment at approximately 40 miles per hour. The car lurches into the midnight air as it flips back toward the highway, landing on all four wheels on the shoulder of the roadway.

The final resting place of Buford's Corvette after the accident

During this process, Buford, who is not wearing a seat belt, is ejected through the Corvette's open T-top and lands about three feet behind the now stationary vehicle. Danny Browder, a nearby resident, has heard the crash while watching TV, describing the noise assounding like a jet taking off. He steps outside his home to see what had happened, howeverwhen he sees nothing, he gets in his car thinking it might be an accident just over the hill on the highway. Arriving at the crash site he sees the vehicle and a body just behind the Corvette on the shoulder of the road. Flames can be seen coming from the car's engine compartment as well. Browder immediately returns to his residence to call authorities for help.

After making the call, Browder returns to the scene of the accident where he finds Jason Hollingsworth and Dwana Pusser, who have moved Buford's body approximately one hundred feet from the burning car. Buford Pusser, who the media called "a Living Legend," is now dead.

"Lady A", Buford's girlfriend, was to have a date with Buford the following day. It would be the first time she would have seen him in quite some time as they had gone their separate ways.

She was curious about why he wanted to see her now as he was a national hero, someone wh could have his pick of women..., so, why her and why now. He has told her that he wanted to take her to Pickwick Lake.

After agreeing to the date, she began to question Buford's motives. The night of his fatal accide "Lady A" would write a letter to her mother, one that she would leave in her room for her mother find in case she didn't come home. Knowing Buford as she did and knowing many of the things he ha done as sheriff, she began to fear for her life, afraid that she might end up like Pauline. Buford w famous now and she wondered what steps he might take to protect his new found fame and fortune. Sl had no idea that the note she was writing would not be necessary as Buford would soon die this ve night.

With his death came all sorts of stories, many claiming that the state line mob had finally succeeded in killing Buford. The movie "Walking Tall" had drawn much attention to the former sheriff and his alleged battle with the state line syndicate as the production company said it was Buford's "true story." Even Buford had contributed to the media hype by claiming the movie was eighty-five to ninety percent true. This media hype led the masses to believe that Buford had actually been assassinated. So, what is the truth regarding Buford's death?

First, think of who had motive to kill Buford in August of 1974? The state line had been quiet for eight full years. Louise Hathcock was dead as was Towhead White. W.O. Hathcock had been out of business at the state line for years, even before Buford became sheriff. Howard Bunch had lost his license to distribute alcohol ten years earlier in March of 1964. Bunch and W.O. Hathcock had purchased the state line properties from the IRS after Buford killed Louise Hathcock. They sold these state line properties years before the accident, so who was left that might benefit from Buford's death? What would the motive be for anyone to kill Buford?

To confuse matters even more, James Smith, Bobby Floyd's future son-in-law, would come out with an alleged deposition after Buford's death claiming that Nimbo Price had contacted him about splitting a contract to kill Buford. This too fed the masses with conspiracy theories as they were convinced that the state line was still alive and active.

So, who was Nimbo Price? He was Towhead's protege, a Towhead wannabe. He was young and ambitious and wanted to be a part of the criminal world. He was a low life who seemed to look for trouble. He had been arrested at one time and charged with rape and was released from jail when Howard Bunch posted his ten-thousand-dollar bond. Nimbo would be shot by Junior Smith when Price would attempt to break into Junior's trailer that was located behind the El-Ray Motel. Nimbo had shot the lock off to gain entry to the trailer and was lucky to survive after being wounded.

Nimbo would be killed on Sunday June 8, 1975 in a shootout at the home of Tommy Bivens. According to Bivins, Nimbo was friendly enough when he arrived at Tommy's home, however the situation escalated quickly. There are two stories regarding the cause of the shootout between Bivin's and Nimbo. Barbara Bivins would write that Nimbo thought that Tommy was involved in and was somehow responsible for Towhead's death five years earlier and was out for revenge.

The other story was that Tommy had allegedly made derogatory remarksabout Nimbo's sexual preferences. Regardless of which story, if either were true, Tommy Biven's would send Nimbo the hereafter, shooting him four times with two .38 caliber slugs hitting Nimbo's chest. Bivins was cleared of any wrongdoing in the shooting.

James Smith would claim he met with Price on August 16, 1974 at Catherine's Club in Selmer. He would tell that while at this club, he overheard Junior Smith and Skeet Adkins discussing a "front end man" in Memphis and Smith apparently conjured up a plot where state liners were planning to kill the legendary sheriff. James Smith claimed that he overheard Junior Smith ask Skeets if he had gotten the money together and he assumed they had discussed money with Nimbo.

Smith would say in the alleged deposition that a few days later he once again met with Nimbo, this time at the Thunderbird Motel in Jackson. According to his statement, Smith waited in the car as Nimbo went into a motel room and returned shortly thereafter with ten thousand dollars. Nimbo told him that that Ed Gillock, Ed Shaw, Junior Smith, Cotton Collins, and "a man" from California were in the room.

Smith went on to say that he noticed that Nimbo had front end parts, explosives, rope, tools, and a master set of GM keys etc. in the car. Smith stated in this alleged deposition that as soon as "it was over" Nimbo would split the money with him for his assistance in killing Pusser.

On August 20, 1974 Nimbo allegedly called Smith again telling him they needed to meet in Eastview. Smith was informed that whatever was going to happen would take place between Collierville and Adamsville and that Smith would be the getaway driver. Smith went on to say that he did not go to Eastview to meet Nimbo, but rather attempted to contact Buford who he knew was in Memphis at that time, meeting with executives from Bing Crosby Productions.

Smith would go on to claim that he and his fiance Camilla Floyd called every Holiday Inn in Memphis to reach Buford. Having no luck, he claimed he called the McNairy County Sheriff's Office as well Buford's parents in an attempt to warn Buford of the impending assassination attempt. Smith, however, would claim he did not reached Buford in time.

He would go on to say that he ran in to Nimbo in Corinth after Pusser's death and Nimbo asked why he had not shown up for the event. Smith claimed, "something had come up" and Nimbo seemed to be okay with his response, however about the same time Smith's mobile home was shot up by parties unknown.

Smith would say that he and Camilla first fled to Mexico for safety reasons after the home was shot up, later moving on to Florida where he and Camilla were married on June 12, 1975. While in Florida, they learned that Nimbo had been killed by Tommy Bivins.

Now, does any of James Smith's story make sense? Why would anyone wait so long to kill Pusser as Smith claimed? The state line days were in the rear-view mirror. Better yet, why would Junior Smith be involved as he and Buford had a long running relationship as both a friend and a business partner? Ed Shaw? What would have been his motive, he ran a restaurant in Shiloh in Harden County, a place I am told that Pusser often frequented. Ed Shaw's name has little if any real connections to the state line story.

Skeets Adkin's? Why would he pay someone to have Pusser killed as James Smith suggested? How would he benefit from Buford's death?

Ed Gillock is another name that does not seem to have any known connections with the state line, however, he was elected to the Tennessee State Senate in 1969. Having been born in Savannah, he may well have known Ray Blanton of Adamsville who would later become governor of Tennessee.

Cotton Collins was a small-time player at the state line, who most have never heard of. This leads to the question as to why Collins would be involved in a plot to kill Pusser?

While the James Smith "deposition" is an interesting read, one must keep in mind that while living in Florida, Smith announced that he was writing a book to expose those who were involved in Pusser's death. He named a lot of names and pointed fingers at various people but none of it ever stuck to those individuals. I have no idea who was behind this alleged deposition or if it even was a legal document.

While one writer claims it is an "FBI Deposition" I have serious doubts as I have had a copy of the deposition for several years and some individuals mentioned in the report were still alive at the time the deposition was written. It is a practice of the FBI to redact names of living individuals from such reports that are made public. This "deposition" has no redactions, making it very suspect.

Camilla Floyd, Smith's wife' would tell me in one of our discussions that Howard Bunch gave the gun used in the ambush, to her father, Bobby Floyd. Floyd was to then give the gun to Buddy Strickland, an employee of Howard Bunch, to refinish. She claimed after the gun was refinished, Bunch decided it might be a liability to have the gun in his possession as it could link him to the August 12th ambush. Before his death, when asked, Strickland allegedly told Camilla Smith that "the gun would never be found," suggesting it was at the bottom of the lake near Pickwick Dam. Over the years, from the time that Buford was elected sheriff to the present day, NONE of these people named have ever become serious suspects of the TBI regarding either the alleged ambush of August 12, 1967 or the death of Buford Pusser seven years later.

Others have written books regarding Pusser's life and using the questionable "Smith Deposition" as well as the writings of Camilla Floyd Smith to name Howard Bunch, W.O. Hathcock and Bobby Floyd as being involved in the ambush, Bunch and Hathcock as the planners and financiers and Bobby Floyd as the driver of the Cadillac used to ambush Buford. George North and Dewitt Curtis were the two shooters according to one writer.

So, ask yourself...if James Smith and his wife Camilla Floyd Smith and storytellers that I have mentioned knew all of this, why didn't the TBI also know? How is it that a writer seems to know every word spoken by Buford and Pauline that fateful morning?

The same applies to Buford's death as many, to this very day, claim that Buford was murdered by the state line mob even though they cannot name anyone in particular who had that kind of vengeance for Buford. One author who calls others "storytellers" would fabricate a story that a deer ran onto the highway causing the fatal accident without mentioning that Buford's blood alcohol level was .18 at the time of the accident.

Buford's death would be thoroughly investigated by many. The Tennessee Highway Patrol would investigate the accident and parts of the car would be sent to the FBI to search for signs of sabotage..., nothing would be found. Helen Pusser would use Dwana's trust inheritance to investigate Buford's death, hiring specialist with General Motors just to learn that no signs of sabotage were found.

Helen Pusser went to the next step in looking for murderers that did not exist, spending over one hundred thousand dollars of Dwana's trust fund to have a con artist investigate Buford's death. Private investigator Larry Britt lived lavishly on Dwana's money, finally concluding that Buford had been poisoned by parties unknown prior to his fatal accident. According to Britt, someone had slipped a drug into Buford's drink which caused muscle relaxationwhich caused the fatal accident.

Britt wanted to have Buford's body exhumed so that he could be examined for traces of this drug, with Helen Pusser filing documents to have Buford unearthed. Carl Pusser and John Pusser objected however to the disinternment and were successful in seeing that the exhumation did not take place.

Helen Pusser would be taken to court for using Dwana's trust fund monies for this investigation and would lose control of Dwana's financial affairs.

Trooper Paul Ervin summarized Buford's crash most accurately as he told me during an interview that the cause of the accident was too much car, too much speed and too much alcohol. He assured me there were no signs of sabotage to the vehicle and there was nothing to suggest

that Buford was the victim of a murder plot.

Ervin would also tell me that he turned in his accident report into his supervisor who returned to Ervin, asking for revisions, without telling the Trooper what was wrong with the report. Ervin had completed the original report accurately which included statements from people at the accident scene that night as well as statements from people who had seen Buford at the fairgrounds before the accident. He turned the report in several times more after making minor revisions to the document only to have his supervisor return it to him each time. Finally, Ervin removed Buford's BAC (blood alcohol content) from the report and it was immediately accepted. It seems as though, now that Buford was a national hero after the release of the mostly fictitious movie "Walking Tall," the state of Tennessee didn't want the public to know that Buford died as the result of being a drunk driver with a BAC of .18.

Buford was, and still is today, idolized by many who saw a movie that hardly showed any factual events. People in the 70's were looking for a hero, but never learned the true story of Buford Pusser or the state line, a story where there were no heroes. The sad part is that the players in the real story had family members they left behind. These people also paid a price as they were judged for the acts of their relatives.

McNairy County also paid a price as many outsiders accepted the "Pusser Legend" as fact when it gave the county an undeserved black eye as it made the entire county appear to be evil. The truth is that many counties were much like McNairy, they just didn't have a movie made about them.

I make no judgments of the people involved in the real story. I am only conveying the story that so many others have ignored. It is now up to you, the reader, to make your own decisions about Buford and others. At least now, you have the facts, at least as best we know them as they were given to us by people who were there and lived their own parts in this real story. Again, these were people from both sides of the story.

Buford's death was simply an act of fate. No one was ever officially named as a suspect in his death. The people who benefited from his death were people who made movies and storytellers, writers who care little about facts, who give us books with little truth.

Trooper Paul Ervin as he looks inside Buford's burned out Corvette

**You can see the skid marks the car made as it crossed the center line and
a gravel parking lot before hitting an embankment on Lawton Rd**

This is the straightaway on Highway 64 immediately before the crash site. Buford's speed at the time of the accident is said to have been approximately 135 miles per hour. Highway 64 was a two lane highway at the time of the accident. Many people would come to visit the crash site to see where Sheriff Pusser died.

This is another view of where Buford's corvette came to rest and burned.

Burkeen's Towing Service with Buford's burned out Corvette.

Historical marker at the crash site

Newspaper story reporting Pusser's death
(Memphis Press-Scimitar)

182

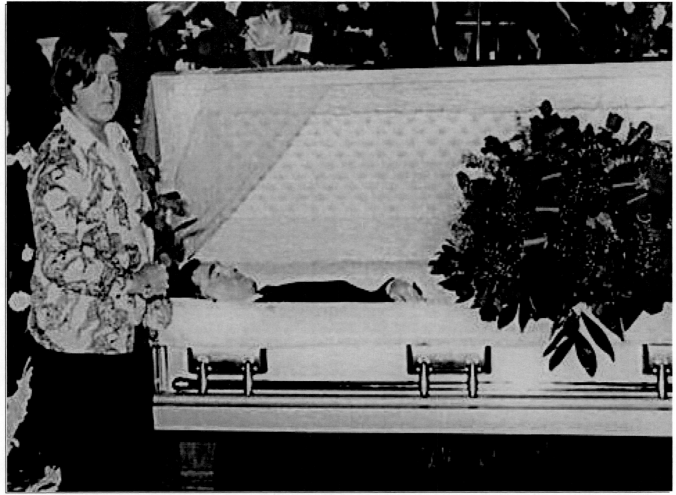

Like so many other innocent children, Dwana Pusser would suffer the loss of family members as she would lose both of her parents in the telling of this story. Sadly, so many of us forget that the children from both sides of this sorted tale were left to deal with the aftermath of the Pusser Legend and the state line. They were the ones who would suffer for the sins of their parents.

(photo: private collection)

Chapter 19
"The Truth has no Agenda"

My mantra has always been "the truth has no agenda." If you are a true student of history, you simply look for the best information you can find on whatever subject that you are researching. You try to properly vet the information as best you can and finally come to a conclusion as to if history has been recorded correctly.

The problem with history is that it is often recorded improperly and much of what is recorded often lacks all the facts needed to make a proper evaluation of an event. Other times, the inaccurate recording of history has more to do with poor research or the writer having his or her own agenda incorporated into the story.

A good example of this kind of research is the assassination of President Kennedy. History tells is that President Kennedy's death was the result of an assassination by a lone gunman, Lee Harvey Oswald. This was the conclusion of the "Warren Commission Report." This Commission was sanctioned by President Johnson as a report to reveal the facts of the assassination to the American people.

The problem with this report was that the commission had an agenda as President Johnson wanted a report that would indicate that JFK's assassination was not the result of a conspiracy involving more people than just Oswald. Johnson got the report he wanted.

Now, after several decades, people realize the Warren Report does not reflect what really happened that fateful day in Dealey Plaza. The problem is the omissions of information contained in the report as well the tampering and manipulation of the evidence and witnesses who were not heard. Today, the majority of American citizens understand the Commission got the report wrong about how and why Kennedy was killed. This is due to Warrens Commissions total disregard for the truth as they had an agenda.

Does this sound familiar? Most books and movies about Buford Pusser and the state line were composed with the same disregard for the truth as an agenda was involved. That agenda was to make Buford a hero.

So what is the truth about many of the events that make up the Pusser Legend?

The truth is that he was never as good of a sheriff as he has been made out to be, while the state liner's reputations were embellished as well. Because of improper handling and the manipulation of information, we may never have many of the answers we are all looking for. So many years have now gone by that most of the people who knew the real story have passed away and much of the evidence has been forever lost. It seems that all we can do now is look at the evidence we do have and examine it as carefully as we possibly can. Most importantly, we should proceed with no preconceived agendas as so many from the past have done.

I will begin this chapter by saying there is no doubt that Buford Pusser did some good while he served as Sheriff of McNairy County, most sheriffs do, if for no other reason than most want to be re-elected. I personally do not believe that people are all good, or for that matter, all bad.

Stories are told about the good things Buford would do, such as seeing a lady who was short on cash at the grocery story. He is said to have reached in his pocket and gave her a one hundred dollar bill. Back in those days, one hundred dollars was a good bit of money so this was a very generous and thoughtful act.

Buford is said to have helped with youth sports and helped teenagers race their cars in a proper and safe manner. He was also known to stretch the boundaries of his duties as sheriff such as when he whipped John Grant, more commonly known as Flag Pole," with a switch after Grant had abused his wife and children. After that whipping it is said that Grant never abused his wife or children again. On the very day Buford died in a horrific car accident he had volunteered to work in a dunking tank at the county fair as part of a fund raiser. But most people don't know however that Buford had a "dark side" as well, often, a very dark side.

Having met and interviewed so many of the real players in this story, I now find it difficult to believe in the "Pusser Legend" as it has been told through the years. Some people will undoubtedly say I have it all wrong as much of the information in this book comes from those who committed crimes and in some cases, the information came from their family members. Some will even suggest that all of these people lied about Buford.

These same people will of course continue to believe in Buford and his legend even though official documents, photos, interviews, FBI reports and much more suggests that Buford often crossed the line from good to evil. Many people often see only that which they wish to see.

Buford, and many of the people who have written about him, have had a habit of embellishing stories of events in his life, indicating that Buford, nor these writers were not above manipulating information and telling lies to those who would listen to them.

Buford would be caught in a lie or an embellishment regarding his past as I learned the story of him watching as Louise Hathcock beat a young sailor to death at a state line establishment was a fictitious account of the actual event.

I located the family of this sailor and learned that he was not killed at the White Iris as Buford had claimed so many years ago. Kenneth Wayne McCoy actually died on November 6, 2012 of natural causes having lived a long and productive life after he was attacked by Towhead White...not Louise Hathcock as so many have reported. This information came directly to me from his sons Earl and Kenneth McCoy Jr.

McCoy, upon completing naval flight school transferred from the Navy to the U.S. Marine Corp in the late 50's and later served as an aviator during the war in Viet Nam. Once leaving the Marine Corp in the late 60's he started a business which still operates today under the management of his son Kenneth Jr.

Some Pusser apologists will say Buford didn't know that the sailor had not died as he had claimed, yet he continued to tell the story after he learned the truth. Why?

Buford, would claim that in February 1957 he was beaten, cutup and robbed at W.O. Hathcock's Plantation Club on the Mississippi side of the state line. Oddly, he never offered any evidence that this event had ever taken place and no witnesses have come forward to back his claim. I haven't found a single person who saw him with the 192 stitches he claimed it took to close his wounds from the attack. Why would people accept this claim to be true without seeing any evidence at all? I have to ask, why did Buford tell such a story?

You would think that in a small town of Adamsville, friends, neighbors, old high school classmates..., someone,..., anyone would have noticed Buford being all stitched up about the face and head had he been attacked as he claimed. Keep in mind that Adamsville was indeed a very small town at that time, having a total population of only 1,046 residence three years later in 1960 according to the U.S. Census Bureau. You would of course think that surely, people in a town of this size, one where everyone knows everyone else as well as their personal business, there would be someone who would have remembered Buford walking around with 192 stitches in his head and face and would have been appalled and demanding justice for Buford...., but no. Not even the Pusser Home and Museum has any evidence that such an attack ever took place.

The movie WALKING TALL, as well as Buford himself, suggested that after being beaten, cut up, robbed and left for dead during a visit to the Lucky Spot (Plantation Club), he would later return to get his money back and dispense a little justice of his own. By his own admission to reporter Ellie Grossman, he later stated that he had indeed returned to the club with two friends, where W.O. Hathcock was beaten and robbed by the three men. Buford would go on to tell Grossman that he and his two friends did indeed commit perjury when they testified in court, during their trial for robbery by falsely claiming they were nowhere near the Plantation Club or the state line on the night in question.

Then there is the truth about Buford and the death of Louise Hathcock. Hathcock's autopsy report is another example Buford playing loose with the truth. Three pathologists in the Memphis office of the State Medical Examiner reported the cause of her death as required by law having completed their work. They indicated that she had two gunshot wounds to the posterior of her body and one from the anterior or front of her body, more specifically to her head. Buford however would have us believe that he was facing Louise as shots were fired as he claimed Hathcock kept raising her gun to point it in his direction. These doctors had no motive or reason to give false information regarding the cause of her death..., they simply documented the facts as they were. Writers however would continue to tell a different story, even after the report was made public. They, after all, were trying to maintain Buford's hero status.

Further, it was Buford himself who gave the order of the shots he fired that day, saying the first shot was to her neck and shoulder area, while his second shot was to her torso. It wasn't until the discovery of Hathcock's autopsy report that we learned that these shots came from behind. Also catching our attention, is that we now know from Buford's own statements that the third shot was to her head as she lay on the floor. The fact that, Buford accounted for his first two shots means she was already on the floor when she was shot for the third time. The timing of the third shot is also evidenced by the fact that some of her teeth were embedded in the carpet, having been blown out the back of her skull. Her teeth being embedded in the carpet as they were, could only happen if her head was already on or very near the carpet when this shot was fired.

To add to this, Howard Carroll and another person were in the back of the motel office and heard Buford's .41 magnum fire before Hathcock's .38 revolver as it sounded. On top of this is the trajectory of the projectile fired by Hathcock's gun as it does not match the circumstances of the shooting as described by Pusser himself. These would not be the only times the true story would be altered to benefit Buford's reputation.

What about the stories of Buford being shot eight times and stabbed seven times? Many of the attacks on Buford have been in question by others over the years as no other McNairy County Sheriff was ever exposed to the number of stabbings and gunshot wounds Buford claimed to have suffered while he was sheriff. When you place these attacks into proper perspective, only the gunshot to his chin, suffered in the alleged ambush of August 12, 1967, was considered to be serious.

Keep in mind that there was only one witness to any of these alleged attacks, and that witness, McNairy County Corner Ward Moore, would clearly state that Buford was not stabbed in a confrontation as he claimed to have been.

Moore would even confront Buford's uncle Ben when he overheard him telling people that Buford had been stabbed while Buford was trying to stop a moonshiner from fleeing. When Moore asked about the origin of this story, Ben Pusser, understanding that he had been caught telling this lie, told Moore that he told such stories as they helped Buford get votes at election time.

In the January 1967 incident where Buford stopped a car and was shot at point blank range, none of his wounds were life threatening as doctors kept him in the hospital only the night of the shooting for observation purposes. Buford wanted people to think it was Towhead White who had shot him. Most people who knew Towhead believe that had it been White who pulled the trigger that night, he would have used something other than a .25 caliber handgun, to kill Buford, especially since Buford was a good size and physically fit. This story, as such, is now in question as well.

Even in the alleged August 12th ambush where Pauline was killed and Buford was hit in the chin, medical personnel at Baptist Hospital in Memphis thought his wound appeared to be self inflicted.

When you examine the Hamilton shooting in 1968 you find that although Buford claimed to have been wounded in a gunfight, he received no medical attention for his wound. This shooting, like all of the shootings where he was wounded, or claimed to have been wounded, were all without witnesses to verify his story. Many people, after examining the facts as we now know them, believe that Buford's wounds were most likely self inflicted.

And what about the allegations that Buford accepted payoffs? Buford would claim he refused payoffs. Buford did not leave written receipts behind with those who paid him as that would have left a paper trail for state authorities to follow. It is certainly worth noting however, that many people including even his friends such as Paul Moore would tell me they paid Buford. Many paid him to be allowed to sell something stronger than beer while others would pay to sell beer without a county issued permit. Why would so many falsely admit to making payoffs to a sheriff?

All one has to do is look at the poor relationship Buford had with the states Alcohol Beverage Commission to know there were problems with Buford as they stopped inviting him to raids in his own county. All too often, information about the raids would leak out. Of course Buford would claim it was all political as he was a Republican and they were Democrats.

Such payoffs goes beyond club and beer joint operators making payoffs as moonshiners and bootleggers would tell me about how they paid Buford as well.

Pauline's death? When some people hear that Shirley Smith and Barbara Bivins overheard Buford threaten Pauline's life just hours before she was killed in the alleged ambush, they still refuse to believe the story is true. They refuse to listen, saying the accusations come from the state line side of the story. Most of these same people however don't know how to respond when they hear of Lavon Punk, the wife of Deputy Peatie Plunk, telling about hearing a gunshot at the Pusser residence, only to learn about three and a half hours later that her best friend Pauline had been killed in an ambush meant for Buford. Most people don't even know that Buford and Pauline were separated at the time of her death or that she was leaving Buford that very day or that she had threatened to report his corruption to the TBI.

I wish I had started my journey ten years earlier so I could have interviewed even more of the real players before so many had passed on. I am grateful that I was able to find and interview as many as I have. I often wonder why no one else has looked at both sides of the story as I have.

It seems that most of the people who have previously written about the Buford have been little more than "storytellers", writing novels as if they were sitting there with these people as they made their plans to assassinate Buford, some even giving direct quotes of what was being said. These novelists have, in my opinion, done a great disservice to the real story as well as to the history of McNairy County by being so careless with their stories.

I look at these writers and think they had the very same opportunities as I have had to find as many of the real players as they could as they wrote their stories. I ask myself why they would want to tell such falsehoods, and why they didn't investigate the Pusser Legend as I have rather than getting much of their stories from other writers before them.

No, I don't know for certain who pulled the trigger and took Pauline Pusser's life. What a I can tell you with a high degree of certainty however is that Buford Pusser was not forthcoming with the facts of how the alleged ambush went down on that fateful Saturday morning.

He kept changing his story about the location of the disturbance he and Pauline were responding to. He failed to tell about being separated from Pauline over their marital issues. He failed to give us an honest answer at that time why Pauline was with him that morning as they were having marital problems and were separated. Buford never told us that Pauline had threatened to divorce him and report his corruption to the TBI. He failed to disclose that he had met with a party in the state maintenance lot in Eastview just hours prior to the ambush, where he gave rifles to a man driving a car with Oklahoma license plates..., and the list of lies, embellishments and omissions go on and on.

Why were other writers not finding this information as I did?

In any other investigation, a person with a list of omissions such as these would be considered the prime suspect in the death of their spouse.

There were other things that happened while he was sheriff which Buford would not tell us, such as Chief Deputy Jim Moffett quitting his job after Buford shot and killed Louise Hathcock.., information I received from Moffett's son O'Neal. According to O'Neal Moffett, his dad left his job for almost two weeks after the Hathcock shooting, before he was eventually coaxed back to work by Buford.

Keep in mind that Jim had told his wife and son, after the Hathcock shooting, that if anything ever happened to him, they didn't need to look any further than Buford. This makes you wonder why he made such a statement and what he knew that he felt he could not tell anyone.

Questions

<u>**Was Buford involved in Pauline's murder?**</u>   In my opinion, the evidence that is available to us suggests that yes, Buford was involved in a murder plot that resulted in the death of Pauline Pusser. Buford's actions before, during and after the alleged ambush make it clear that something was amiss around the time of her death.

<u>**Did Buford have motive to murder Pauline?**</u>   It is a well known fact that Buford was having multiple extramarital affairs at the time her death, and many people have declared that he was accepting payoffs from club and beer joint operators as well as moonshiners and bootleggers. The fact is that two witnesses overhead Pauline threatening to report this corruption to the TBI. This information could very possibly have sent him to prison and thus gave him motive to get rid of Pauline. The fact that she had threatened to divorce him, also gave him motive, as in a divorce, he may have lost custody of Dwana, his only known biological child. This would certainly have happened had he gone to prison.

<u>**Were others involved in Pauline's death?**</u>   While we can't be sure, again, look at the evidence for possible answers. After Pauline had made the threat to expose his corruption, he is seen in Eastview just hours before the alleged ambush giving rifles to a man in a car with Oklahoma tags. What was the purpose of Buford meeting someone in the middle of the night to give them firearms? Was this man involved with Pauline's death just a very few hours later? Why was it necessary for Buford to chase his girlfriend away to do so? Was he afraid she might see the gun exchange and later put two and two together when she heard of Pauline's death?

There are also the calls allegedly made that night to both the Sheriffs Office as well as Buford's home to report a disturbance near the state line area. If it is true that such calls were indeed made, it suggests others may have been involved as they were executing a plan to lure Buford to the ambush site..., or give him a cover story for being near the state line that morning. If no such calls were made, why did both Buford and his father lie about this? If the calls were made from the state line area, they would have been on the Corinth telephone exchange and long distance calls to Selmer, making them easy for investigators to trace.

Did investigators ask Buford why he took the convoluted route to get to the alleged disturbance? Is this possibly why he changed to location of the alleged disturbance to being on New Hope Road?

Buford certainly could have had the assistance of others at the ambush site, but there is no way for me to say with any real certainty that he absolutely did. However, consider how he first said he got a good look at the shooter who was only about five feet away from Buford as shots were fired, only to later change this story as well. Why did he find it necessary to change his story?

Buford would have you believe that Kirksey Nix was involved, however when he was shown photos of Nix, he said he wasn't sure if Nix was indeed the the shooter. He then said that he would have to see Nix in person to be sure. After Investigator Warren Jones found that Nix was incarcerated in the Oklahoma City jail, he drove Pusser several hundred miles to Oklahoma City for the in person identification. Pusser still insisted he couldn't be certain that Nix was the shooter.

It certainly could be that Nix, being a native of Oklahoma, could have been the man that Buford met in Eastview and was observed driving a car with Oklahoma tags and receiving guns from Buford. It is also possible that Buford, knowing he couldn't pull the trigger to kill Pauline himself, had Nix or some other accomplice there to do that job for him, as well as to wound Buford to make the "ambush" look real. Now the question is, did Pusser simply protect Nix by not identifying him as the shooter? Had he identified Nix as the shooter, Nix could have then turned the table on Buford and implicated Buford in planning Pauline's death.

<u>What about Buford's actions?</u> Consider the fact that Pauline's best friend stated during our interview that she heard a gunshot coming from the Pusser residence that night as Pauline was said to be gathering her children along with some some personal items. She was leaving Buford then and he was losing control of this situation. This may have been his last good opportunity to prevent her from telling the TBI what she knew about his illegal activities giving him motive to take drastic action.

On top of this we have a recording of Beverly Maxwell telling of her conversation with Diane, Pauline's oldest daughter. The recording was about a conversation they had while Diane and Maxwell were attending junior college in Henderson in the late, 60's, long before WALKING TALL was even a dream.

Maxwell tells that Diane was awakened by a disturbance at the Pusser residence. She was afraid to look out her bedroom door. Things got quiet and she finally heard the front door open.

As Diane looked out a window, she saw Buford carry Pauline from their residence to his car and watched as he placed her in the front passengers seat. She goes on to say that Diane told her that Buford went back toward the house to retrieve Pauline's shoes which had fallen from her feet. She described how he placed them in the front floorboard. This description matches the placement of the shoes shown in one of the crime scene photos..., Pauline's shoes sitting there, clearly on an angle as if they had been placed there rather than Pauline having removed the from her feet.

As I have stated before, Buford took a rather convoluted course as he drove to the state line, using back roads through Stantonville and Michie to finally arrive on New Hope Road and near the state line area. Why didn't he take highways 64 and 45 to get to the state line? A better question is how did the ambush party know that he would be taking the odd route he chose todrive that morning? Was he avoiding driving through Selmer with Pauline in the car, possibly unconscious or even dead? What if someone had seen seen them or stopped them for some reason? Why was the ambush party behind the church on New Hope Road? Why were they not on Highway 45 or 64? Was all of this per-planned and prearranged? Was it all a set up to make it look like a real ambush?

The shell casings found on New Hope Road..., why were found on the roadway in a pattern that did not fit the shooting as had Buford described it to have happened? Were these casing planted there in an attempt to make the ambush look authentic?

And what about Buford's actions at the state line, showing a handful of Pauline's brain with her wedding ring stuck in it..., telling Albert Kiddy, look what they have done? Why would a wounded man take the time to do this, show it to someone and then drive away? Was it all for show, a desperate attempt to make things look real and gain public sympathy when this story was later passed around and repeated in the community?

Why did Buford turn north to Selmer and the small medical facility there approximately 12 mile away, rather than turn south to Corinth and the much larger and better equipped hospital there about ten miles away? Did he do so to avoid crossing a state line and possibly involving the FBI in the investigation?

Why did he stop just north of the Shamrock and leave abruptly when he heard sirens coming from the Mississippi side of the border? Was Buford afraid that the arriving help might take him across the state line?

What about Towhead White? Many people suggest that Towhead orchestrated the

ambush from his prison cell. Theories suggest that White made contact with the outside world while incarcerated at the Leavenworth Federal prison in Leavenworth Kansas and ordered the "hit" on Sheriff Pusser.

There are several things to consider here. First, federal prisons usually monitor all communications an inmate has with the outside world regardless of whether the communication is by phone, mail or in person visitation, making it somewhat unlikely that Towhead was involved with the August 12, 1967 ambush. I'm not saying it couldn't happen, but it is somewhat unlikely.

Such suggestions made by Pusser advocates make for interesting discussion on forums and certainly spice up a book which is one reason we continue to hear this theory. What evidence however, is there that such a "contract" was put out on Pusser from inside a prison? I know of none and it seems to be nothing .

Did Buford kill Towhead White as revenge for the death of Pauline? Over the years many people have said that Buford was on the roof of the EL-Ray Motel and shot White when he returned to the motel rather late on the night of April 3rd in 1969. Towhead was living in Clarksdale at the time and had made the trip to Corinth presumably to conduct some business concerning his juke box business.

It is true that Pusser feared Towhead, especially after Buford had shot and killed Louise Hathcock at the Shamrock Motel on on February 1st of 1966. Buford thought that White would be seeking revenge for the death of Hathcock.

It is interesting to note that when Buford shot and killed Russ Hamilton on Christmas day, 1968, Pusser explained in newspaper reports that he was armed that day as Towhead had been released from prison, adding that Towhead had sworn to kill him.

As I stated earlier, when Towhead escaped from prison at Maxwell Air Force Base in December of 1967, Buford was said to fear that White escaped prison to find Buford and kill him.

Many believe that when Buford was shot in January 1967 as he stopped a speeding car near the state line, that his gunshot wounds were self inflicted as a means to spur local, state andfederal authorities into making Whites capture a priority.

I would agree with the suggestion made by many researchers that had White been the shooter that night, he would have used something more powerful than a .25 caliber handgun to kill Buford. Many researchers suggest that White would have considered a .25 caliber as anything but the right weapon for such a task.

Tishomingo County Sheriff insisted that it was Glen Alexander, aka "Bluetick" that was on the roof of the El-Ray that night, not Pusser. Alexander and Junior Smith were indeed good friends at that time and Blue Tick was indeed a dangerous man.

On the night in question, Bluetick and Junior Smith both fired shots into Towhead's car, snuffing out White's life. While there is no evidence that Buford was present, many believe that Smith and Bluetick were shooters involved in a "murder for hire" plot and were working for Buford. I honestly have no idea why Sheriff Bishop thought that Buford had White killed. I would have to think he had some information for Bishop to make such allegations against another sheriff.

With all of this having now been told, I hope everyone has a better understanding of the people and events in this story. It is my hope that readers can understand that there were no real heroes in this story, just people living their lives in a way not really that much differently than we do today. Regardless of which side of the story you look at we are talking about people most of whom took advantage of their positions regardless of which side of the story they came from.

In my opinion, Buford wasn't as good a man as books and movies made him out to be and the state liners weren't as bad as they were said to be either. I hope everyone can see this now. Regardless, let's keep in mind that it was the children on both sides of this story who have paid a heavy for the sins of their elders through these stories being told as incorrectly as they have been for so many years.

The Truth Has No Agenda The truth simply is what it is. The truth is always
without feeling or opinion. Truth in inanimate and without life. I tried to keep this in mind as I wrote this story.

Like others before me, I have no smoking gun, no written confession to display and no video recording to offer as absolute proof of some my beliefs. What I do offer is research. Now, I ask you what Buford had to offer you other than his story? For that matter, what have all the novel writers really offered you? Did they interview people from both sides of the story as I have? Did they piece the different parts of the story together to show you a more complete picture as I have attempted to do? Did they disclose to you Buford's "dark side" in the same fashion as I have? Did they connect the dots, the different events together as I have? Did they do any real research of their own or did they simply rely almost exclusively on the inaccuracies reported by others before them as they gathered information to give their opinions? Do other writings have the look and sound of sameness as other books before them? In short did they make a reasonable effort to determine if Buford's story was even anywhere close to being true?

I know of no other person who has researched the real story as I have. This is why I titled my book, BUFORD PUSSER: "The Other Story".

Hathcock
Documents

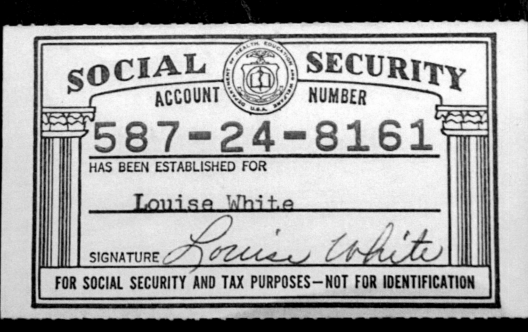

Top License:

STATE OF TENNESSEE — OPERATOR'S LICENSE — ORIGINAL — NOT GOOD AFTER July 1, 1959

24144009 — DAY OF ISSUANCE 11 17 58 — OCCUPATION H-Wife

DATE OF BIRTH 3 19 19 — RACE SEX W F — COLOR OF EYES Brown — COLOR OF HAIR Brown

HEIGHT WEIGHT 142 5 4 — CONDITIONS None

PRINT OR TYPE NAME: Laura Louise Hathcock (FIRST NAME / MIDDLE NAME / LAST NAME)

STREET AND NUMBER: Rt. #5

CITY OR POST OFFICE: Corinth, Miss.

SIGNATURE OF OPERATOR: Louise Hathcock

CUT OFF ALONG DOTTED LINES

ACCOUNTING NUMBER O No. 0116892

(signatures) Gov. of Tennessee / Commissioner of Safety / J. J. Burks County Court Clerk

DRIVE SAFELY

Middle License:

STATE OF TENNESSEE — OPERATOR'S LICENSE — ORIGINAL — NOT GOOD AFTER JULY 1, 1965

9 30 63 — 2983847 — OCCUPATION Motel & Rest.

COLOR OF EYES Brown — COLOR OF HAIR Brown — DATE OF BIRTH 3 19 19 — RACE W — SEX F

WEIGHT 151 — HEIGHT 5 4 — CONDITIONS None

PRINT OR TYPE NAME: Laura Louise Hathcock

STREET AND NUMBER: Rt. #2

CITY OR POST OFFICE: Michie, Tenn.

SIGNATURE OF OPERATOR: Laura L. Hathcock

CUT OFF ALONG DOTTED LINES

EXPIRES FIRST BIRTH DATE MONTH AFTER JULY 1, 1965

ACCOUNTING NUMBER O No. 0126613

(signatures) Gov. of Tennessee / Commissioner of Safety / J. J. Burks County Court Clerk

DRIVE SAFELY

Bottom License:

DRIVE SAFELY

TENNESSEE — OPERATOR — LICENSE

LICENSE NO.	EXPIRATION DATE	HEIGHT	WEIGHT	EYES	HAIR
3372266	03 19 68	505	150	BR	BR

R	S	COND.	DATE OF BIRTH	ISSUE DATE	BLOOD TYPE
W	F	1	03 19 22	11 15 65	

CONDITION CODES
1 CORRECTIVE LENSES
2 AUTO. TRANSMISSION
3 KNOB ON STEERING WHEEL
4 OUTSIDE MIRROR
5 MOTORCYCLE ALSO,
6 MOTORCYCLE-5 BRAKE H.P.
7 MOTOR SCOOTER
8 MOTORCYCLE ONLY
9 ALL OTHER:

WHITE LOUISE A
RT 2
MICHIE   TENN

SIGNATURE OF OPERATOR: Louise A. White

THE PERSON WHOSE SIGNATURE AND DESCRIPTION APPEAR ON THIS LICENSE IS HEREBY LICENSED TO OPERATE A MOTOR VEHICLE IN TENNESSEE SUBJECT TO THE LAWS OF TENNESSEE.

GOVERNOR OF TENNESSEE   COMMISSIONER OF SAFETY

NOT GOOD UNTIL VALIDATED

Note that the top and middle drivers licenses were issued to Laura Louise Hathcock, issued 1958 and 1963, while the License at the bottom was issued on Nov. 15, 1965 to Louise A. White.

196

C. P. J. MOONEY
LAWYER
900 COMMERCE TITLE BUILDING
MEMPHIS, TENN.

December 27, 1965

Mrs. Carl White
Route 2
Michie, Tenn.

In re: Carl Douglas White

Dear Mrs. White:

I have examined the indictment in the case above
and the record of the court proceedings on August 26,
1965, and September 14, 1965, before Judge Clayton and
the record of the proceedings in the same case the 24th
of September, 1965, before the same Judge, all of which
occurred at Aberdeen. Frankly, from what you have sent
me, I know you want an honest opinion. I see no
irregularity. I suggest that if you have correspondence
from Mr. White pointing out claim of errors that do not
appear in the record, please forward the same to me.

Very truly yours,

C. P. J. Mooney

CPJM/M

C. P. J. MOONEY
LAWYER
900 COMMERCE TITLE BUILDING
MEMPHIS, TENN.

Mrs. Carl White

Route 2

Michie, Tennessee

In this letter from an attorney, Louise was obviously seeking legal assistance in getting an appeal on Towhead's prison sentence. Notice that both the envelope and letter are addressed to "Mrs Carl White." also note the date on the letter is 12/27/1965. Did Louise and Towhead marry after Jack's 1964 death?

197

December 22nd, 1965

Re: Carl D. White

Mr. Taylor-

In regards to our nice telephone conversation last week, I am enclosing the information that you so kindly ask me to do.

Carl Douglas White, an inmate at Texarkana, Arkansas, is serving a 3-year term for conspiracy to operate a whiskey still.

The sentence was imposed by the United States District Court for the Northern District of Mississippi, Eastern Division, Judge Claude Clayton presiding. There was some five or six parties involved in this and all of them entered a plea of guilty.

No doubt, he was technically guilty, but was not one of the principles. The still was to be operated by other parties. The still was captured and destroyed before operation began.

One of the principles who was to operate the still I believe received a three-year sentence; one either a year or fifteen months, and all the other suspended sentences.

I would like very much to see White's sentence ~~~~~~~~~~~~~~~~
~~~~

Mr. Taylor, if I am out of order in asking this, I feel sure that you would inform me so, but if you can be of any help in getting this sentence reduced, I will greatly appreciate same.

Carl is a close, personal friend of mine and if I didn't have confidence in him, I certainly would not try to seek this favor at the present time.

I plan to be in Santa Fe the latter part of February next year and will certainly drop in to see you nice people. I wish for you and your family a nice 1966 and that we all may have peace and contentment. (God knows we all need it).

Will personal regards, I am

Sincerely,

Another piece of correspondence from Louise where she continues to seek a remedy to Towhead's imprisonment in connection with the "Three State Moonshine Operation." Here she portrays herself as White's "close, personal friend" rather than his wife. This letter is dated 12/22/1965.

February 6, 1965.

Mr. Cary Stovall
Attorney at Law
Corinth, Mississippi

In re: Mrs. Louise Hathcock

Dear Cary:

After careful consideration of the matter, we have come to the conclusion that we can not represent the above named person in connection with a recent proposal of Internal Revenue Service to assess her a large additional tax as transferee deriving from Jack Hathcock, now deceased.

The obligation of Jack Hathcock represented by a certain notarized $ 40,000.00 note payable by him to his Mother, and represented to us by him as being a valid obligation of his for money received, which representation was relied on and used by you, Robert and me in connection with a conference at Atlanta, Georgia, with certain personnel of Internal Revenue Service, is now being denied by Mrs. Louise Hathcock. This denial results in two things: (1) it would have to be revealed to representatives of Internal Revenue Service at any future conferences if we continued in this case, and (2) this would cause them to be doubtful of any and all other representations, which in turn makes it very doubtful that much, if any, relief could be expected in the amount of tax proposed to be assessed.

In short, we do not feel that we could do Mrs. Hathcock any good, and in having to reveal her change of the position with respect to the $ 40,000.00 note, more harm than good would result, in our opinion.

An extra copy of this letter is being sent for you to give Mrs. Hathcock if you wish.

Cordially yours,

M. M. WINKLER AND ASSOCIATES,

By

Certified Public Accountant.

MMW:ds

In this document Louise is referred to as Mrs. Hathcock

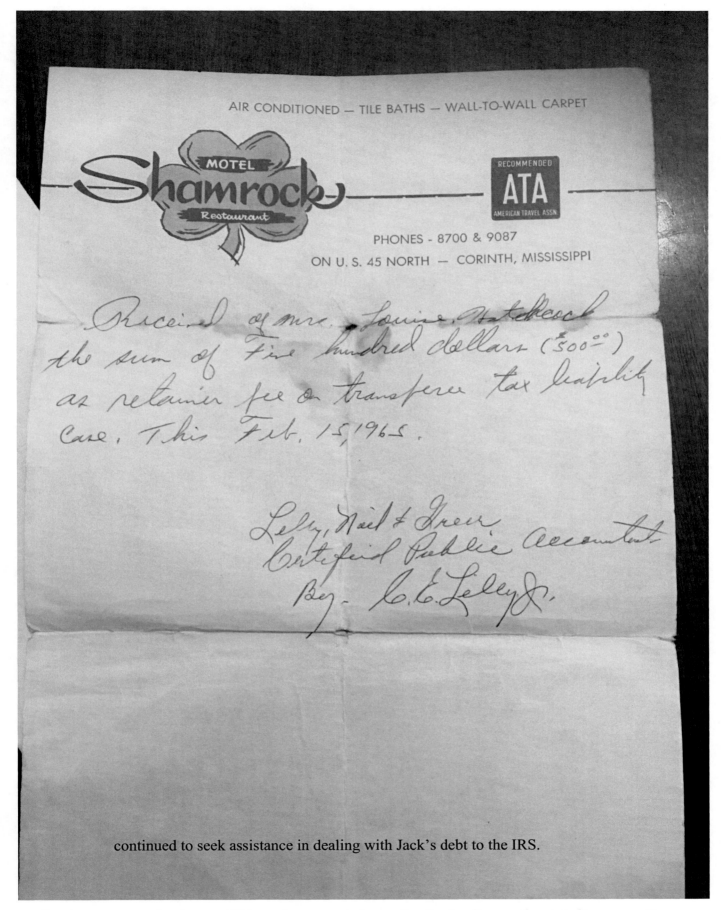

AIR CONDITIONED — TILE BATHS — WALL-TO-WALL CARPET

Shamrock MOTEL Restaurant

RECOMMENDED
ATA
AMERICAN TRAVEL ASSN.

PHONES - 8700 & 9087

ON U. S. 45 NORTH — CORINTH, MISSISSIPPI

Received of Mrs. Louise Hatchcock the sum of Five hundred dollars ($500⁰⁰) as retainer fee on transferee tax liability case. This Feb. 15, 1965.

Lelly, Nail & Greer
Certified Public Accountant
By - C. E. Lelly Jr.

continued to seek assistance in dealing with Jack's debt to the IRS.

Louise gets a receipt from a CPA as she attempts to resolve the tax lien on the state line properties.

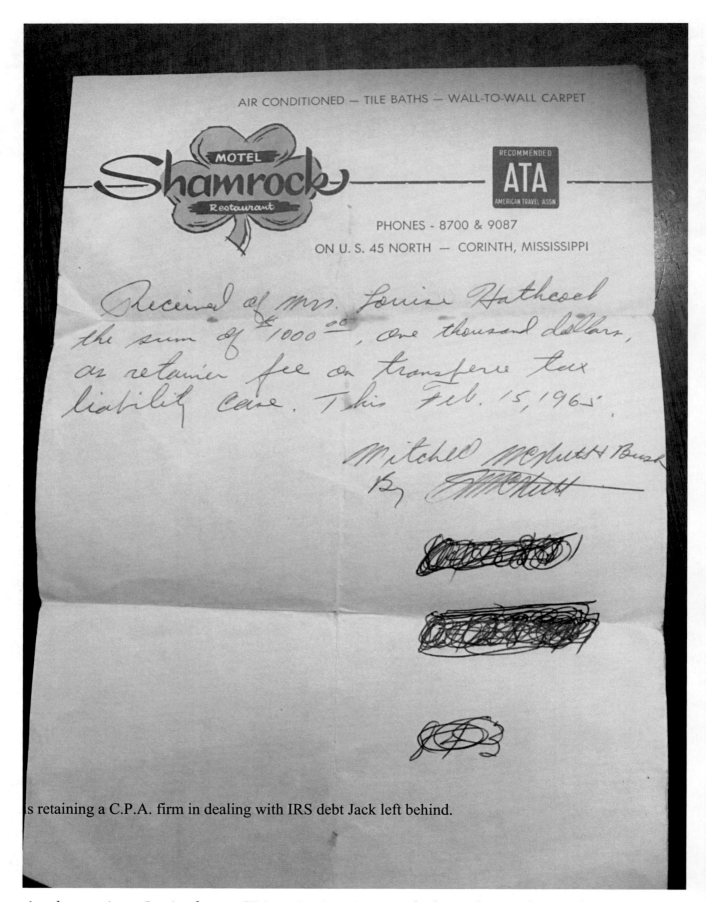

AIR CONDITIONED — TILE BATHS — WALL-TO-WALL CARPET

MOTEL Shamrock Restaurant

RECOMMENDED **ATA** AMERICAN TRAVEL ASSN

PHONES - 8700 & 9087

ON U. S. 45 NORTH — CORINTH, MISSISSIPPI

Received of Mrs. Louise Hathcock the sum of $1000⁰⁰, one thousand dollars, as retainer fee on transferee tax liability case. This Feb. 15, 1965.

Mitchell McNutt & Bush
By

is retaining a C.P.A. firm in dealing with IRS debt Jack left behind.

Another receipt to Louise from a CPA as Louise tries to settle the tax lien on the state line properties.

BILL OF SALE

9-22-65

For value received the undersigned has sold, assigned and transferred to

R L Scott

Corinth, Mississippi, the following described chattel, together with all attachments thereto and equipment thereof, which is now in my possession, which is unencumbered and is the only property of like kind owned by me and described as follows:

Dec 1962 GMC ½ Ton Pickup For The Sum

of 1150⁰⁰ cash

PJ11192A

x Harry D Bivins

STATE OF MISSISSIPPI
COUNTY OF ALCORN

Sworn to and subscribed before me this 22 day of Sept. 1965

Haskel Pusey

RANKIN-CORINTH

My Commission Expires January 15, 1968

ABC-2 Rev.: 2-1-65	ALCOHOLIC BEVERAGE COMMISSION STATE OF TENNESSEE COUNTY McNAIRY	NO. 831

CITY OR TOWN Selmer ___ DATE JAN-14, 1966

NAME OF PERSON Louise Hathcock

ADDRESS Shamrock Motel 45 HWY 45

THE ALCOHOLIC BEVERAGES, LISTED BELOW BY BOTTLE SIZE, WERE SEIZED OR RECEIVED FROM THE ABOVE NAMED PERSON AS CONTRABAND.

NUMBER OF QUARTS ___ FIFTHS ___ PINTS ___ ½ PINTS 2,088

REMARKS: NON TENN TAX PAID

I CERTIFY THAT I HAVE DELIVERED A COPY OF THIS RECEIPT TO THE ABOVE NAMED PERSON AND THAT THE ABOVE GIVEN COUNT OF LIQUOR IS ACCURATE AND ACCOUNTED FOR.

White Copy to Person Found in Possession of Liquor.
Pink Copy to Alcoholic Beverage Commission.
Canary Copy for Officer's or Agent's File.

NAME James Bivins
OFFICER OR AGENT

A.B.C. agent.
TITLE

Top: a Bill of Sale involving Tommy Bivins found in Louise's personal documents
Bottom: A receipt from the State Alcohol Beverage Commission for illegal liquor seized in a raid on the Shamrock. 2,088 half pints were confiscated during the raid.

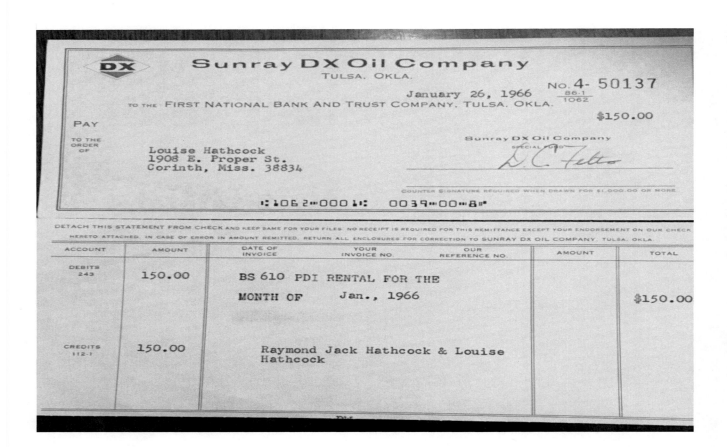

A check for rent payable to Louise Hathcock by Sunray DX Oil Company in the amount of $150.00. The date on the check is January 26, 1966. This was just days before Buford killed Louise. Louise apparently never had an opportunity to cash or deposit this check before her death.

Also found in her private documents was Louise's Gulf credit card

OFFICIAL

SEARCH WARRANT

STOLEN PROPERTY

THE STATE OF TENNESSEE

vs.

Louise Hathcock

Issued this ....1st.... day of

Feb. , 19 66 , and delivered

to Him Moffett

on this 1st day of

Feb. , 19 66 at 10 o'clock AM

for execution.

Judge of General Sessions Court.

OFFICER'S RETURN

Came to hand same day issued. Executed as commanded by searching the within described premises and the defendant and by reason of such search I found the following described personal property, to-wit:

which property was taken and delivered to the said

This the day of , 19

Sheriff.

D. S.

The search warrant for the Vogel's property which led to the death of Louise Hathcock

No._____

OFFICIAL
Search Warrant
INTOXICATING LIQUORS

THE STATE

Louise Hathcock
_____
_____
_____

Issued this **1st** _____ day of
Feb. _____, 19 **66** and delivered

to **Jim Moffett** _____

on this **1st** _____ day of

Feb. _____, 19 **66** at **10** o'clock AM PM XX

for execution.

_____
Judge of General Sessions Court.

OFFICER'S RETURN

Came to hand same day issued. Executed as
commanded by searching the within described
premises and the defendant and by reason of
such search I found the following described

intoxicating liquors:_____
_____
_____
_____

which were taken before the Judge and then
by his order delivered, to the Sheriff at the
County Jail.

This the_____day of_____, 19____

_____, Sheriff.

_____, D. S.

_____ D. S.

A second warrant, this one for intoxicating liquors that Buford Pusser was to serve on Louise Hathcock. Hathcock was killed in a questionable shooting during the service of the two search warrants. Her autopsy report indicated that she had two posterior gunshot wounds and and one anterior gunshot wound to the head. Two people in the backroom of the motel office say they heard Sheriff Pusser's .41 magnum fire before hearing the single report of Hathcock's .38 Smith & Wesson. Neither man was called to testify before the grand jury investigating Hathcock's death.

Photos

**Remembering McNairy County and the state
line area as it once was...**

W.O. Hathcock operated the Plantation Club on the Mississippi side of the state line. He claimed he never knew why Pusser hated him so much. There is no evidence and no witnesses to verify that Buford was ever beaten, cut up and robbed at the Plantation Club.

Buford's political nemesis Clifford Coleman

Tishomingo County Sheriff James Bishop arrested Towhead White for the "Three State Moonshine Operation" sending him to federal prison for three years. This was something Sheriff Pusser was unable to accomplish while White operated in McNairy County.

Jim Moffett (retired) would tell that he was never in so much
as a fight when he served as Buford's Chief Deputy

TBI Investigator Warren Jones (retired) had deep suspicions
regarding Buford and his possible involvement the death of
Pauline Pusser

Paul David English was portrayed as "Pinky Dobson in "Walking Tall Part Two". English was shot by Buford and partially paralyzed after escaping from the McNairy County Jail

State Medical Examiner Dr Jerry Francisco (retired) would tell me about Louise Hathcock's autopsy report, a document that the grand jury investigating her death was not allowed to see. The report revealed she was shot twice in the back by Buford Pusser before being shot in the head as she lay on the floor.

Sheriff James Dickey points to the spot where Jack Hathcock collapsed and died after being shot in Louise Hathcock's private living quarters at the Shamrock Motel.

This old and blurred photo is of a fourteen year old Bobby Anderson would enter room #1 immediately before Jack Hathcock was shot multiple times. Towhead White would push Anderson back into room #2 so he would not witness the death of his uncle, Jack Hathcock, as he was shot and killed.

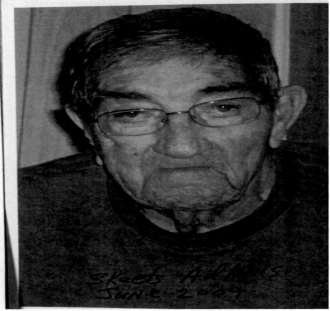

Skeets Adkins would be interviewed by Jerry Heacock of the Condo News, telling Heacock of Pusser's corruption. I would interview him in 2009 and his story about Buford had not changed.

(photo: Private Collection)

Fannie Belle Barker would return to Corinth MS after illegal operations in Phenix City Alabama were shut down, however, she would not engage in operating a brothel again.

(photo: Barbara Bivins Collection)

Buford's real life attorney Loyd Tatum would play the role of the prosecuting attorney who was trying Buford for the robbery of the "Lucky Spot" in the 1974 movie "Walking Tall".

Loyd Tatum as the prosecutor in "Walking Tall"

Junior Smith

"The Old Hickory Grill" was operated by Jr and Shirley Smith
(photo Private Collection)

Willie B's was called "Willie Rae's" in the movie "Walking Tall". Unlike
so many others, this building still stands at the time of this writing.

Moore's Place, a favorite hangout of Buford's, still
stands as well. I interviewed Paul in 2009 & 2012.

The White Iris as it appeared in the 60's. This is where Buford alleged that he witnessed Louise Hathcock beat a sailor to death with a hammer, This is another myth that has been debunked.

Naval Aviator Kenneth Wayne McCoy is the individual Buford claimed he saw Louise Hathcock kill with a hammer at the White Irs. The photo (left) is McCoy in the time frame this was alleged to have happened. The photo (right) is McCoy in 2012 prior to his death due to natual causes. The story was meant to embellish the Pusser Legend. Another misrepresentation of the real story.

(Photo:Courtesy of Earl McCoy)

Inside the "White Iris". Lots of stories are told about happenings that took place here.

Another look inside the White Iris

McNairy County Sheriff James Dickey

McNairy County Sheriff James Dickey was killed in a single vehicle accident just two days before election day paving the way for Buford Pusser to become McNairy County Sheriff at age 26. Many believe his death was not an accident.

Sheriff Dickey was ejected from his vehicle and
pronounced dead thirty minutes later.

Author Mike Elam standing beside the tree that was struck by Sheriff Dickey's car.
(Photo: Mike Elam)

W.O. Hathcock's "Plantation Club" on the Mississippi side of the state line. Buford Pusser claimed to have been assaulted and robbed there in February 1957. No police reports, medical records or even witnesses to the event were ever found to verify his claim. He claimed it took 192 stitches to close the wounds to his head and face, however, no one recalls seeing him with such injuries. In "Walking Tall" the Plantation club was called the "Lucky Spot." The diagram of the club was made from the memories of those familiar with the building. Note that there is no casino as was shown in the movie. That was another misrepresentation in the movie WALKING TALL.

W.O. Hathcock (left) who operated the Plantation Club with Walter Flanagan (right) who managed the Rustic Inn in Corinth Mississippi. Contrary to popular belief, Flanagan was about the only person who came from Phenix City Alabama and was active in the state line area.

(Photo: Courtesy of Dennis Hathcock)

Jerry Heacock of the Condo News was one of the first people to publicly recognize the Pusser Legend as a Hoax

Volume X   No. 8   January 21, 1981

"Walking Tall" Sheriff was no hero
Buford Pusser Legend a Hoax

[Author's note: Buford Pusser was killed shortly after midnight on August 21, 1974, when his Corvette - possibly going 150 miles per hour - went out of control and crashed into an embankment on Route 64 near Adamsville, Tenn. The story which appears in this paper, of which I am the publisher, might not have been written except for the fact that a new series of "Walking Tall" is currently appearing on television and the "real Buford Pusser" is soon to be told in a book I'm writing, not about Pusser but about an outlaw, "Towhead" White, with whom Pusser was closely involved. I've spent nearly a year researching this true story and I see no reason not to expose the myth of Buford Pusser, here and now, since this current re-emphasis of his heroics contradicts the facts as I've found them].

By Jerry Heacock
For nearly a year I have been involved in researching the life of a notorious Mississippi outlaw, Carl Douglas "Towhead" White, who made his mark on the Mississippi/Tennessee state line, most of it in McNairy County, Tenn., where Buford ... er of "Walking Tall" fame was Sheriff from 964 until 1970.
I can unequivocally state - the only thing "tall" about Pusser was his height, six-four.
His legendary acts of heroism, his dedication to uphold the law, his fearlessness, and his loving ... on to his wife, Pau ... ... thing mo ... in ... ommemorating the date, August 12, 1967, when ... auline was killed and Buford Pusser's jaw ... ha ... during an alle ed "amb ... " by outla ...
eorge Cust ... s!
The death of Pauline was either a masterful overup by Tennessee authorities or the world's orst homicide investigation.
In June of 1980 I became intrigued by the ersistent stories and attributes of the now dead, famous, charming, handsome, rough, tough ...

One of the first articles to dispute the Pusser legend

Buford Pusser, False Hero

Mister "Walking Tall" Buford Pusser shown standing in the back yard of his home in Adamsville, Tenn. Why this man ever ...

The first article to catch my attention and make me question the legend. I made contact with several people mentioned in this article.

Several people have written articles and regarding the "Pusser Legend" and we now know it to be a highly embellished story. People such as Jerry Heacock, of the Condo News, Camilla Wilson of the Dayton News, along with others such as newspaper reporter Ellie Grossman and author Barbara Bivins would all call foul on "Walking Tall" being a "true" story.

Camilla Wilson (left) and Barbara Bivins (right), much like Jerry Heacock wrote about all of the embellishments regarding the "Pusser Legend."

Towhead White when he first arrived at the
state line and went to work for Jack Hathcock
(Photo from Barbara Bivins collection)

A young Jr and Shirley Smith would operate the Old Hickory Grill
(photo: Barbara Bivins collection)

Eddie Bond (right) would record several ballads about Buford Pusser. He and Buford would form both a business and personal partnership

W.R. Morris (left) would write Buford's biography. Buford would later claim he hardly knew Morris even though he signed a contract giving Morris the rights to his printed story.

Buford would run for the office of sheriff in 1964. At the age of 26, he would become the youngest sheriff in Tennessee.

According to author Barbara Bivins, one of Buford's first acts as sheriff was to visit the Shamrock to secure payoffs for his "protection services." He kept increasing his fees as time went on.

	WAGE AND TAX STATEMENT **1965**

County of McNairy
Howard Moore Judge
Selmer, Tenn.   62-6000755

Type or print EMPLOYER'S identification number, name, and address above.

Copy C—For employee's records

INCOME TAX INFORMATION			SOCIAL SECURITY INFORMATION		
Federal income tax withheld	Wages paid subject to withholding in 1965	Other compensation paid in 1965	F.I.C.A. employee tax withheld	Total F.I.C.A. wages paid in 1965	
$ 213.40	$ 4,917.16	None	$ 174.12	$ 4,800	

Type or print EMPLOYEE'S social security number →   409-56-5267

Buford Pusser
Adamsville, Tenn.

Type or print EMPLOYEE'S name and address above.

Keep this copy as part of your tax records.

FORM W-2—U.S. Treasury Department, Internal Revenue Service

During Buford's first full calendar year as sheriff (1965), he earned $4917.16
in wages, yet he lived a lifestyle that far exceeded his sheriff's income.

Jim Moffett would be the first Deputy Buford would hire.
Moffett would be almost 14 years older than Buford. A
little known fact is that Moffett, upset with the unnecessary
killing of Louise Hathcock, quit his job as Chief Deputy
after Buford shot Hathcock twice in the back. A little less
than two weeks later he returned at Buford's request. Moffett's
son Oneal was the source of this information.

Peatie Plunk would be the second Deputy that Buford would hire.

Dave Lipford would be one of the first black deputies to be hired, a very controversial hire during the 1960's.

Buford would hire his father, Carl Pusser, to be a Jailer. Carl would earn a reputation as a cruel deputy as one temporary inmate claimed that Carl would beat a prisoner's feet as a form of punishment to the point they could hardly walk.

Inside the McNairy County Jail

Kirksey McCord Nix Jr to this day will not say if he was involved in the alleged August 12th ambush in which Pauline Pusser lost her life.

Drewry's Steak House as it stands today. Nix, Towhead and many others were known to have dined here. It was one of Corinth's finer dining establishments at the time. It stood next door to the El-Ray Motel.

The Smith Deposition

James Smith was the son-in-law of Bobby Floyd. Smith was alleged to have knowledge of certain state line activities and would claim that this knowledge would bring him death threats. Smith claimed that he and his wife Camilla Floyd Smith had to flee to Mexico for their safety, claiming that their home in Mississippi had been shot up after he failed to act as a driver in the alleged Pusser assassination in 1974.

Upon eventually leaving Mexico behind, James and Camilla relocated to Florida where they were married. After some time had passed and Smith claimed they felt safe, Smith publicly announced his intention to write a book regarding his alleged knowledge regarding the state line and the illegal activities there. As far as I know, he never followed up in writing this book.

What is apparently credited to him however, is the following alleged deposition in which he gave names and discussed alleged events including the alleged assassination plot of Buford Pusser in 1974. As far as I know, his claims were never vetted or taken seriously.

Some authors have referred to the following as an "FBI deposition." I personally have my doubts that it is an official document as claimed as it is not on letterhead, it is not signed by Smith and it contains no redactions. It has been a long standing policy of the FBI to redact the names of persons still living before a document of this nature can be released to the public. There were no such redactions made to this document while several persons mentioned within were still very much alive at the time it was released.

Still, while the document is an interesting read, James Smith is a name you rarely if ever heard of in connection with state line. Is it a true deposition? I have my doubts.

During 1962 and 1963 while attending schools at
Corith Junior High, it became less difficult for me to
do the absurd and or as often commit criminal acts as
would be rubbing elbows with sons and daughters of the
more socially accepted families. Subsequently, I became
involved with persons who would steal various items and
as often have buyers for such items. Being young and
knowledgebly indigent (as my only excuse or defense) I
sought various ways to become superior in every criminal
act or endeavor. It was during these times I was able
to become more accepted in the illegal circles from
which I was able to begin buying liquor and handguns at
the early age of 15 and 16 years old.

In May of 1963, two other fellows and myself set
out stealing cars one evening and eventually wound up in
Missouri apprehended in stolen vehicles. We were apprehended while on our way to St. Louis to make sale of the
same vehicles to a dealer I had met only days previously.
Subsequently, we were tried, convicted and sentenced for
a period of time in the State of Missouri. Later we were
transfered back to Mississippi and tried, convicted and
sentenced to Columbia Training for an undetermined period
of time. Upon my release I soon later resumed a part of
criminal activities which once before had been a financially
rewarding way of life. After a short period of time I

(1)

joined the army. Neglecting to mention my past criminal
record and not giving a true and accurate account of my
age along with my unwillingness to conform to a number of
militarily accepted ideas and not having been paid for a
period of over three (3) months I went AWOL. After a
period of one hundred (100) and some odd days later I
turned myself in at Millington Naval Air Station in
Memphis, Tennessee and asked to be discharged. Later
I was discharged and resumed my association with criminal
elements in N.E. Mississippi. It was during that period
of time I came in closer contact with both Toehead White,
Nimbo Price and shortly after Bill Garrett. After having
achieved a record of criminal involvements, my total
acceptance in criminal areas was more or less expected.
Being unable (more like unwilling) to conform to a
more decent way of life, I sought the easy ways to make
larger amounts of money fast. Subsequently, I became
very closely involved in every operation that Bill
Garrett was in contact with. Thinking perhaps that eventually I would become a free agent.

Later I went to Kenosha, Wisc. following my involvement with a girl and her family from Kenosha. Myself,
being one to frequent bars and taverns I came in contact
with an associate of Toehead White's. On one occasion this
associate (De Al Martino) and I went out drinking. At this

time we went to Morelli's ship yard where upon he removed
a body from the trunk of his car and threw it into the lake.
I became frightened of what had happened and of any possible
criminal involvement I may have had and decided it was best
for me to leave Wisconsin. Being without funds, I attempted
to steal some merchandise so that I might afford to leave.
My attempts were foiled by Kenosha Police. Upon my release
to make restitution and pay $500.00 fine, I fled the state
of Wisconsin and hopefully any possible involvements that
I might have resulting from my knowledge of involvements and
association of De Al Martino.

During 1967-1969 I worked with Garrett painting and
dismantling stolen cars and removing numbers from other
stolen merchandise. These cars come from all areas but
rarely from within the N.E. Mississippi area since this was
too close to our operation, often they would come from Memphis,
Chicago, Atlanta, Birmingham, and various other places.

Around May 1969 I began flying with Garrett. Garrett,
Eugene King, Billy Joe Woddal, Ira Newton (Slim), and others
were doing burglaries on airports, such as taking naviga-
tional aids from planes and tools and parts from aircraft maintenance shops, also shoe factories, marinas (boat docks etc.)
I also learned to fly while we were involved in this. As a
result of getting involved in flying I became aware of the contact:
persons [   ] (who) dealt in stolen

automobiles and other hot merchandise. (Dr. Kelly Segars who issued flight medicals and certificates to Garrett and myself). Furthermore they were never caught while commiting these burglaries.

In July 1969 Garrett and I flew to Lexington, Tennessee where we picked up some stolen cars. While Garrett flew the plane back, I along with another man towed the cars to Adamsonville, Tenn. where Garrett met me. We all went to Ed Shaws Restaurant at Shiloh National Park where upon the man who drove back from Lexington went into the restaurant and returned with a large amount of money he had gotten for the cars.

I first met Buford Pusser during 1969 at the McNairy County Airport. At this time I had drifted away from my work with Garrett and was now employed by J.C. Phillips as a flight attendant. I was doing legitimate work although Phillips was a minor fence and occasionally would take hot merchandise from Garrett since Garrett had gotten so deeply in debt to Phillips for flying time etc. Occasionally would fly to McNair Airport to pick up automobile or airplane parts. When I first met Pusser he offered to pay me for information about minor crimes in McNairy County Tennessee and surrounding areas. He said he wanted to go for a ride in the plane which surprised me since I didn't actually have my license yet. Pusser said he knew I had gotten a raw deal from Bill Garrett and Sheriff Grady Bingham of Alcorn County, Miss.

concerning some stolen goods I bought, which were intended for
Garrett. Garrett had turned me in for stealing the goods and
Sheriff Bingham beat me up while in jail. After this beating and being
released on bond I went to McNairy County, Tennessee to look
for a man who sold me the stolen goods, since I had told
R.C. Matlock, one of Pussers Deputies about what Bingham and
Garrett had done I figured this was the only way Pusser
could have known about the "raw deal". At any rate I had
given R.C. Matlock a $200.00 check to help me find the man
who sold me the stuff. (no results) Buford and I flew for
about 20 minutes during which time I consented to give Pusser
the information he wanted, mostly because I was fed up with
Garrett and also because of Pussers' promise to make it worth
my while. In all up until 1970 when my contract with Pusser
diminished he gave me about $150 to $200 for information.

Pusser and I usually met at the State Line Road or near
what is now the Torch Club. My mother, (Sandra Launderwille
Bauer) from Vienosha, Wis., Kathrine Thacker and Jerry Foust
were the only ones who knew I was giving information to Pusser.
In the Spring of 1970 Pusser gave me an Honarary Deputies card
which among other things, entitled me to a cheap cup of coffee
at local restaurants. If Phillips and Garrett were aware of
me having the card it would not have bothered them since these
cards were easy to come by and didn't necessarily indicate a
closeness with the law. As mentioned supra my contact with

Pusser diminished in the last half of 1970, particularly after 8-31-70 - the date his term as sheriff expired. At this time I was developing an interest in the law exforcement as a result of my contract with Pusser.

In the latter part of 1970 I left Phillips and went pipelining, a legitimate business until returning to start school at N.E. Miss. Jr. College in the fall of 1971. Sheriff Ralph Lambert had been elected sheriff and was to take office January 1, 1970 at or about this time I was a clerk at Booneville Police Department Booneville, Prentiss County Miss. while attending school soon after Lambert took office he made me an honorary deputy. On July 4, 1972 I was appointed tax collector and City Marshall in Burnsville and later Police Chief subsequently I left Booneville P.D. but still was an honorary deputy with Alcorn County. During this period of time old friends such as Garrett started coming around asking for favors but I had nothing to do with them. In a conversation that nobody knows about, I told Pusser that Buddy Strickland (a resident of Burnsville) had the gun that killed Pussers wife (August 12, 1967). Strickland worked for Howard Bunch who was the leader of Alcohol Traffic in N.E. Miss. Bunch was also the owner of the Shamrock Motel and Restaurant on the State line and at one time employed Red Brewer. In Ala. custody to manage it for him. Bunch also

owned and operated a liquor store in Corinth, Miss. At
this time I did not know of any plots to kill Pusser although there were always rumors around stateline joints.

As mentioned in the previous praragraph while working
in Burnsville I saw Pusser once maybe more. I felt like
Pusser was using me to get at criminals in Miss. near
Burnsville, ones that would be beyond his jurisdiction
even though at the time he was out of law enforcement.
Pusser would also give me tips to help me rise politically
such as telling me who and where to check for what.

In the fall of 1973 there was a political upheaval in
Burnsville which resulted in my leaving office and returning
to Corith where I returned to school. There once again
I returned to work for the Booneville Police Department at
NE Miss Jr. College. However, because of the death of Art
Murphy in March 1973 and a Grand Jury inditement for
embezzelment, I was fired form Booneville P.D. subsequently
I was unable to continue my work and study at NEMJC.

Art Murphy was the Police Chief in Corith. While I
was visiting there on March 3, 1973 he was killed. Jerry
McDaniel captain of the police had told me earlier in the
evening that Murphy would be killed (see deposition) and
and Deputy Austin had told me to keep quiet about it. I
obliged. McDaniel killed Murphy, but McDaniel was released
within hours since Sheriff Lambert said it was self defense.

(7)

He immediately went to Chicago upon his release.

I later told my mother, Murphy's daughter and the Mayor of Burnsville what happened. Furthermore I went to Ron Windsor, the county attorney and asked him to make me a special investigator, which he did. This angered several people in law enforcement who knew what had happened even though I tried to brugh it off as having nothing to do with Murphy's death.

I believe the people responsible for Murphy's death decided I knew too much and that they had to get rid of me more than once my murder was attempted. Once by throwing bolders down from the overpass through my windshield. Also, I was shot and did chase Bailiff James E. Timbes home. Since it was he whom I believed to have shot me. During the chase I did temporarily lose control of my car and was unable to apprehend same. However I did see water returning to a mudhole in his driveway when I arrived at his residence. Also I observed lights being turned off. I was off work for three(3) days. A charge of embezzlement had already been brought against me as a result of a car I had purchased from Bailiff Timbes in Burnsville which happened to have a county radio in it. Although I got a bill of sale, this embezzlement charge was brought in what I am sure was an attempt to get me back into Tishomingo County, Miss. where they can deal with me.

Because of this charge and the concurrent political upheaval I had to leave Burnsville and returned to Corith in the fall of 1973 as mentioned supra. When news of this embezzlement

(8)

charge became known I was dropped from the Booneville
Police Department and had to quit school due to lack of
money.

While in Corinth I couldn't live at home with
mother and family for safety reasons so I stayed at
Corona Plaza Motel and Noel Motel.

In late 1973 Pusser visited me at this Motel (Red,
Lee Glidwell, (Nimbo's girl) (Sue Wooley) Restaurant Hostess
should be able to attest that Pusser visited me. Also
my mother and present wife were aware of some meetings.

Around Mid 1974 I saw Pusser again at Coleman's
Bar B. Q. in Corinth. This Bar BQ was and is situated
on Hwy 45 N at 7th Street. It was at this time I
advised him that Nimbo had called me concerning spliting
a contract on Pusser's Death with him. Pusser told me to
"stick with " to see what developed. I never saw him again
until the night he was killed and that was the time he
was on TV in Memphis signing a contract with some people
concerning a new movie.

Catherine Thacker or Mrs. Harris were two persons who
should have seen us together during this meeting.

On July 25th or 26th, 1974 Nimbo Price came by my
mothers house and told her he and I were meeting in
Henderson, Tennessee, But he didn't show up as scheduled
on July 26th or 27th we met in Jackson, Tennessee at the
Thunderbird Motel. I had gotten there before Nimbo and

(9)

239

had rented a room under the name of Jack North. At the
time I was driving my wife's car. While we were there I
met Cotton Collins who haggled with Nimbo about money in
the parking lot. Later that night I returned to Corinth.

About a week later Nimbo and his girlfriend met me
at Null Bros. Garage where he told me it was "coming
down soon", apparently refering to Pussers death. Later
that night we went to a tavern in Tennessee.

On or about August 16, 1974 Nimbo contacted
me at my mother's and we went to Catherinn's Club in
Tennessee to do some drinking. While there I overheard
Jr. Smith the owner of the Old Hickory Grill and murder
of Towhead and Skeet Atkins discussing a front end man in
Memphis. They knew that Pusser was coming back from
Memphis and Jr. asked Skeet if he had gotten the money
together. I presumed they discussed money with Nimbo.

We went home. A few days later returned to the
Thunderbird Motel in Jackson. At this time Nimbo drove
a green or brown 69 Chevy. While I waited in the car
Nimbo went to a room to get the money. I jotted down
the license numbers of several cars in the parking lot.
In paticular, I remember spoting Cotton Collin's car.
When Nimbo returned to the car, he had $10,000 and said
that Ed Gillock, Ed Shaw, Jr. Smith, Collins and a man
from California were in the room. Incidentally, Nimbo
had a set of GM master keys, explosives, rope, tools,
front end parts, etc, in his car while we made this trip.
He told me that when it was over he would split the money

(10)

240

with me because I was supposed to drive the get away car.
We returned to Corinth.

On August 20, 1974 Nimbo called and said to meet
him at Eastview, Tennessee in McNairy County at 6 or
8 PM. He said it was going to happen between Colliersville
and Adamsville.

I did not go to Eastview ; rather I tried to contact
Pusser who I knew, was in Memphis. My wife and I called
every Holiday Inn in Memphis as well as the McNairy
County Sheriff's Office and Pusser's parents, but could
not reach him. On one of these calls I did identify
myself (McNairy Co?) Later I saw Nimbo in Corinth after
Pusser's death and he wanted to know what had happened
to me. I brushed it off, saying something had come up
and I couldn't make it. We had some drinks and seemingly
the matter was forgotten. (Approx. the same time our trailer
was shot up and Camilla went to the hospital for her nerves.
Her Dr. advised her to get out of that stupid town before
she had a nervous breakdown.) After these incidents , we left
for Mexico where Camilla got a divorce from her husband. On
or about 4-30-75. After a while we returned to Corinth
and then left for Florida where we were married 6-12-75
While in Florida I learned Nimbo had been killed by
Tommy Bivens. Armsted, an investigator, claims that Nimbo
came to Bivens to kill him due to remarks made about
Nimbo's sex habits and that Bivens had acted in self-
defense. I know that the substance of these alleged

(11)

241

remarks were untrue and I believe that it is a fact that
Nimbo's gun was never fired.

Since learning of Nimbo's death, we have been on
the run ever since. It is my belief that those people
that had Nimbo killed also want me silenced because I
know too much.

Interesting Items

The source stated that [   ] of Columbus, Miss., was seen there by [   ] knows him and that he is a gambler.

The source stated that [   ] heard from some of the people hanging around the state line, but not from LOUISE HATHCOCK, that 48% of the business is owned by the Gold Coast Syndicate, that is by some gamblers from around the Gold Coast of Mississippi.

The source said i[   ] WHITE would end up by killing LOUISE HATHCOCK. She claimed she could give no further information concerning the allegation concerning the Gold Coast Syndicate.

On 1/19/65, [   ] of the Little Rock Office, advised SA [   ] that CARL WHITE, who is also known as "TOWHEAD", manages the Shamrock Motel, Corinth, Miss., and had moved his fencing activities to the White Iris Restaurant at Selmer, Tenn., where WHITE has a "fix" with local law enforcement officers.

This source reported that as of 1/13/65 the following individuals were hanging out at the restaurant and believed to be staying at Selmer, Tenn.

[   ]

pounds, [   ] place of [   ] unknown, reportedly resides in a motel, name unknown, at Selmer, Tenn. It was stated that he recently was hospitalized for gunshot wounds, place unknown. He is supposed to have been shot with a .38 calibre through the left thumb and right shoulder with one bullet. The source described [   ] as a safe man and a gambler and said he was driving a 1965 Bonneville Pontiac convertible with Tennessee license, number unknown.

COVER PAGE

The "Fix" in with local law enforcement…. paragraph 4

The gambling at the White Iris Restaurant has stopped for an unknown reason and the principals involved has scattered.

The gambling activities consisted of a "razzle" game which is actually a confidence game whereby a victim is swindled out of his money.

The operator of the "razzle" game uses a cup and from six, eight or ten dice and a pool table cloth with various squares reflecting odds of the game. It is played by counting the ones and sixes on the dice and you win or lose through a combination of numbers. The victim of the game is actually "out counted" or the dice are secretly turned over by the operator to bring up the desired combination. The dice are turned over by the operator when he conceals them with his hands while in the process of counting the numbers on the dice.

This restaurant was operating 24 hours and the confidence game operators were always on duty. Each victim was screened very carefully. They would primarily concentrate on a man accompanied by a woman with an out-of-state license tag. They would actually check the cars for the license tag, clothes hanging and other signs to indicate that the potential victim was actually a tourist traveling through the area. They would also pick on a man as a victim if he were by himself, but would never take on two men. They would draw from the potential victim through conversations as to where he was from and where he was going. If the victim appeared to be a legitimate tourist, the sign was given and when the customer started to pay his bill his woman companion would win a free throw of the dice and always won a box of candy, and thereafter be entitled to another throw. If the victim declined to continue and would leave with the box of candy, the restaurant did not lose any money because the cost of the candy was figured into the meal. If the victim continued to play, the operator of the "razzle game" would take all his money.

ROY ALLEN and an individual known a= [   ] were the operators of the "razzle game."

"Razzle Game" at the state line

I have known "Towhead" White for a good many years and
I have prosecuted a good many subjects, and in my opinion
he is one of the most dangerous men that I have known. I
believe him to be one of the most dangerous persons in this
entire area. The place of the slaying, the Shamrock Restaurant and Motel (formerly the 45 Grill) has been a hangout for many years for hoodlums traveling out of Illinois
and Kentucky into the Mississippi, Alabama, and Florida
area. White is, in my opinion, the number one candidate for
the list of subjects for the organized crime and racketeer-
ing program. It is my recommendation that he be added to
the list and that all effort be exerted to bring him to the
bar of justice.

As a sidelight, former Sheriff James Dickey, at the time
of his death, was being considered by his office for prosecution for conspiring to violate the Internal Revenue laws with
reference to the moonshine whiskey business. Our case report
clearly indicates that Dickey was in the moonshine business.
I do not know Dickey's successor in office; but if he is per-
mitting "Towhead" White to operate in his county, then I am
confident that White has made the necessary arrangements to
operate. Former Sheriff Dickey's death occurred in the
vicinity of the Tennessee-Mississippi state line during the
early morning hours; and it appeared that he left the highway
at high speed and hit a tree.. Because of our knowledge of
his activities and especially his association with the Hathcock's and White, we think it is entirely possible that his
death may have been as a result of unnatural causes.

I apologize for writing such a long letter with respect
to the matter. I could write ten pages concerning White alone.

Prosecutor discusses Dickey's Unnatural death and possible payoffs to Buford re: "Fix"

CASE NO. A66-104

OFFICE OF THE CHIEF MEDICAL EXAMINER

COUNTY McNairy

858 Madison Avenue
Memphis, Tennessee 38103

AUTOPSY REPORT

NAME OF DECEDENT __Louise Hathcock__   RACE __W__ SEX __F__ AGE __40__

HOME ADDRESS _____ __Selmer,__ __Tennessee__
                          NUMBER OR STREET   CITY OR TOWN   STATE

COUNTY MEDICAL EXAMINER __Harry Peeler, M.D.__

ADDRESS __Selmer, Tennessee__

DISTRICT ATTORNEY GENERAL __Will T. Abernathy__

ADDRESS __Selmer, Tennessee__

ANATOMICAL DIAGNOSIS __Distant gunshot wounds, multiple__

CAUSE OF DEATH __Distant gunshot wounds, multiple__

NARRATIVE OF FINDINGS __Cause of death in this instance was due to a distant
gunshot wound of the head(3A) which entered the left lateral angle of
the chin and exited through the parieto-occipital area of the skull(3B)
causing multiple fractures of the skull and lacerations of the brain.
An additional distant gunshot wound passed through the left lateral neck
from back to front (2A & 2B). The third distant gunshot wound passed
from left to right through the upper abdomen lacerating the spleen and
liver. Left post axillary line (1A) to right anterior chest (1B)__

__Blood alcohol - 0.23%   Urine alcohol - 0.22%__

The purpose of this report is to provide a certified opinion to the County Medical
Examiner and the District Attorney General. The facts and findings to support these con-
clusions are filed with the office of the State Medical Examiner.

2-18-56   J. T. Francisco,   M.D.
                                858 Madison Ave.   Memphis, Tennessee

Page from Louise Hathcock's autopsy report, description of wounds

CHART # 15

411

A66-104

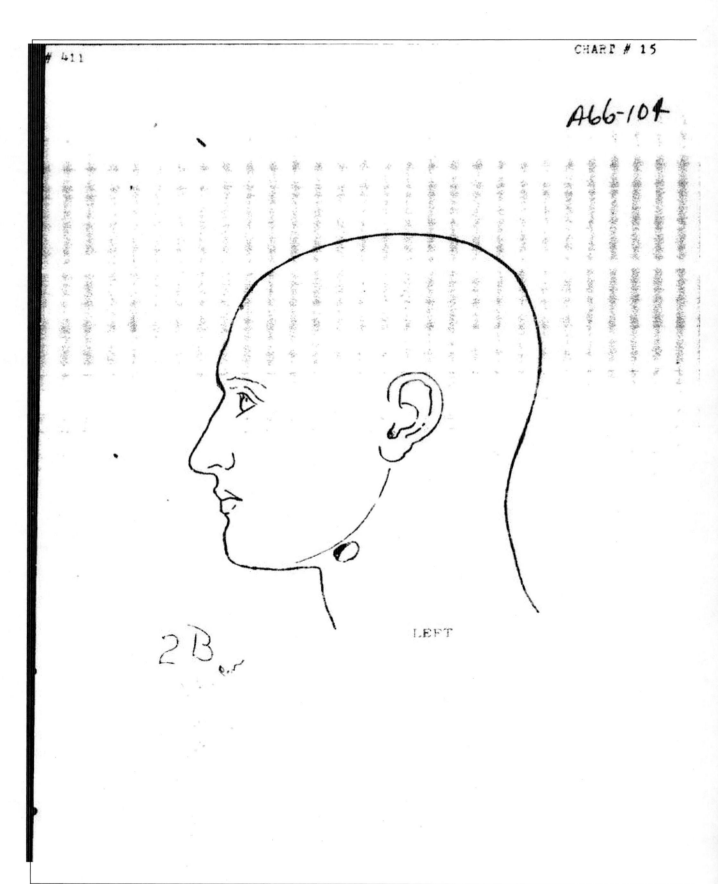

2B

LEFT

Entrance wound of Buford's third shot as Louise lay dying on the floor

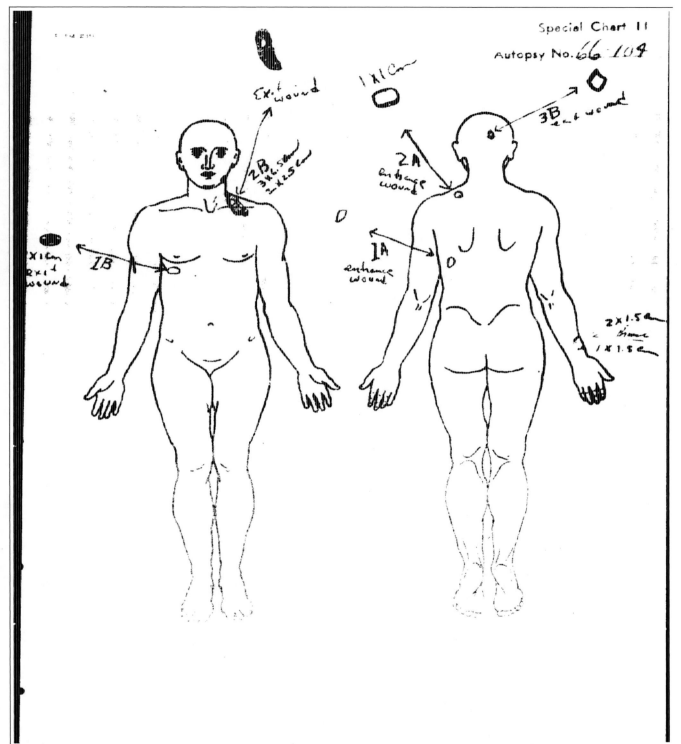

Special Chart 11

Autopsy No. 66-104

Exit wound

2B 3×1.5cm 2×1.5cm

1×1cm

2A entrance wound

3B exit wound

1A entrance wound

1B

×1cm 2×1 Exit wound

2×1.5cm time 1×1.8cm

Hathcock autopsy report **Exit** wounds on diagram (left).... **Entrance** wounds on Diagram Right

249

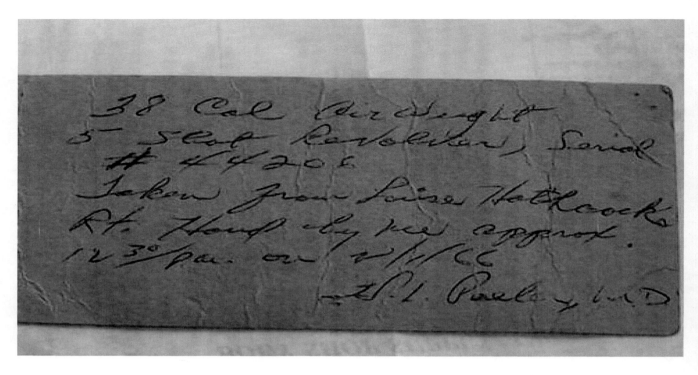

Evidence Tag for Louise Hathcock's revolver after she was killed at the Shamrock Motel. Notice it was signed by McNairy County Medical Examiner Harry Peeler. Notice that the gun was still in her hand after she had been shot three times. Was it planted there?

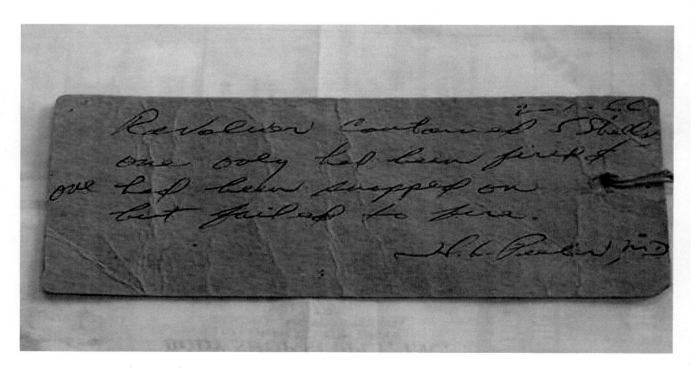

The backside of the evidence tag showing only one round fired.